Power to
The People -
Ernie Goff

ELSIE FOX

Portrait of An Activist

by
Karen Stevenson with Elsie Fox

iUniverse, Inc.
New York Bloomington

Elsie Fox
Portrait of An Activist

iUniverse books may be ordered through booksellers or by contacting:

iUniverse
1663 Liberty Drive
Bloomington, IN 47403
www.iuniverse.com
1-800-Authors (1-800-288-4677)

COVER PHOTO: Watercolor portrait of Elsie Fox, 1939, by artist Cecelia Corr, a fellow activist for peace and civil rights.

ISBN: 978-0-595-51856-2 (sc)
ISBN: 978-1-4401-0909-6 (dj)
ISBN: 978-0-595-62064-7 (ebook)

Printed in the United States of America

iUniverse rev. date: 12/18/2008

For Elsie

"When I give bread to the poor, they call me a saint. When I ask why people are poor, they call me a Communist." —Dom Helder Camara

Contents

Acknowledgments

Early on my daughter Ann provided creative and wise consultation and enthusiastic support. My writing group patiently plodded along with me through drafts and re-drafts. Friends read the manuscript and offered gentle critiques and encouraging words. Clay Scott gave a listening ear and kind support. Kathy O'Brien shared her expertise in sorting through a tangle of endnotes and smiled at just the right times. Glenda Pearson at the University of Washington dug in dusty archives and my cousin, Lynn Montgomery, took the time to be my research assistant in Seattle. James Gregory at the University of Washington, head of the research project about Communism in the state of Washington, unwittingly provided a wealth of knowledge to loose Elsie's memory. Catherine Powell at the Labor Archives in San Francisco found photos and pertinent information regarding Elsie and Ernie. My husband Mike believed in me. Thank you … and gratitude to all.

And to Elsie, thank you for trusting me with your story.

FOREWORD

I met Elsie Fox for the first time a few years ago. A friend had told me she was someone I should get to know, so I drove out to Miles City to see her. We spent the better part of a day in her modest trailer, drinking tea and talking. I returned to see her the next day, and we picked up the conversation where we had left off. Since that first visit I have found excuses to go out to Miles City on several more occasions. Elsie would talk for hours about her life, but her narrative was more than a simple recounting of events. She constantly strove to make her past experiences relevant to the present, and she often interrupted her stories to challenge me.

"What do *you* think?" Or, "What would *you* have done in my place?" Or, "What do *you* think the government's role should be in that situation?"

She told me the stories you will read in these pages: of her dirt-poor childhood on the Powder River, a childhood filled with hard work, and with long, dusty cattle drives, and with loneliness; and peopled with itinerant horse traders and cattle thieves.

You will also read in this remarkable book about Elsie's time in Seattle during the Depression, of her later move to San Francisco, of her political awakening – and its consequences.

"I became a political progressive," she told me. "You can call me a radical if you like. I have sometimes been ostracized for my political beliefs. But if you are passionate about seeking the truth, being ostracized is part of the package!"

Still, Elsie confesses to feeling depressed and frustrated at times.

"I always had the perspective that the world would get better, that it *must* get better," she said. "I dedicated my life to that belief. And it has been a tremendous disappointment to me to realize that, on the whole, the world has not gotten better. But then that feeling of depression and despondency turns to anger, and that anger turns into action. Because if we don't take action when there are problems in the world, then what are we?"

I called Elsie the other day, to get her thoughts on the 2008 presidential campaign, and was pleased to find her—at 100 years of age—as curious, forceful, passionate and intense as always.

"This country seems so passive!" she told me, her voice shaking. "So many Americans seem content to let things happen to them! Sometimes I think my countrymen believe history is something you watch on television! They seem to have no idea that they are making history! They have no idea that their very lack of engagement is helping to shape history! I am so angry!"

Then she paused, took a breath, and chuckled.

"I'm forgetting my manners," she said, sweetly. "How are you, my dear?"

And that is Elsie in a nutshell: impassioned citizen of the world, and attentive friend; able to grasp the big picture, and appreciate the small.

I asked her once if, after all her experiences, she ever felt isolated in Miles City. She laughed at the question.

"When I was a little girl," she said, "there was a little ditty we used to sing in Sunday school. 'Brighten the corner where you are.' And I have found that I have been able to do that. So no, I don't feel isolated at all. Wherever there are people, life is interesting."

By Clay Scott

Clay Scott is a freelance writer and radio producer. He spent several years as a foreign correspondent for ABC News and Christian Science Monitor Radio.

October, 2008

Helena, Montana

PREFACE

Ninety-eight year old Elsie Fox leaned into the microphone and surprised the crowd with her strong voice. "I want to voice my appreciation for all of you that are here today." Dressed in a long, black skirt with a gold and black vest and matching earrings, Elsie stood behind the podium on a raised platform in a city park in Bozeman, Montana, on Mother's Day of 2006. She was the guest speaker at a peace rally, which had attracted a large crowd of all ages.

"I also want to voice my appreciation for Montana Women for Justice and Peace. Their aims embody the tradition of Jeanette Rankin. They are fast becoming spokespersons for we, the people. Let's give them a cheer that can be heard up the mountainsides of the Gallatin Valley!" She waved her arm in the air yelling, "Hip, hip, hooray! Hip, hip, hooray!"

The crowd reacted to this white-haired, less-than-five-foot-tall woman by following her lead, and their shouts resounded loudly in the warm, May air. She held yellow index cards, which had key lines of her speech printed in bold, black letters big enough for her to read, yet, Elsie was determined to deliver her speech, not read it.

Elsie began her speech after the crowd settled on the lawn under the fir trees that towered overhead. "I was born in 1907. I remember when my mother voted for the first time in 1914. She put her shoulders back and said with pride in her voice, 'I voted today!' This event was only made possible by the actions of thousands of women known as the suffragettes. They chained themselves to courthouse pillars. They tirelessly marched and protested and petitioned throughout the country until women won the right to vote."

Elsie continued, "I was a young woman living in Seattle during the Depression of the thirties. I saw the crash. I saw the banks close and people losing their jobs and being evicted from their houses. I saw industry stop. I saw the country stop. I saw people go hungry! I saw fear. Fear of hunger is almost as bad as hunger itself. I saw people go without health care. I saw racial discrimination among black people, immigrants, women, and the elderly. I saw unfair labor practices. Does all this sound familiar? President Hoover told us that the benefits of big business would trickle down to the people. Sound familiar? And what did we, the people, do?"

Elsie knew how to work a crowd. She was an experienced agitator. Her voice grew stronger as she emphasized key words.

"*We, the people*, marched from one end of this country to the other to demand change. We marched ten-thousand-people strong down Main Street of Seattle—demanding work and food. Incidentally, the man who led that march later became my husband. We pooled our resources and drove our tin lizzies and took boxcars and thumbed rides to Washington DC to demonstrate on the Capitol Mall.

"*We, the people*, educated the working class by publishing a newspaper, the *Voice of Action,* and distributing it door to door.

"*We, the people*, organized Townsend clubs after pensions were lost when the banks closed and discussed ways to provide security for the working man's future. This was the beginning of Social Security.

"*We, the women*, boycotted silk stockings. We knew that Hirohito was flexing his muscles dangerously. We knew that the scrap iron Japan was buying from us could very possibly come back to this country in the form of bullets, which it did. But we made ourselves heard.

"*We, the people*, united to help our neighbors. People had no jobs—no money to pay the rent. Evictions were common. I saw, in my own neighborhood, the sheriff taking the little furniture and sorry belongings of a family out the front door and neighbors, on the other side of the truck, taking it off and returning it through the back door. *We, the people*, fought back.

"What were the results of our actions? If there is one thing I want to make clear today, it is that Social Security, Unemployment Insurance, bank reforms, and the New Deal came from the people! The Works Progress Administration was established by the insistence of people who wanted work and not charity. FDR got these ideas because he *heard the voice of the people* from the grass roots of America!

"That's the way it happened, folks. We did it then; you can do it now! It's not going to happen through politicians of both stripes in Washington DC. In the spirit of the suffragettes a century ago, *we must unite in a common cause*!

"I want to end with a quote written by Pastor Neimoeller, a Protestant Minister in Germany who survived the concentration camps:

> First they came for the Communists and I didn't speak up because I wasn't a Communist. Then they came for the Jews and I didn't speak up because I wasn't a Jew. Then they came for the Catholics and I didn't speak up because I was a Protestant. Then they came for the trade unionists and I didn't speak up because I wasn't a trade unionist. Then they came for me and by that time there was no one left to speak up for me."[1]

Elsie paused, and her gaze swept over the crowd. The challenge came as she pounded her fist on the podium.

"*We, the people,* must have solidarity ... unity! The voice of action must be heard ... *by the people, for the people, from the people.* We, the people, can take back our country! We can make a difference! *We can win!*"

The crowd, seven hundred strong, leapt to their feet with cheers and applause. Elsie Fox stepped off the stage and was surrounded by people eager to meet her. Several young men in their early twenties shook her hand and started asking questions about her life and the details she had mentioned in her speech. The *Nation* later posted her speech on their Web site in the Moral Compass section. Elsie stepped out of the forgotten pages of a history book that day, shook her fist, and called for people to wake up, remember, act, and make a difference.

98 year old Elsie - Mother's Day Speech, Bozeman, Montana

Introduction

When Elsie Fox stepped up to read at the open mike event at the Custer County Art Center in Miles City, Montana, I saw for the first time the woman who would eventually inhabit my life with the force of her will. She walked briskly to the front of the room and waited for someone to adjust the microphone down to her size. Elsie wore a black, mid-length skirt that flared at the bottom revealing stylish boots. Silver earrings bobbled below her upswept, white hair, and the rings on her fingers sparkled as she held her manuscript. Rouge added color to her cheeks, softening her sharp nose, and her lips were tastefully painted with bright lipstick. The person next to me leaned over and whispered, "She's over ninety years old!"

Elsie read her story about growing up "dirt poor" on a remote ranch in eastern Montana at the turn of the last century. She told about a runaway team of horses and a one-room school. She described her childhood home—a sod-roofed log cabin with no electricity or running water. I had heard similar hard-luck stories from elderly people in the area, but her almost exotic appearance and the flair with which she spoke suggested there was more to her story. Afterwards, over coffee and cookies, I introduced myself, and we talked briefly. It would be years later that I would really get to know Elsie.

Elsie and her 1976 Gremlin

Elsie drove a yellow, 1976 Gremlin, which was easy to spot among the pickup trucks, SUV's, and family vans that were the norm in Miles City. Everyone in town knew if Elsie was out and about blocks away just by recognizing her car. Despite her age, she got around.

Elsie sold her car when her eyesight began to fail and relied on friends or a taxi to take her places. On occasion, I would take her to the grocery store. I trailed behind Elsie that first shopping trip, pushing my cart, anxious to help her. She turned to me and said, "Don't you have your own shopping to do, dear? I'll meet you at the checkout stand," and off she went.

Twenty minutes later, I pulled up behind Elsie at the checkout stand. She turned to me and said, "Dear, would you please watch my cart? I forgot something." I was happy to finally be of some help and pushed her cart toward the clerk as Elsie hurried over to the counter where lottery tickets were sold. It didn't take long before she came back, ticket in hand. "I buy one every month. I plan to build my dream house when I win!" She chuckled and stuffed the ticket in her purse.

One Friday evening, I met Elsie—never one to pass up a good time—at the local bookstore where musicians played and sang for an appreciative audience. During an intermission, I went to greet Elsie, who was sitting in the front row. With simple hellos out of the way, she obviously had something other than pleasantries on her mind. "So … what do you think of the impending invasion of Iraq?" she asked.

I muttered something about it being terrible. "Well, I have the most fantastic idea, dear! Wait until you hear this ... and I think it will work!" I sat down beside her while she continued excitedly. "I'm very concerned about this present military escalation. When you're my age, you don't sleep a lot and have time to think. So as a result, I've come up with a brilliant idea. Now listen to this." She put her hand lightly on my arm while sitting on the edge of her seat. "It will take the women of the world to stand up to war. The *women* have to unite to stop this insanity. We'll call it WOW: Women Opposed to War." She swept her hand in front of her, rings flashing, like a talk show host introducing a famous guest. "Now visualize this—we'll get as many women as we can and form this great line. We'll stand, arm in arm in a line that will stretch for miles and miles between the two armies. We won't have guns or weapons—just women standing for peace! I think it will work! I mean, how could they shoot at all us women?" I noticed that her pronoun usage while relaying her idea had turned plural. "Don't you think that's a great idea?" I gave her a thumbs–up, and she sat back and smiled. "Now, who can we get to see this idea through?" Elsie asked, and she wasn't kidding.

The autumn day that I first visited Elsie at her home has remained vivid in my memory. Elsie was ninety-eight years old when she phoned me wanting my help with a community health project that she was involved in. She asked me to come visit her. Home was a trailer that sat on a corner lot of a tidy, established trailer park. A white picket fence outlined the perimeter of the lot. The faded green trailer, with thin aluminum siding and little or no insulation, looked to be from the seventies. It was small—about twelve feet by sixty feet—with an enclosed particleboard porch that doubled as an entryway and storage room. Potted flowers and tomato plants lined the deck, which looked out to a small yard and the next door trailer. I rang the doorbell.

Elsie graciously greeted me and motioned toward a wicker rocking chair. As she fixed tea, I glanced around the living room. I was intrigued with what I saw. On the wall in front of me, a silk screen wall hanging—a monochrome of gold and brown—presented an intriguing scene of a river and a woman with flowing hair that floated in the sky with a crescent moon. A Chinese pastel of running horses hung above the television set while a herd of figurine horses graced the top of a small shelf in the corner. Worn, orange cushions in a black, bamboo frame served as her sofa. "It has a minimalist, European feel to it," Elsie explained about the sofa. "It was in my apartment in San Francisco." A big, copper-engraved plate hung on the wood-paneled wall behind the sofa. She later told me it was from Iran. She handed me a cup of tea, then settled onto the sofa. The trailer's outside appearance seemed to echo her homestead beginnings while the art on her walls and steaming cups of tea before me hinted at the middle of her story—the one I sensed at the art center years earlier. A dozen questions surfaced, but Elsie had business in mind.

She explained her role and the possibility of mine in the new community health center. She was direct and businesslike. "Here is a piece of paper and pen. You might want to take notes." Satisfied she had gotten what she wanted out of me—a promise to help with signage for the community health center for low-income people—she sat back and said, "Now, tell me about your life."

Her directness circumvented the usual chitchat and caught me off balance. I felt like I had just been given a topic for an impromptu speech, and the judges sat expectantly alert. Elsie's calico cat, Mia, jumped onto the sofa. Elsie absentmindedly stroked Mia as she waited for me to begin. I managed to sum up my homegrown, Montana background in short time—growing up on a wheat farm, my widowed mother raising three children and later my husband and I living on a remote, southeastern, Montana ranch, where we raised our three children, and I taught eight grades in a one-room school.

After I finished, Elsie pushed aside a pile of markers and notepads and set her teacup on the coffee table. A magnifying glass sat on top of a stack of *New Yorkers,* and local newspapers littered the glass top. A confusion of books spilled out of the bottom of the table—Howard Zinn's *A People's History*, Marx's *The Communist Manifesto,* Fodor's *India,* and numerous western history books.

"Now, I'll briefly tell you about my life." I knew the beginning—the remote ranch and log house. She had almost a century of living behind her, and I thought I'd be there for hours. Mia jumped onto the floor as Elsie folded her hands in her lap and began. It may have taken five minutes, or maybe it took two hours—poverty, single-mother struggles, the Roaring Twenties. "I was a flapper in the twenties … that doesn't mean I was promiscuous, but it doesn't mean I was a virgin, either!" Bootleg-whiskey and speak-easies, radicalism and the labor movement, intrigue, suspense, conviction, and a cause—this was nothing like the stories my homesteader grandparents had told me. Elsie finished by saying, "I think I've led a rather interesting life, don't you?" It had been an interesting afternoon, indeed.

I began to visit Elsie off and on. One afternoon, she told me about her memoir writing project. For several years, she had been writing about her life, and when her eyes began to deteriorate, she had spoken into a tape recorder. Several friends had transcribed her tapes. "I just need someone to help me put it altogether." Then she asked if I would be willing to "put it all together." I must have said yes because when I left her trailer that afternoon, I carried a big box to my car. It was filled with a jumble of cassette tapes, transcriptions, records of family history, books on the Cold War and the labor movement, newspaper clippings, and old photographs.

"We'll be seeing a lot of each other, dear!" Elsie chimed as I stepped out the door onto her deck. A metal, cutout figurine of Kokopilau—the bent-over flute player of Hopi Indian folklore, who had a reputation as a trickster—with red, yellow, and blue plastic streamers tied to his feet, was mounted on the railing of the deck. The streamers waved in a gentle breeze, and the trickster, with his story telling flute, seemed to dance in celebration. I put Elsie's life, all ninety-eight years of it, on the passenger seat of my car and drove off.

I started meeting with Elsie once or twice a week. She sorted through her memory like I sorted through the mounds of documents in the box. One day, I phoned her to arrange our next meeting and fill her in on recent developments. "Good news, Elsie. I heard from the FBI. They acknowledged receiving my request for your files." I heard her familiar chuckle.

"Are they going to charge you anything, dear?"

"I don't think so," I replied.

"Well, they'll send you a bill when it takes a truck to ship it all." We both laughed at the thought.

I continued the update saying, "I found the 1973 newspaper article about your trip to China in the archives of the library, but I'm still looking for the Silver Shirt article you wrote for the *Voice of Action.* I think the year was 1935." Elsie had a hard time remembering specific dates, which left me to do the detective work.

I glanced at the time. She planned to watch the president's State of the Union address, and I didn't want to keep her. We arranged our next visit. "Well, I play bridge on Wednesday, and I swim on Thursday, so Friday will be fine for you to come over." She took a deep breath and continued, "I am very interested in the president's speech tonight. Everyone in the world is against the war in Iraq, and I want to hear what he says about it!"

I replied, "I'm not going to listen to the speech tonight, Elsie. It's the same, old rhetoric, and besides, I already know the state of the union—it's a mess." The daily news proclaimed the dire truth of global warming, corporate power gone amuck, and conflict spreading all over the planet like a plague. I told Elsie, "I think I'll read a good book instead."

There was silence on the line. I wondered if she was still there. Then I heard her take another deep breath. "Now, dear, I know you know this. My whole life has been involved in politics."

"You live and breathe it, Elsie."

"Well, then, you'll understand what I'm going to tell you. It's our *duty*, dear. When I think of all those young men and women being killed in Iraq … it just breaks my heart. But this is the bottom line: *I* am the one responsible." The image of this hardly five-foot-tall, white-haired, elderly woman bearing the responsibility of the war startled me. She had more to say. "This is *my* country. This is a *democracy,* and the *people* are ultimately responsible. We mustn't lose sight of that, dear." She did not sound preachy or self-righteous, simply matter-of-fact. "Now what haunts me to this day … when I remember the Nazis … here were these enlightened German people. How could a people as cultivated, intelligent, and wonderful as the German people let that happen?" She paused slightly, then, lowering her voice so I had to strain to hear, she said, "Well … now we know. Now we know."

I came to realize that Elsie's story had as much to do with the present as with the past.

PART ONE—1536 TO 1924

CHAPTER 1:

The Early Years

Elsie Gilland Fox's family tree on her mother's side can be traced to France in the 1500s. Her descendants were Huguenots—French Protestants who threatened the status quo in Europe. It all started with Martin Luther daring to question the practices of the Catholic Church when he hammered his theses to the door of the Wittenberg castle church in Germany, for all to see. The great Protestant Reformation was born and spread to France.

The Catholic French government, in turn, hammered their edict on a wall in 1536, urging the extermination of the heretics (i.e., Huguenots). But the number of Protestants grew, and a religious war devastated France for decades. Then Henry IV proclaimed the Edict of Nantes in 1598, which ended the war and allowed religious freedom. Along came Louis XIV. He hammered another edict on top of the last one, and persecutions of the Huguenots resumed. Hundreds of thousands of Huguenots fled France during the sixteenth and seventeenth century, and those who stayed—half a million—were tortured and killed. Many of the Huguenots who were working class people—artisans, craftsmen, physicians, silversmiths, weavers, teachers, merchants—escaped to the colonies in the New World. France lost her best craftsmen. As a result, the gap between rich and poor became wider and wider. Some theorize this was the cause of the French Revolution. Elsie's ancestors fled to the Americas somewhere in that time frame. Perhaps Elsie's independent spirit originated from that rebellious gene pool that defended liberty and justice for all.

The earliest family record in the United States originated in South Carolina, where many Huguenots settled. According to family research, some of Elsie's descendants sailed to America on the *Globe* after a wave of Huguenot persecutions in France in 1620. Valentine Nash, Elsie's great-great-grandfather, was born in 1795. He was a farmer and merchant and married Mary Hodges Anderson. They moved to Georgia, where their daughter Elizabeth, Elsie's great-grandmother, was born. The Nash family eventually settled in Sabine Parish in west central Louisiana in the town of Many. Valentine lived to be at least ninety-five years old, and the family was well respected as original settlers in the area.

Elizabeth Nash met and married Louis Gay I, and among their eight children, Elsie's grandfather, William Hannibal Gay, was born in 1846. He served in the Confederate Army in Company H, Thirty-sixth Arkansas Infantry during the Civil War. William Gay married Elsie's grandmother, Rosa Cross, in 1872.

Rosa Cross was one of ten children born to Harris and Mary Griffy Cross. They lived in Arkansas and farmed one thousand acres of cotton, where they owned 127 slaves. They lost everything during the Civil War. In 1872, William Hannibal Gay and Rosa Cross moved to Morrilton, Arkansas, a town fifty miles northwest of present-day Little Rock. A booming railroad town, it had a population of three thousand and offered plenty of opportunities for farmers and merchants. Macie Madeline Gay, Elsie's mother, was born in December of 1876 in Morrilton. Macie's brother, Harris Hannibal, otherwise known as Bud, was born in 1880.

Macie's earliest memories, related to Elsie in later years, were visits to her wealthy uncles, Louis III and Felix, in their fancy colonial-style mansion home in Robeline, Louisiana. Felix and Louis had a thriving business in the railroad town as dealers of wines, liquors, and cigars. There were plenty of visitors and parties in the two-story, antebellum home with a veranda that wrapped around the entire house. Macie recalled her visits as an exciting time for a little girl. She remembered in particular waking up in bed while servants brought breakfast on small trays. They poured coffee with plenty of cream into a small, delicate cup.

On those occasions, Macie's father loved to dress his little girl in dresses adorned with lace and petticoats. The skirts were stiff with starch, and her father paraded her among the guests. As a young girl, Macie tasted prosperity and elegance. Her appreciation for stylish clothes and her refined manner stayed with her all of her life. Elsie recalled her mother always looked glamorous, even in the simplest of dresses, despite the hardships she later endured in her life.

Macie's father died from pneumonia at the age of thirty-six when Macie was four and Bud was three months old. William did not enjoy the financial success of his brothers and left Rosa with little monetary resources to draw upon. Work opportunities were limited for women, particularly a widow with a baby and a young daughter. One might wonder why her wealthy brothers-in-law didn't help. Maybe they did. Or maybe it was pride that forced her to remarry. Probably, it was more a matter of survival than love that prompted Macie to marry soon after her husband's death.

Elsie recalls years later that Macie and Bud only referred to their mother's second husband as "Old Smith." Smith favored his son, Leo, who Rosa bore before she died. Bud was nine and Macie thirteen when their mother died in 1889 at the age of thirty-four. Smith was a short tempered man when it came to Macie's children. Rosa could protect Bud and Macie when she was alive, but it was another matter after she died. Smith looked upon his stepchildren as extra mouths to feed, and his resentment played out in his foul temperament.

Despite the fact that Rosa's mother, Mary Griffy Cross, moved in to help with the children, Smith treated Bud like a servant, beat him on occasion, and expected him to bring in money to earn his keep. At the age of twelve, Bud quit school after the fifth grade and got a job plowing the cotton fields for five dollars a month. It was a reprieve from the misery of enduring Smith at home. Grandma Cross must have provided some buffer between Bud, Macie, and Old Smith, but life in general was wretched. Elsie was unclear as to how long Mary

Cross helped with the children, but she had enough influence to see that Macie went to school.

A young girl's education at the end of the nineteenth century prepared her for a genteel life in the home. Macie learned manners and the proper use of eating utensils. She learned elocution, the piano, and the basics of reading and writing. By the time she was twenty, Macie had the skills to become a proper wife.

In 1896, Frank Gilland, a thirty-three-year-old horse wrangler, delivered a trainload of horses from Montana to Morrilton. A tall, dark-haired man with charming airs, Frank told stories of an exciting new country open for settlement "up north" in Montana. Frank befriended Macie, and a short courtship ensued before they married on July 1, 1896. The newlyweds boarded a train to Montana. It was Macie's one-way ticket out of town.

Macie, Elsie's mother

CHAPTER 2:

Montana Bound

Parcels of land in present-day, rural Montana are oftentimes referred to by the first owner's name, which may date back to the homestead era in the early part of the twentieth century. It was a necessary point of reference to avoid confusion when land claims frequently changed ownership. Names like Aunt Mamie's Draw and Brewster Place still define a physical place regardless of the present owner. Frank and Macie's destination in southeastern Montana was Tibbit's Place. Since the 1880s, Frank Gilland had worked breaking horses for a British man named Tibbit, who had squatter's rights on a piece of land. When Tibbit left the country in 1893, Frank stayed and went into partnership with William Leitner, breaking horses. He filed for Tibbit's homestead on the Powder River, twenty-five miles south of what became the town of Broadus in southeast Montana.

When Macie and Frank came to Montana in 1896, they got off the train at Rosebud, Montana, a hundred miles from the homestead. Frank had a contract to break horses, which meant they would spend the summer at a horse camp south of Rosebud. After the contract was filled, they would move to the Powder River property and finish filing for Tibbit's Place.

Macie's first view of Montana, when she stepped off the train at the Rosebud train station next to the Yellowstone River, must have taken her breath away. The lack of population and the immense expanse of prairie and sky were in stark contrast to Arkansas. Macie and Frank climbed into a horse-drawn wagon and continued their journey to the horse camp. The trail wound its way through open grasslands and crossed shallow, muddy, creek bottoms. Sandstone rocks, eroded by wind and rain, stood like sentinels on top of the hills splashed with the bluish green hue of sagebrush, and spiky, cactus like yucca plants hinted of an arid climate.

After their arrival at the summer camp on Sweeney Creek, Macie discovered there were no neighbors or settlements nearby—just a new husband, his partner, and the horses. Elsie speculated that the sight of a large herd of horses grazing on the prairie and the sound of them galloping on the open range must surely have impressed Macie. Stunned may have been a more accurate description.

One could speculate that fear was also an initial reaction to her new home. Frank would be gone most of the daylight hours working horses. He told Macie to carry a gun when she went to get water from the creek because of Indians in the area. Just seventeen years earlier, Colonel Custer and his men had been massacred by the Sioux Indians at the Little Big Horn, fifty miles away. Despite the fact that the Indians were all on reservations, mythic fear and suspicion of their race continued. Macie carried the gun under her apron but was more afraid of the gun than the Indians.

Macie's schooling did not serve her well in Montana. She knew where eating utensils were placed on a properly set table and how to engage in dinner conversation. Marksmanship or wringing a chicken's neck was not in the curriculum of the finishing school. Macie proved to be adaptable, however, partly due to the fact that her choices were limited. Leaving her table linens and wedding dowry packed in her trunk, she set to work cooking and washing clothes in a pot on a fire pit while her husband and partner roped and broke horses one at a time throughout that first summer.

The heavy demand for horses at the turn of the century made for a lucrative business, and Frank and his partner took advantage of the bonanza. Horses were used in farming and freighting and as saddle horses, carriage horses, and cavalry. Between 1895 and 1907, hundreds of thousands of horses were sold, due in part to the Spanish American War and the Boer War in South Africa. In addition, in 1889, not only did Montana become a state, but a Montana-bred horse named Spokane won the Kentucky Derby. Everyone wanted a Montana horse. Gilland and Leitner contracted a certain amount of horses to halter break and sold them in Miles City, a bustling town on the Yellowstone River east of Rosebud that had access to the railway for shipping.

At the end of the summer, after their contract was fulfilled, Frank and Macie loaded their wagon and traveled to the Powder River Country, where they moved into Tibbit's Place. The logs were caulked with mud, and the roof was sod. Learning from other ranch women, Macie dusted calamine, a white chalky powder, on cheesecloth and hung it on the walls and from the ceiling in an attempt to make the rooms look more civilized. But when it rained, the water came through the sod roof, mixed with the calamine, and made a muddy mess. Her uncles' Southern mansion was a distant memory.

The homestead was in prime ranch country. The Powder River ambled through their claim and supported large meadows of native grasses, providing excellent grazing land. Ponderosa pine trees dotted the hillsides on either side of the river. The hills converged to form draws where chokecherry bushes, sumac, and wild plum trees grew in the folds of the earth, nourished by underground springs. Moorehead, a post office and general store, was located twelve miles from Frank and Macie's cabin. The nearest neighbor was at least that many miles away.

When Macie became pregnant that first year of their marriage, she traveled back to Morrilton for the birth of her baby. Her grandmother was there to assist in the birth, and Macie also looked forward to seeing her brother. Bud's life had not improved. Not wanting to endure life with Old Smith, he slept under house porches in Morrilton and stayed with an uncle. Macie made plans to bring Bud back to Montana.

Her first child, Frank Jr., was born in November of 1897 in Morrilton. As soon as she felt the baby was old enough for the long, train trip to Montana, Macie boarded the train in February, accompanied by Bud. Frank offered Bud a job breaking horses that summer at the horse camp on Sweeney Creek.

Bud learned quickly how to handle horses under Frank's tutelage—it was a skill that would serve him well. He became known for his riding skills all over southeastern Montana. Taking advantage of the long daylight hours, Bud and Frank spent the summer of 1898 breaking hundreds of horses. Frank promised to pay Bud twenty-five dollars per month plus room and board. At the end of the summer a Canadian buyer bought six hundred head of horses for six dollars a head. Frank and his partner collected the money, but Frank never paid Bud. Maybe Frank assumed room and board were enough pay.

After the horses were sold that fall, the family moved back to Tibbit's homestead. Frank bought horses from Granville Stuart, a noted Montana rancher, near Lewistown almost three hundred miles away. In October, Frank and Bud drove the horses from central Montana to the Powder River country, crossing the Musselshell, Yellowstone, and Tongue rivers. Bud, in desperate need of new clothes, would confiscate discarded clothing in bunkhouses at various ranches in the area as they drove the horses south. Finally, Frank gave him a few dollars when Bud pressed him. That spring, Frank promised to give Bud a raise to thirty-five dollars a month, but again, he was never paid.

Despite his less-than-generous brother-in-law, Bud flourished in the wide-open, eastern Montana country. He honed his roping skills and could ride most any horse he swung a leg over. Bud's strong work ethic in a country where horses meant money laid a sturdy foundation for his future.

Macie gave birth to her second child, Lucille, nicknamed Girlie, in August of 1899. The addition of one more child to the Gilland family was not the only major change that occurred that year. Frank's partnership with William Leitner came to an abrupt end.

Leitner discovered that Frank had sold some horses and pocketed the money without telling his partner. Horses were selling for thirty dollars a head due to the heavy demand from the Boer War being fought by the British in South Africa. Elsie imagined the contentious scene, described by her mother years later, when William Leitner arrived at the ranch after discovering the ruse: "I can imagine how mad he was at my father. I imagine it like this: He rode his horse into the yard, got off, and stood yelling for his cheating partner to come outside. 'Get out here, Frank Gilland, you lily-livered son-of-a-bitch!' He more than likely threatened to kill him. Horse thievery was a serious crime in those days." The result of the fracas was that Frank packed up his family and left Powder River Country in the fall of 1900. Before they left, Elsie's father promised to turn the deed for the ranch over to Bud and gave him, in lieu of lost wages, four cows and four calves.

CHAPTER 3:

A Lot of Trouble

In 1900, the Gillands moved from town to town, state to state, and Frank worked at whatever job interested him. They traveled by train to Cedar Rapids, Iowa, where Frank had a job breaking horses. Gold fever still burned in the West at the turn of the century as a result of discoveries in Alaska, Nevada, and Montana. In 1905, after the stint in Iowa, Frank took his family to Kendall—a gold camp in central Montana not far from Lewistown. A thriving town, Lewistown consisted of livery stables, saloons, restaurants, and hotels, all sprouting around the gold mine like mushrooms. The family lived in a tent, and Frank drove a team of horses and a wagon to Lewistown to pick up beer and deliver it to the saloons at the camp. Months later, after hearing of a new gold discovery in Tonopah, Nevada, Frank planned to try his luck at striking it rich or at least find a better job in another thriving town. Unwilling to continue this nomadic life with young children, Macie made plans to return to the ranch where Bud was running the operation without Frank's help.

They parted ways with Frank's promise to return to Powder River with his fortune. Macie bought a train ticket to Miles City and departed with her two young children. There was no regular transportation from

Miles City to the Powder River ranch. Macie had to inquire around town, in stores, and in saloons to see if anyone was going in that direction. While waiting for a ride, they stayed in a boarding house.

Soon Macie's financial reserves were falling short, and she needed money. Macie broke down in tears when explaining to Mrs. Loveridge, the woman who owned the boarding house, about her predicament. "Young woman, you're in a lot of trouble aren't you?" Mrs. Loveridge responded. "I know how you can get some money. There's a man who lives at my boarding house. He makes tamales during the day and delivers them to the saloons at night. I know he needs help making the tamales." Macie went to work making tamales and made enough money to pay for her room and food. A week later, she and her children found a ride to the ranch. After that episode, whenever Macie cooked tamales for her family, it was cause for celebration and a retelling of the lucrative tamale business in Miles City that provided money while she looked for a way home.

Frank drifted back to Powder River now and then but never with a fortune and he never stayed for any length of time. On December 4, 1907, Macie delivered a baby girl in the two-room log cabin on the ranch. She was attended by their neighbor Mrs. Yarger. Mr. and Mrs. Yarger and their family of seven children had moved from Missouri to the Powder River country earlier in the year. They buried four of their children in less than two weeks when diphtheria claimed their young lives. After Macie gave birth, Mrs. Yarger asked if she had a name in mind. When Macie said she hadn't picked a name yet, Mrs. Yarger asked if she would consider naming the baby after one of her daughters that had perished. Thus Macie named her new baby Elsie Mary Gilland. Elsie remembers visiting the gravesites of the Yarger family years later—there were markers sticking out of the earth and the plot was enclosed by barbwire to keep the cattle out.

Elsie Gilland - 1 year old

Frank's questionable business practices and itinerate lifestyle weighed heavily on Macie, and when she discovered he was also illiterate, she understood why he had not completed filing his claim on Tibbit's homestead. At some point before Elsie's birth and after Macie's return to the ranch, she completed filing the papers on the 160 acres and, remembering the promise Frank made, signed the deed over to Bud.

Frank saw Elsie for the first time when she was eighteen months old. He didn't stay long before drifting off to another boomtown, looking to strike it rich. Elsie has very few memories of her father, yet at an early age, she innately knew her father was the cause of her mother's struggles. Because of Frank's prolonged absence, Macie relied more and more on Bud for everything. She must have felt like a burden to her brother and decided to give Frank one more chance.

Macie, Frank, and the children moved to LaPine, Oregon, in one more attempt to make the marriage work, but Frank showed no signs of settling down and taking responsibility for his family. Macie finally obtained a divorce in 1911when Elsie was four years old.

Macie, just like her own mother, Rosa, found herself single with young children and no income at a time when social services were decades away. The owner of the livery stable, a man by the name of Bogue, offered to ease Macie's predicament. He volunteered to adopt Elsie. Macie must have been horrified by the proposal since the answer to Bogue was a definite and quite possibly a defiant "No!"

Elsie, about 3 years old (Holmboe Studio, Miles City, Montana)

Another man, who happened to be a widower, took an interest in Macie. He may have honestly been attracted to her, but a widower with a young son had more than romance in mind—he needed a housekeeper and a mother for his son. Frank Jr. and this man's son were the same age and did not get along. Even though he offered marriage and even if Macie had feelings for this man, her children came first. Maybe the specter of Old Smith still loomed in her memory, and she didn't want to repeat that episode with her own children. Macie opted to go back to Powder River where she would swallow her pride and look to Bud for support.

Bud recalled, in an autobiography he wrote in 1931, that when Macie and her children returned to the ranch in 1911 and looked to him for support, "it added a lot to my expenses but made me a much more comfortable home." He probably remembered his sister buying him a one-way train ticket from Arkansas to Montana, and now it was his turn to return the favor. In later years, he referred to Macie and her children as his second family.

Elsie never saw her father again. In later years, Elsie's sister, Girlie, kept in touch and visited their father. Elsie and Frank Jr., remembering the pain their father had caused their mother, never attempted any relationship with him. Elsie's father's lineage became an unknown branch on the family tree—one she never bothered to research. Elsie was asked when her father left the family, and she replied, "The answer is … he never arrived."

CHAPTER 4:

Eastern Montana Ranch Life

Bud concentrated on expanding his ranch by filing on nearby homesteads. Bud also hired out to other ranch outfits in the area—breaking horses or herding cattle and spending his hard-earned money on cows and land. Elsie recalled an early memory of her uncle rounding Bird Butte on horseback, driving a cow he had just bought. "He built up his ranch one cow at a time," she said. "And his hard work paid off. The Gay Ranch became one of the most successful ranches in the state and is still in the family over one hundred years later."

Uncle Bud on the Gay Ranch - 1930's

Macie filed on a desert claim in 1905, which Bud bought from her years later. He built a shack on the land to fulfill the legal obligations of the claim and later replaced it with a four-bedroom home when Macie and the children returned to the ranch in 1911. The terms of the desert claim required them to plow, plant, and irrigate at least twenty acres. It was the beginning of gardens in the area. Macie, with the help of Bud, planted all the vegetables they would need and canned them throughout summer and into fall. They also had a root cellar where they stored the jars of produce as well as root crops like carrots and potatoes. Frank Jr. helped his uncle on the ranch and worked for other ranchers to earn money. In the winter, he trapped coyotes and wolves and sold the pelts. Life fell into a pattern as predictable as the seasons for Bud, his sister, and her children. Work occupied a better portion of the year, but entertainment was a needed and welcome diversion.

It was miles between ranches, and social occasions were rare. People worked hard putting up hay, calving, branding, and maintaining the daily routine of an isolated ranch. So when the opportunity presented itself to hold a dance, it was a social event not to be missed. Frank and Girlie, who attended the one room school and were in the upper grades, looked forward to the dances with great anticipation. For the adults, it was a way to catch up with the neighbors and enjoy a bit of frivolity. Elsie's early memories of childhood include the country dances.

After a long summer of work, the first dance of the season was six miles away at Thoets' ranch, where a spacious barn provided dance space. It was fall, and the weather was cool. On the day of the dance, Elsie started feeling sick with a sore throat. Frank and Girlie were desperate—they knew Macie would not go if Elsie was sick, and Macie wouldn't let them go without her. Frank and Girlie begged Elsie not to tell their mother how badly she was feeling. Spurred on by underlying resentment of always being excluded from her older siblings' activities, Elsie commanded a dear price for not telling Macie about her condition. She charged Girlie a pretty hair bow, and Frank was charged a little, pearl-handled knife. Elsie thought of more booty throughout the day, and by the time the family loaded in the wagon for the dance, Elsie had not complained once and was tickled with her profitable venture. The flatbed wagon was pulled by their workhorse team, Snip and Kid. Frank and Girlie sat up on the driver's seat, and Elsie and her mother huddled under blankets on the wagon bed with their feet resting on hot rocks.

As soon as they arrived at the dance, Elsie cried and told her mother how sick she was, but there was nothing to do but lay her on a bed loaded down with coats. Macie plied Elsie with hot soup and doted on her the rest of the evening while Frank and Girlie danced the evening away.

Elsie recalled the music at the barn dances was something she would never forget—an out-of-tune violin accompanied by an out-of-tune piano or a wheezy pump organ with a guitar or two on occasion. The musicians played polkas, schottisches, waltzes, and square dances. "Turkey in the Straw," "Red Wing," and "Red River Valley," were just a few of the familiar tunes that accompanied the dancers as they twirled, clapped, and stomped despite the out-of-tune instruments. After the midnight supper, in the early hours of the morning when the musicians became tired, Elsie remembered lying on a bench, feigning sleep, and hearing the wail of the music sounding disconcertingly like coyotes in the distance.

In 1913, when she was six years old, Elsie started first grade at Bay Horse School—a one-room school across the Powder River and a mile from the ranch. Frank and Girlie rode horses to school with Elsie riding double behind Girlie. In the spring, when the river was high and difficult for a horse to navigate, they walked to school and used Frank's handmade boat to cross the river. Frank spent his spare time one summer building a boat by soaking boards in water and putting weights on them to get the right curve. His ability to use his hands to invent and fix things was a lifelong skill.

In the fall, after Bud sold the steers and old cows, they would take the wagon to Moorehead twelve miles up river to buy supplies. It was a treat for Elsie to go to the country store. She remembers big jars filled with candy that was layered with chocolate and white and pink filling. A large bin held the peanuts. The flour and sugar came in big, cotton sacks with the brand stenciled in red or black. At home, when the sacks were empty, Macie used them as dishcloths, and the stenciled lettering faded with continued use.

Planting potatoes with her uncle was a fond, childhood memory for Elsie. She treasured any time spent with Uncle Bud—maybe it was from a yearning for the father she never had. She recalls Bud with the reins to the horse loosely draped around his neck so his arms would be free to guide the plow. Elsie's role, which made her feel important and needed, was to walk about a yard behind him and drop pieces of potato into the freshly plowed ground. Bud was never hesitant to chastise her if she did something wrong and withheld any physical contact in the way of hugs or a pat on the head. Despite his lack of affection, she respected him.

Summers on the ranch were carefree for Elsie. She tagged along with her older brother and sister as often as they would allow. They would ride their horses to nearby Bloom Creek and pick buffalo berries, plums, and chokecherries and put them in used flour sacks. Macie made jellies and syrups from these native berries, and they filled the shelves in the root cellar.

When Frank was not working for Bud, young Elsie followed him like a puppy. As a result, he taught her how to shoot at an early age. Rabbits were the main targets, and they supplied the family with another source of meat. Rabbit hunting led to an interesting episode later in Elsie's life when she was a blossoming teen.

Frank also showed Elsie how to fish. He would set her up at a fishing hole while he went to another one up or down the river. Elsie had fond memories of being by the river—concentrating on casting and reeling and watching the line when a fish took the bait. She was aware of the summer sounds of the wind rustling the cottonwood leaves, the cicadas whirring, and her bait plunking on the water. Chickadees chirped in the chokecherry bushes, and meadowlarks sounded on the open meadows. Fishing had a lifelong, restorative effect on Elsie.

The ranch animals provided sustenance for the family and needed constant care. Chickens were a necessity since the hens provided eggs as well as meat. Cleaning the chicken coop was Elsie's chore—one she disliked immensely. Using old curtains that she dug out of a box, Elsie made a veil and draped it over her head, pretending she was a nun suffering penance as she performed the smelly chore. She wonders to this day how she was familiar with nuns and the concept of penance "being the heathen ranch kid that I was."

Elsie's sense of determination and fair play was shaped in her early childhood by watching her mother deal with everyday challenges. One of those challenges was milking the cows. The milk cows were not the typical Guernsey or Swiss breeds. A range cow would be designated a milk cow because it had an extra-big bag. Bud herded the recalcitrant cows back to the ranch and corralled them. A range cow had very little contact with people, so standing still and letting someone pull on her teats long enough to get a bucket of milk took some convincing. Macie had the idea that the cow would respect her more if she looked like a man. One of the few times Elsie remembered her mother wearing pants was when she milked the cows. She put on overalls and, authority in stride and bucket in hand, approached the rangy bovine, planning to intimidate the cow into submission with her manly outfit.

After she milked the cow and separated the cream from the milk, Elsie's mother made ice cream for special occasions. The ice cream was made in a bucket where everyone took turns cranking the handle until it was too hard to turn. Then they opened the lid, and Bud or Macie pulled the paddle out, dripping with ice cream. Everyone got a turn scraping the paddle clean. The effort from beginning to end was worth the results. The milk cow, according to Elsie, never did get the message of the pants: "She was ornery no matter what the mode of dress."

Elsie didn't have to put on a pair of pants to stand up to one of her classmates at the one-room school she attended on the Powder River. Elsie relayed the following story to drive home her point. "Bay Leitner was from Bay Horse Creek. Bay was an energetic, naughty boy. He teased me by pulling my curls at every opportunity. I did not take this lying down. I fought back by hitting and scratching. After one of these bouts, our teacher, Mabel Helm, took us together in a corner. She scolded us for fighting and particularly warned me of the dire consequences of blood poisoning Bay might get from my scratches. I remember glaring at Bay and thinking, 'Wait till I *really* scratch you!' I thought blood poisoning wasn't such a bad idea!"

Classmates Paul Traub, Elsie, Bay Leitner-Bay Horse School, about 1913

CHAPTER 5:

The Runaway (written by Elsie)

It was a fall day—a Saturday. Uncle Bud decided that Frank should return a plow we had borrowed from the Leitners, whose ranch was across the river and up Bay Horse Creek about four miles. Of course, I wanted to tag along. Frank asked Bud if I could go; Bud hesitated, and then said okay. I was in seventh heaven having my big brother all to myself.

Frank harnessed our team, Snip and Kid, to the wagon, and we took off. Snip and Kid were no ordinary team. They were high-spirited and hard working—beautiful, bay Belgians with black manes and tails. Frank or Bud worked them all day to plow the virgin prairie, but once they were brought back to the barn and unharnessed, they would be just as spirited and snorty as when they had left that morning. We all loved them and respected them for the work they could do and still have spirit left at the end of the day.

Frank and I crossed the river, went past our schoolhouse, and took off up Bay Horse Creek. As we neared Leitner Ranch, we had to go through a barbed wire gate. Frank put the reins around the brake, got down, opened the gate, and then took Snip by the bit to lead them through. The axle of the wagon hit one of the gateposts, and that's all it took!

Snip and Kid, startled by the sound, began to run, leaving Frank in the dust. The sense of freedom and fun increased their speed. I was terrified, and Frank was equally horrified knowing the danger I was in as he watched the team race away at top speed. I remember my reaction: The first thing I did was what I had observed the cowboys do … swear, with the same results. Then with all my eight-year-old strength, I pulled back on the reins, which didn't affect their forward momentum in the least. Snip and Kid showed no signs of slowing down. We raced across the countryside, headed for the creek bed, and all I could do was try to keep from bouncing out of the wagon. The team left the road, veered to the right, and went over the four-foot creek bank. I bounced around but stayed in the wagon. I remember the impact of the wagon swinging violently left as it hit the creek bank. They left the creek bed and continued their race on the road that, by now, was going uphill. This was my break as even Snip and Kid had to slow down. I had bounced to the back of the wagon bed, and as it slowed, I saw my chance to jump.

Meanwhile, Frank had been running at break-neck speed, spurred on by genuine fear of what would happen to me and thoughts of the raking over the coals Mother would give him. When he saw me jump, he sank down beside the road, utterly exhausted.

The team and wagon continued on to Leitner Ranch and went through the barnyard close to the house, but they had slowed considerably at this point. A dog came out, barked, and set Snip and Kid off again. They gathered speed and plunged into a muddy creek bed, where the wagon got mired in the mud, which finally stopped them.

You can imagine the excitement all this caused for the Leitners. Mrs. Leitner hugged and kissed me and said with a southern drawl, "Honey, the Lord saved you!" I was a heathen ranch kid who had never been to church and replied, "No, he didn't! Nobody saved me! I saved myself!"

Elsie, about 8 years old (Holmboe Studio, Miles City, Montana)

CHAPTER 6:

Change

Bud continued to manage and build the ranch; Macie dealt with putting food on the table and household chores. Monday was wash day, and Tuesday was ironing day. Macie would build a big fire in the stove and fill an oblong pan with water to heat on the stove. The dirty clothes were put in the boiler. She would then shave the Fels-Naptha bar soap into the boiler and stir the scalding clothes with a heavy wooden stick. The next step was to put the clothes in the washing machine—a half-barrel sitting on a pedestal with a manual crank agitator. Bluing would be added to the white clothes to make them whiter. Afterwards, the clothes were put through the wringer mounted on top of the washer and hung on the clothesline near the house.

The family had very few changes of clothes, so Macie washed them frequently, which caused them to wear out faster. The children would also outgrow their clothes, causing Macie to worry about the cost of buying more clothes. As she put the worn clothes in the boiler, Macie would mutter, "We'll give them a lick and a promise." Oftentimes, the children wore damp clothes to school because they didn't dry during the night, and there were no extra school clothes in their closet. "Mother could rub a living out of nothing," Elsie remembered.

The one-room school only went through the eighth grade. A daily commute by horse to the nearest high school was impossible due to the long distance. When Girlie graduated from the eighth grade, she went to a boarding school in Rapid City, South Dakota, and Frank worked around the different ranches instead of furthering his education.

Elsie no longer had the company of her older brother and sister on the walk to school. In the winter, Elsie's teacher, Mabel Helm, boarded with them, so during the winter months, Mabel and Elsie walked together. They made trails through the snow, and one can imagine little Elsie and her teacher chatting while they trudged along. One sunny day, a fresh snow, like a layer of goose-down feathers, covered the ground. Miss Helm surprised Elsie by flopping down on the snow. She moved her arms and legs side to side and then eased herself to a standing position. With giggles and smiles, Elsie followed suit. It was the first time she had ever made a snow angel.

In 1915, Macie had a roof over their heads and food on the table but no extra income for the other basic expenses for her family. She had to ask Bud for money to buy the necessities of clothing for her children. Elsie recalled that incident ninety years later. "One of the earliest memories I have is hearing my mother cry. Mother stood on the screened porch by the back door of our ranch house. She didn't know I was around the corner. I was frightened by the sobs that racked her body. 'I *have* to ask Bud for money. I *have* to!' I was seven years old, and despite my young age, I sensed her humiliation." Another seed was planted in Elsie's psyche during childhood and emerged in her adulthood as solid conviction: she would never rely on a man for money.

Macie began to feel like even more of a hindrance when Bud began courting Mabel, Elsie's teacher. She knew Bud's desire to have his own family, so once again, Macie was looking for options. Elsie was seven years old when Macie met Jack Miller, a nearby rancher, at a dance, and they began courting. He bought Macie gifts of clothes, and when he learned she played the piano, he bought her one. He loved Macie and genuinely wanted to make her happy. They were married in 1916, and Macie and Elsie left the ranch that had been their refuge for so many years and moved to Jack's ranch.

The first year that Macie and Jack were married, Jack sexually abused Elsie. Elsie remembered the incident with clarity. "Jack and I were in the kitchen while Mother was elsewhere in the house. I remember we were by the stove. He was holding me and began fumbling with my panties. I sensed that Jack was doing something he shouldn't be doing, and just then, Mother came into the room. She told me to go out and play." A person can only speculate what Macie did next. She probably didn't waste much time weighing the odds. She had managed as a single parent, thanks to the refuge of Bud's ranch, but now she didn't have that option to fall back on. "I'm sure Mother told him she would kill him if he ever touched me again. And he never did." There was little interaction between Elsie and Jack—Macie saw to that. Jack became a nonperson to Elsie for the rest of her life. "It was like he didn't exist," she said.

"Those early, impressionable years affected us the rest of our lives. I think a girl raised without a positive father image is left at a disadvantage when she starts to date. My Uncle Bud was a positive force in my life, but he never hugged me. I had no physical contact with him. And then came Jack. … I've asked myself why Mother stuck with him, but Jack had given her the only security after years of insecurity. After we moved to Seattle, he would bring his paycheck home and hand it over to Mother. She stuck with him even after the neighbor ladies came to her house and told her of Jack's pedophilic ways. Her decision to stay with him reinforced in my mind that I would *never* rely on a man for money." Self-reliance became Elsie's mantra.

Elsie began the path to womanhood at an early age, and she remembers the experience with clarity. "I began my menstrual periods when I was eleven. I remember how startled I was when I saw blood on my long johns. Of course, I asked Mother what was happening. She didn't offer any satisfactory explanation whatsoever. I wonder if this was customary for that time? How backwards such a situation was—not explaining to me what was happening in my body. I went through all the major things that most young women go through with cramps and depression—I just dreaded the whole set up.

Elsie in a WWI uniform (Anderson Studio, Miles City, Montana)

"Tampons were not available until the late 1920s, so we used cloths or rags and soaked them in a jar with cold water before putting them in the washing machine. It was quite a process. We folded the rags and safety pinned them in front and back to an elastic band we called a belt. I sewed the belt so it would fit around my waist." With the arrival of puberty, more changes were in store for Elsie.

Her nuclear family was growing and changing. Girlie married a local rancher and lived in Eastern Montana all her life. Frank worked on the ranch for his Uncle Bud, which he thought he would do the rest of his life. It shocked him to realize that Bud wanted his own family and the ranch. Elsie found out later that Bud suspected Frank had some of the same unscrupulous characteristics of their father. Distrust in Frank's character was something Bud couldn't shake. There would be no room for Frank on the ranch, so he left for Chicago to break horses during World War I. He joined the navy when he was eighteen and traveled the world. Perhaps Bud's instincts were right. Frank developed problems with gambling and went from one bad business venture to the next. He was obsessed with money, which Elsie blamed on watching their mother struggle with financial security. Elsie was loyal to Frank his entire life just as Macie was loyal to her own brother. Loyalty in Elsie's family was quite possibly born from adversity.

Elsie graduated from the eighth grade when she was twelve years old. Macie, not willing to send her off to a boarding school and always protective of her youngest child, decided that she and Elsie would move to Miles City for her high school years.

Teen-aged Elsie sitting on Uncle Bud's porch

CHAPTER 7:

Miles City High School Years

Elsie was twelve years old when she started high school in Miles City in the fall of 1920. Skipping a grade at the one-room school may have been convenient for the teacher, but it propelled Elsie out of childhood and into puberty. Maybe for that reason, Macie decided Elsie was too young to attend a boarding school like her older sister.

Macie rented an apartment in Miles City and worked numerous jobs to supplement their income during Elsie's high school years. One job involved cooking and cleaning for two bachelors who owned a hotel on Seventh Street and the movie theater on Main. Elsie explained, "They were certainly entrepreneurs, devising all sorts of schemes to make money. One plan they devised was an inducement to get people to come to the movie by having a drawing for a live chicken. The drawing was rigged of course. They drew the ticket stub, and lo and behold, it was my number! I remember walking down the aisle, presenting my ticket, and being handed a squawking chicken. It ended up in Mother's cook pot for the two young men, Mother, and me to eat the next day. I've never entirely believed in raffles as a result."

With the new decade that became known as the Roaring Twenties, the Victorian Age was ending, and young women were becoming liberated. An advertisement for a movie in the 1924 high school newspaper showed a seductress with her dress strap falling off her shoulder while she smoked a cigarette. Elsie started smoking in her high school years—a habit that would continue for thirty years. She and her friends smoked punk—a dried wood with a very acrid smelling smoke. "We would also sneak tobacco, bags of Durham, from grownups. I learned at a very early age to roll my own cigarettes. Mother disapproved, but I was determined to smoke and did so secretly."

Clothing styles changed dramatically during the decade of the twenties. Girls rolled down silk stockings that accented knee high skirts. Short, bobbed hair replaced long locks. Movie stars began to set the fashion, and teenagers, as usual, mimicked the big city trends. "We wore unfastened overshoes, hence the term 'flappers.'"

Women were becoming liberated in other ways besides hairstyles and dress. In 1920, the Nineteenth Amendment was ratified to the U.S. Constitution, which guaranteed women in every state the right to vote. Women had been given that right in Montana in 1914. Elsie remembered her mother voting for the first time: "She squared her shoulders and said with a great deal of pride, 'I voted today.' Women nationwide could vote, and they were no longer second class citizens." Her mother's pride planted another seed in Elsie's life that blossomed into political activism later in her life.

Elsie hung out with a gang of friends, not unlike today's teens, but she had to reacquaint herself with her classmates every fall because in the summer, Macie and Elsie returned to Jack's ranch. Yet she never had trouble making friends. "I got good grades, not excellent, but good. I participated in basketball in school." A yellowed high school newspaper that she saved for eighty years tells more. According to her senior high school newspaper, the *Spotlight*, Elsie belonged to chorus and participated in class plays. *Prince Charmin* and *Maid on the Bamboo Screen* were two such plays. The annual dance, called the Hop, where girls wore taffeta and lace, took place in the spring. The paper documents more than Elsie remembers. The class prophecy noted Elsie's long, naturally curly hair: "Elsie Gilland is another expert in the world of beauty, endeavoring to teach the art of the permanent curl." Elsie did not follow the bobbed hairstyle until after high school. That may have been the reason "Elsie Gilland's quaint Quaker ways" were willed to Agnes Nugent, an underclassman in the 1924 school newspaper. Her curls are evident in her senior class picture, where she's looking directly at the camera with dark curls spilling down her neck.

1924 Senior Picture, Custer County District High School, Miles City, Montana

Through the eyes of a young girl from an isolated ranch, Miles City was a lively, exciting place. There were a multitude of saloons that had grown up with the town, dating back to the end of Custer's Battle of the Little Big Horn when Ft. Keogh was established. Miles City sported a movie theater, corner grocery stores, clothing and hardware stores, and drug stores with soda and ice cream counters. There were Ford Model T cars co-mingling with horse-drawn wagons, and in the winter, there was an ice skating rink where Elsie remembers placing crack the whip with her friends. It was a big city for Elsie.

One Sunday, sitting in the Presbyterian Church, Elsie's mind began to wander. She looked around and realized everyone was Caucasian—not only in church but in the entire town. She remembered her uncle and mother telling stories of the black people that populated Morrilton, and she wondered why there were none in Miles City. While the pastor's sermon droned on, Elsie was lost in her own imagination and remembered family stories. She tried to visualize the black woman that suckled her mother and Bud when they were babies. She pictured a large, kindly woman with the little white baby at her breast. Elsie puzzled at her mother and Bud's derogatory remarks about all black people. She remembered the story her mother told of going to Morrilton to visit relatives, and a black woman noticed Macie and called her by name. "Macie, I remember you when you were a baby. I had you on one side and my own Sadie on the other," and she laughed and laughed. Macie related her humiliation by the woman's air of familiarity, as if they were related. Elsie imagined herself being born black. Would her mother have given her away? Instead of being influenced by her mother and uncle's negative prejudices, it only sparked Elsie's curiosity.

Elsie's curiosity about the world may have begun with a prune peddler. "In the fall, a prune peddler came in a horse-drawn wagon to the ranches along the Powder River, selling his wares. His wagon was set up as a display and storage space for dried apples, apricots, and prunes and spices like cloves, allspice, and cinnamon. The smells were heavenly inside that wagon. The peddler was Lebanese and as exotic looking as the spices he sold. I was mesmerized by this foreigner. And I wondered … where did he come from? I wanted to go there!" Elsie was ready to venture out of the corner of the world where she spent her childhood. Miles City was merely a stepping stone.

Throughout Elsie's high school years, Jack dealt with the consequences of a prolonged drought followed by the terrible winter of 1921–22. Her Uncle Bud stepped in to help one year by buying a house for Macie and Elsie to live in during the school year. Jack borrowed money to buy hay at exorbitant prices. In March, after the cows ate all the expensive hay, a spring snowstorm blanketed the new grass with deep, heavy snow. Most of the cows died. Jack, along with many ranchers in the area, faced financial ruin when the banks foreclosed on him. Jack lost the ranch the year Elsie graduated from high school in 1924.

Economic circumstances triggered the move that started Elsie's journey far from the Powder River country. After sixteen-year-old Elsie graduated, Jack, Macie, and Elsie packed their few belongings and boarded a train for Thermopolis, Wyoming. Jack had developed arthritis, and he was hoping the hot springs at Thermopolis would provide relief. Upon arriving, Macie immediately found a job managing a number of apartments. Jack started a job working in the oil fields, and Elsie found employment working as a maid at a big hotel. Although she hated the job itself, that first paycheck marked her start in obtaining financial independence.

Part Two—Now And Then

CHAPTER 8:

Coming of Age

Meeting with Elsie

Our meetings took on a regular pattern. I sat on the floor with my notebooks and tape recorder while Elsie sat on her sofa. There were times when her descriptions of events and details from my research created vivid scenes in my imagination. One particular day, I came armed with notes I had taken at the Miles City Library, where I had read 1920 newspapers on microfilm. I was hoping to jar her memory with details of the time. I commented on all the advertisements for movies.

Elsie replied, "Of course, they were silent movies then. The talkies didn't come out until the end of the decade. That's where we went to hear live music. I admired those screen-side pianists. It was usually a woman piano player, and she sat under the stage watching the film and playing the piano at the same time, matching the music to the action."

"And the movie stars," I said as I leafed through my notes. "Dorothy Gish starred in a film called *Little Miss Rebellion.* There were movies called *Sinners in Silk* and *Forbidden Fruit.*"

I read to her an ad I had copied down: "'Brilliant men, beautiful jazz babies, champagne baths, midnight revels, petting parties in the purple dawn, all ending in one terrific smashing climax that makes you gasp.' Whew!" I said, "That's steamy stuff!"

Elsie smiled and nodded her head as she said, "Rudolph Valentino was in a movie called *The Sheik.*" She rolled her eyes in a swoon. "Now wait a minute … I just thought of something. James Joyce. This talk about actors reminded me." She continued, "You must remember how backward our country was intellectually, and still is, I suppose," her shoulders shook with laughter. Then her eyes narrowed, and she leaned toward me. "We, *our country*, banned James Joyce's books. No book company could sell his books. Now check that out dear, when you're at the library. No one could buy his books because of explicit sexual writing." She paused to catch her breath. "Now you think of abortion."

"Whoa, Elsie, slow down! What are you getting at?"

"You've been listening to the news … how they're trying to ban abortions in South Dakota? And if they do, you can bet they will challenge Roe vs. Wade! Can you imagine?" Her voice rose in pitch and her dark eyes flashed in my direction. "We've gone *backwards* in this country as far as women's rights." Her mind was racing now, and my pen was flying as I tried to keep up with her.

"My mother instilled in me at an early age a sense of dignity. She was a very sensible, realistic woman, but she was also very much a product of her time." Elsie continued, indirectly steering toward the present. "In those days, women were so fouled up because they had this idea that was pounded into their head from the time they were tiny girls that they were here to please men. Their main objective of growing up was to learn how to keep a house and learn about the rudiments of raising children. A girl's whole objective in life was not to develop themselves but to please somebody else. Well, if we are not vigilante, we'll lose what we have gained regarding women's rights!" She sat back against the orange cushions slightly winded. "Oh, and by the way, remind me to tell you about my mother's corsets."

Another pattern to our conversations was established. As she remembered details of the past, not necessarily in chronological order, the present swirled in the mix. Current events were being defined by the historical context of the past century with the clarity of her own experience.

* * * * *

The hot pools of Thermopolis, Wyoming, attracted people for therapeutic relief from rheumatism and arthritis. The hot, underground water was piped into a big outdoor pool as well as into smaller rooms. In the rooms, people sat in pools, not much bigger than a bathtub, shrouded in heavy steam, and the smell of earthy minerals penetrated the air. The only sounds were drips from the ceiling and an occasional splash as someone shifted position. Twenty minutes was as much as a person could handle before taking leave of the soggy heat and jumping into the outdoor pool, which shocked every bodily pore awake. However, when Elsie recalled Thermopolis in the 1920s, it was not the hot pools with their purported curative effects that made the biggest impression.

Elsie arrived in Thermopolis ready to fully experience this Wyoming town. She befriended a Jewish girl her own age, and the two girls were often mistaken for sisters. Elsie's facial features were similar to her Jewish friend's—she had dark eyes and hair and a prominent nose that accentuated her cheekbones. This would be the first, but not last, time that Elsie was taken to be Jewish. "The family fascinated me. They were different from anyone I had ever met. The food they ate seemed so strange with unfamiliar spices. They even talked a little differently. I was intrigued." The lure of the mysterious prune peddler that came to the Powder River country continued to lead Elsie on a road of discovery.

One of the first summers they were in Thermopolis, Jack, Macie, and Elsie found higher paying jobs at the Black Mountain oil field about thirty miles from town. Macie and Elsie cooked for the fifteen-person crew. Everyone lived in temporary bunkhouses, so entertainment that far from town was left to the imagination.

Elsie was the only young woman for miles. Her ranch upbringing familiarized her early on with an array of men, from her brother and uncle to the area cowboys. She felt the same ease in their presence as she did in the shade of a cottonwood tree on a hot day.

Her curly auburn hair cut in a bob, flashing dark eyes, and emerging femininity surely must have caused more than one head to turn among the oil crew, and Elsie knew it. "I loved being made a fuss over and was conscious of their lustful looks in my direction." The crew adopted her as their mascot and even bought her some work clothes to wear—khaki pants and a work shirt. The same working clothes the men wore.

Elsie, about 19 years old

Living on the prairie was second nature to Elsie, and she never lacked for something to do. It was almost as if she was back on the ranch, roaming the draws and river bottom of the Powder River. She acquired a .22 rifle and spent summer evenings hunting rabbits. Eventually, one of the men on the crew asked to accompany her on a rabbit hunt.

"He was a fellow in his forties, which I thought was very old, but he was rather good looking. You can imagine what happened. My curiosity got the best of me, and at that age, I was very curious about sex."

It was easy to imagine the scene: The setting sun illuminated the dusty blue sagebrush as the older man and young woman walked the prairie land. Katydids chirred with the heat of the summer evening. A killdeer skimmed above the grass, calling the intruders away from her nest. Elsie toted a gun but soon lost interest in the dash of a rabbit. They probably talked about guns and hunting as they strolled through the tall prairie grasses. The conversation meandered toward sex. They paused at a small coulee, where branches of a cottonwood tree embraced their intentions by providing a haven of sorts. He politely asked her if she wanted to, and she said yes.

"It was all very considerate, and I looked on it as an adventure. I had no romantic feelings for him, just curiosity about sex. We did meet one other time in Thermopolis at his house. I liked it much better in a bed!"

After summer, Macie insisted Elsie attend the University of Wyoming in Laramie. Macie's life had resonated with struggles for self-sufficiency, and by now, her own path was determined, but she wanted to provide her daughter with a different one. Higher education, Macie reasoned, would give Elsie more options for employment. Elsie lived in a dorm and attended the university for two years. "That's when I really started reading good literature. It was my favorite class as a result of a good teacher. Math gave me problems, and I think that was a result of skipping a grade early on in my schooling. And I remember having many boyfriends." Elsie quit after two years of college despite her mother's protests. Elsie had her sights set on a regular job, a steady paycheck, and financial independence. Change, mixed with a touch of rebellion, defined not only Elsie, but the decade of the twenties.

The nation moved into the twenties with moonshine in hand and hemlines on the rise. Prohibition went into effect in 1920. The Volstead Act enforced President Hoover's Eighteenth Prohibition Amendment, which was deemed "a great social and economic experiment, noble in motive."[2] Yet despite the prohibition law that made it illegal to barter, transport, import, export, deliver, furnish, or possess alcohol, the law was flagrantly violated by a great many people. Americans bought portable stills from any hardware store and converted fermented mash—a yeasty concoction consisting of anything from barley to potato peelings—into their own booze. Elsie, in her early twenties, joined in the frivolity. She marveled at those days as she remembered, "It's a wonder people didn't go blind, given the stuff they made the liquor from! We would go outside the dance hall when the band took a break and share mickeys, which were small bottles of bootleg liquor. If you want to make something popular, just ban it!"

In Elsie's mind, the corset was a symbol of women's confinement. As a little girl, she remembered pulling hard on the laces of her mother's corset—pulling it as tight as she could—while her mother held on to a table or chair. In the twenties, progressive women shed their girdles and loosed the laces of their corsets to shimmy to the new dances. It was the Jazz Age.

Elsie recalled visiting a friend whose older sister played the piano. "Say, listen to this song. It's the new kind of music, and everybody is dancing to it!" the girl said. She broke into a ragtime piano piece and then jumped up and started dancing, shimmying from head to toe and swinging her legs. "It's a new dance. Everybody's doing it!" The unrestrained movement that accompanied the jazzy sounds of the Charleston and the Black Bottom appeared uncivilized to the older generation, while the younger generation, Elsie's generation, embraced it with a ferocity that spread coast to coast.

The famous misquote of President Calvin Coolidge in 1925—"The business of America is business"[3]—seemed to carry some truth in historical hindsight. Improved technology coupled with electricity heightened production rates. "Buy now, pay later" resounded the mantra of the day. Big business rode the surge of capitalism. Through mergers and acquisitions, the first chain stores opened up, including Walgreen Drug Stores and Woolworths.[4] The business landscape became a monopoly of giant corporations that owned railroads and public utilities, which paid big profits in return. Personal debt overtook income.

The booming economy targeted women through new magazines and glossy advertisements. *Reader's Digest, Good Housekeeping, Ladies Home Journal, New Yorker,* and *Time,* as well as true confession magazines, found their way into Victorian parlor rooms for the first time. The magazine images highlighted just one of many ways a woman could explore the meaning of liberation. With a steady job and regular paycheck, Elsie embraced the new styles and fads with enthusiasm.

The economic and political developments of the twenties set the stage for the next decade where Elsie's life would take a radical turn. All over the country, the gap between the rich and the poor widened.

Drought and recession kept the good times from reaching the back roads of America, where half of the population still lived on farms. On the growing industrial scene, despite the fact that companies were making great profits, 5 percent of the population was taking home one-third of the nation's personal income, yet 40 percent of wage earners in the country were earning less than two thousand dollars a year.[5] Coal miners made two dollars a day, and John L. Lewis, president of the United Mine Workers of America, pressed for a militant union despite the government and industrialists branding unions as un–American.[6]

An influx of working class immigrants after WWI alarmed the status quo. The American Legion declared its goal as 100 percent American. A. Mitchell Palmer, the U.S. attorney general, stated, "Too many people have free speech in this country,"[7] referring to the rising voices of workers making demands for better working conditions. In the United States, unions were suspect of being Communist. Elsie, however, was oblivious to the undercurrents of discontent in the nation, which would later direct her life.

After two years in Thermopolis, Macie, Jack, and nineteen-year-old Elsie had saved enough money to continue their journey westward. The booming lumber and fish industries of the Northwest promised employment. In 1926, with enough money in the bank for a down payment on a house, they boarded a train in Thermopolis. Destination: Seattle.

CHAPTER 9:

Ain't We Got Fun?

Meeting with Elsie

After meeting for about a month, we spent several hours one particular afternoon sorting through Elsie's memory until we were both tired. I closed my notebook and put my pen away. Mia, Elsie's cat, wandered into the living room and leapt onto her usual spot on the sofa next to Elsie, who sat in silence with her hands folded prayerlike on her lap. As I stood up, she inhaled audibly, and on the exhale, she said, "Now, did I tell you I was married?"

I stopped and stared at her. "No … you've never mentioned a husband." She had no family photos on her walls, only collected art from San Francisco and her foreign trips. There was no marital evidence in the box I lugged home. "How long were you married?" I asked.

"Twenty-eight years."

I was shocked. That is a long time to be married and not mention him until now. "What was his name?"

"Ernest." She said his name as if it were a stone she let drop from the vault of her memory. She stood, walked to the door, and opened it for me while I stepped over the threshold.

"Well, good-bye dear. I so enjoyed our visit this afternoon." I heard the door shut gently behind me. Ernest would have to wait.

* * * * *

Jack and Macie found a small house in a working-class neighborhood twenty miles from Seattle in an area called Richmond Highlands. Jobs were not hard to find. Elsie found work as a waitress in a café above a drug store on Pike Street—the main street of downtown Seattle at the time. She rode the interurban trolley to and from work.

The café catered to blue collar working men and featured lunch and dinner. Elsie had grown to like a man's attention, but not the kind she found as a waitress. To "make time," the men pinched her too familiarly, and she found their conversation banal and comments lewd. Entering the kitchen made her job more stressful. For sport, the Filipino cooks threw their knives back and forth to each other. Elsie found herself ducking not only their knives but their caustic remarks as well. If she complained to her boss, she risked being fired. There were women on a waiting list for jobs like Elsie's. The situation convinced her to look for an office job.

Elsie enrolled in a night school to improve her shorthand. After filling out an application at the employment agency, she found work in a business office doing stenographic services for a variety of businessmen. One of the businessmen, Tom Jones Parry, owned an advertising agency and offered Elsie a job when he moved to another building. "He was one of the most charming men I've met in my life. I was quite taken with him, not in any romantic sense, but just as an individual. He treated me with the utmost consideration. For example, he would say, 'Miss Gilland, when you have a moment, please come into my office.' I worked for him for fourteen years and became his right-hand assistant."

Elsie, about 22 years old

The wages were good; she loved her job and never returned to school. With her first paycheck, she proudly bought her mother a sewing machine stand. She also opened up a charge account at the best department store in Seattle. Elsie spent part of her hard-earned money on stylish outfits and, for the rest of her life, wore clothes like a badge of independence.

Parry involved Elsie in decision-making aspects of the business. When a new account arrived, they discussed the product and designed the container, advertisements for newspapers and magazines, and even billboards and radio announcements. Elsie recalled, "I loved the creative part and even got to name a candy bar. I called it a Pick-Me-Up, and we advertised it as an energy builder. I even designed the wrapper for it." The burgeoning advertisement business encouraged the nation to buy. "It really is a fascinating business. I remember some of those catchy slogans: 'Next to myself, I like BVDs the best.' Now that is clever. Here's another one: 'Nothing runs like a Deere' or 'Promise her anything but give her Arpege.' It was an exciting, innovative time." Elsie's job was not the only exciting element of her life in 1927.

Prohibition gave rise to speakeasies. Elsie had many dates, usually to a "joint" in someone's house or apartment, where they drank bootleg liquor and danced to live music. A popular song of that time summed it up: "in the mean time, in between time, ain't we got fun!"

Elsie was financially independent and enjoying her work and a full social life. Macie, on the other hand, viewed each boyfriend as a potential husband and was impressed with one in particular. He was a doctor and considerably older than Elsie. "He appealed to Mother because of his social status, which was the furthest thing from my mind. However, he turned me off completely by telling me how great he was in bed. Incidentally, I never found out."

Elsie got pregnant when she was in her early twenties. Alcoholic beverages were legal in Canada, where she and her date and another couple went for a weekend fling. "I didn't particularly care for this young man. He was just a 'good time Charlie.' I knew I was pregnant from the onset. Of course, I had no intention of telling my partner. It was my problem, and I had to solve it. My only thought was to get an abortion. I knew of a medical doctor who performed abortions on the side. I could afford it and made the arrangements. I realize now how fortunate I was to be able to afford a capable doctor unlike poorer women who had to resort to drastic, and often fatal, measures. I know the doctor who helped me had a thriving business on the side doing abortions, and I was much more careful after that."

Elsie's memory of standing behind a curtain when she was a little girl and listening to the story of a neighbor lady hemorrhaging from a self-induced abortion came to the fore when confronted with her own abortion. "Little pictures have big ears," said Elsie. "The women were gossiping about a neighbor woman who had five children and was worn out from it. She was determined to not have any more children, so if she got pregnant, she would abort herself using a pen with a metal quill. She would hemorrhage to the point that every time she took a step, there was a pool of blood. Her husband would then take her to the nearest hospital, which was in Miles City. You can imagine how horrified I was as I listened to these women." The memory was still clear ninety years later.

Before the nineteenth century, Protestants and Catholics allowed abortions until quickening—the moment the fetus became a living organism. The Catholic Church considered forty days from conception as quickening for boys and eighty days for girls.[8] Abortion was commonplace in the United State during the nineteenth century. There were no laws against abortions in the first trimester of pregnancy or until quickening. Full-time abortionists worked in cities—two thousand alone in New York City. More women died in childbirth than the result of an abortion. Before the mid- and late-nineteenth century, the primary health care givers for women were midwives. Eventually, medical care for women moved into the hands of male doctors and so did laws regarding birth control.

Elsie, being sexually active by choice, encountered the difficulty of obtaining birth control for women in an age where laws, determined by paternal congressmen, governed morality. The Comstock law, written by Anthony Comstock from Connecticut, was approved in 1873. Known as an anti-obscenity bill, it regarded any information about birth control as lewd and illicit. Sending contraceptives or any type of information involving birth control through the mail was a crime. Connecticut passed further laws stating that married couples could be jailed for using birth control.[9]

In 1905, when women were beginning to gain a better understanding of conception and birth control, President Theodore Roosevelt attacked birth control. Factories and industries, as well as new farming territories, needed workers. Roosevelt described smaller families as decadent and a sign of moral disease just when waves of immigrants moved into the country from Europe, lured by the promise of a better life. U.S. citizens believed the immigrants were a threat to job security, and their new ideas and strange food, clothing, and traditions were suspect. American families were encouraged to have more children to prove their patriotism. Women's primary social duty became that of motherhood.

Women had gained the right to vote, but liberation was a long time coming. Elsie held in high esteem, and still does, the women pioneers who dedicated their lives to making women's lives better. She spoke of the suffragists with the same admiration she held for Margaret Sanger and the congresswoman from Montana, Jeanette Rankin.

Early suffragists were outraged when moral reformers spoke against abortion and birth control while social moralists preached that sex within marriage was immoral if making babies wasn't the objective. Sex for pleasure was as wrong within marriage as without. Margaret Sanger led the revolution and inspired many young women of the day, like Elsie Gilland, to participate in the charge for change.

Margaret Sanger, born in 1879, had watched her mother die a slow death due to eighteen pregnancies, eleven of which were full-term. Sanger, a nurse, worked with poor women on the Lower East Side in New York City. She tried to save the life of a young woman bleeding to death from an attempted abortion. Sanger saw the grave injustice of the lack of healthcare and birth control for poor people. Wealthy women could afford birth control devices sold in stores and listed as feminine hygiene.[10] Sanger began her crusade for birth control, specifically opposing the Comstock law.

"We didn't have the convenience of the pill like women have now," said Elsie. "We used diaphragms. A doctor fit you, and then you would spread lubricant on it and insert it with a long-handled device. Birth control has always been a struggle for women."

In 1916, Margaret Sanger went to jail for telling women about diaphragms. Yet, while in prison, she continued to educate more women about birth control. Sanger and her husband owned the oil lubricant company Three-In-One and began manufacturing the lubricant necessary for diaphragms. By 1925, she had founded the first U.S. company to manufacture diaphragms. Sanger had a box of diaphragms mailed from Japan to a doctor in the U.S., but it was confiscated under the Comstock law. Sanger took it to court, and in the case *United States v. One Package,* Judge Augustus Hand, a judge with the U.S. Circuit Court of Appeals, ruled the box could be legally delivered. The Comstock law weakened but stayed on the books until the mid 1960s when it went to the Supreme Court. In *Griswold v. Connecticut,*[11] the court's decision, based on a right to privacy guaranteed by the Bill of Rights, nullified the Comstock law on June 7, 1965. Yes, indeed, "birth control has always been a struggle for women"!

Elsie joined the ranks of the suffragists in spirit and recognized that change came from the demands of those that needed it most, and change was just around the corner. The decade of the twenties was about to slam into a new decade—the thirties.

CHAPTER 10:

Gone Red

Meeting with Elsie

I pressed the doorbell and heard Elsie's voice: "Come in, dear." She was expecting me, so the door was unlocked, and I walked in. "You should have gotten here a few minutes earlier. You could have seen me in action." She held up the newspaper and shook it. "I called our congressman and governor about this prescription drug business that's going on, which is only going to hurt senior citizens." An index card sat next to the telephone. The large print spelled out the names of legislators, congressmen, and the governor with their phone numbers. I took the paper from her to read the headlines, but she was ready to start working. "Now then, I have some exciting news. When my housekeeper was cleaning, we found this box of pictures I had forgotten about. There might be some good photos for the book."

She sat on the edge of the sofa and eagerly watched me open the box. I had seen very few pictures of Elsie from the thirties and forties. I leafed through the black and white photographs of the Great Wall of China, rivers, buildings, but there were very few people. "Oh, those are my brother's albums—photos of the places he went to when he was in the navy. I guess it wasn't such a find after all."

Then I picked up some loose photos at the back of one of the albums. I recognized a middle-aged Elsie sunbathing beside a pool and another photo of a man with some Chinese officials. I picked up a black and white photograph of Elsie and the same man on a sailboat. "Is this a picture of Ernest?" She took the photo, went straight to her reader, and positioned it under the magnifier. She steadied the glass over the man and gazed at the image for several moments.

"Huh. I didn't know I had these." She reached up and clicked the reader off. "Yes, that's Ernie." She walked briskly back to the sofa and changed the subject before I could inquire any further about this man, Ernie, her husband of twenty-eight years.

* * * * *

The crash of Wall Street on October 24, 1929, triggered the end of a rip-roaring good time in the nation. Along with the rest of the country, the advertising business that Elsie worked for in 1931 was struggling to survive. Elsie's boss was forced to let all of his employees go except Elsie. At the end of each week, Tom Parry and Elsie would decide how much money each of them needed to take home. He had a wife and two young children. Jack and Macie had lost their jobs and relied on Elsie's paycheck. Elsie and Parry divided the money according to their respective needs for that particular week. It was an unusual arrangement, but Parry was an extraordinary man. Elsie would never forget his generosity and sense of fairness. They were the lucky ones.

One dreary, rainy day, Elsie left the office and walked to the bank to make a rare deposit. On her way back, she found herself on the periphery of a demonstration thousands of people thick, all marching with handmade signs that stated, "We Want Food." She remembers the scene vividly: "Everything was gray—the sky, the streets and buildings, and the people marching … all gray." A gloom had settled on the world.

"I was stunned to see such desperation. They were demonstrating for food! How could this be? One day we were on top of the world; the next day we were at the bottom of the heap. They were marching simply for food. I went back to the office sobbing."

This was a turning point in Elsie's life. "I had never really thought seriously about economic issues until then. I found myself asking some serious questions. What had happened to cause all this misery? I wanted to understand how we, the people of this country, went from prosperity to despair almost overnight. I remember thinking … the fish are still swimming around in the ocean; the trees are still growing in the forest. The workers are still here, but they don't have jobs." Some of Elsie's neighbors—working class people—were being evicted from their homes due to bank foreclosures. Transitory towns, nicknamed Hoovervilles, constructed of scrap material, wood, and collected cardboard, sprang up within the city to house the newly homeless. Elsie asked herself, "What has stopped production, shut down factories, and put so many people out of work?"

The 1932 Bonus March was another event that turned Elsie's life toward politics. One evening, Elsie went to a movie—a diversion from the glumness of the day for millions of Americans, especially since movie theaters had become wired for sound in 1927. The movie may have been *City Lights* starring Charlie Chaplin, which humorously dealt with unemployment problems, or it could have been the fanciful drama *King Kong,* featuring Fay Wray or possibly Cole Porter's *The Gay Divorce*. Before the main feature, the audience watched the usual newsreel that reported newsworthy events around the nation. That evening, the Bonus March was headline news. The audience watched as the newsreel played out. U.S. infantry in tanks and trucks rolled down Pennsylvania Avenue in Washington DC. Soldiers on horseback wore gas masks and were armed with bayonets and sabers. Gas grenades were launched at World War I veterans and their families, which caught their temporary shacks on fire.

Desperate times preempted the scene unfolding on the big screen that night. In the summer of 1932, twenty thousand WWI vets from all over the country had camped out on Anacostia Flats—vacant land near the White House—and demanded the passage of the Veterans Bill. Rumors were circulating that these veterans were part of a Communist conspiracy. The Senate defeated the Veterans Bill, calling for the veteran's immediate dispersal.

Eight thousand veterans remained after the bill was defeated, so President Hoover gave the order to forcibly remove them. General Douglas MacArthur and his aide, Major Dwight Eisenhower, and Major George Patton led the charge. Hundreds were injured and a baby died. The *New York Times* reported the event the next day: "Flames rose high over the desolate Anacostia flats at midnight tonight and a pitiful stream of refugee veterans of the World War walked out of their home of the past two months, going they knew not where."[12] In subsequent years, the veterans continued their fight, meeting at the capitol every summer until public sentiment backed their demands. The Bonus March demands were finally met in 1936, laying the groundwork for the G.I. Bill of Rights, which was passed in 1941.[13]

Elsie recalled, "The scene of the federal government turning on its own veterans is a chilling memory, and I have never forgotten it. I don't remember what the feature movie was, but I do remember leaving the movie theater stunned. The veterans had to rise up before the government paid any attention to them. All the veterans since that time have benefited from their activism, resulting in the G.I. Bill. I'm telling you … change comes from the people. *That* is democracy." Elsie was searching for answers to troubled times—both then and now.

Franklin Delano Roosevelt won the presidential election in 1932 on a progressive platform to create jobs and relieve the country's problems. The following spring, the banking system collapsed nationwide after customers withdrew their funds en masse and hundreds of thousands of people demanded their withdrawals in gold. In Washington State on March 3, 1933, Governor Clarence Martin issued a proclamation closing all banks statewide in order to protect its gold reserves. The closure was called a "bank holiday" and forty-eight states did the same in the next few days. Checks, including payroll, could not be cashed. Only cash was accepted as payment for goods.[14]

Elsie's boss told her to take the day off. "I went home and couldn't think of anything to do but sweep the floor. I had the radio on and listened to FDR's speech, explaining why he closed the banks and that we, as a people, need to have faith and not fear. You know," said Elsie, "my family never went hungry in the Depression, unlike so many people. I always had a job. But the fear of hunger is almost worse than hunger itself. I cried while I swept the floor." The bank holiday in Seattle lasted eleven days.

Elsie went to the public library looking for answers. The librarian directed her to the world economics section. She sat at a small, wooden table and started reading, skimming the contents as she perused her pile of books. Then she came to a small, black book entitled *The Communist*

Manifesto by Karl Marx. "I was fascinated. I read about how world economies change whenever the means of production changes. I read about class struggle and the capitalist system that resulted in more inequality than equality. In this book, Marx predicted what would happen with the development of capitalism and the signs to look for in its demise."

Karl Marx radicalized Elsie Gilland that day in the Seattle library. She determined that the capitalist system was at fault—it failed to provide basic care for the elderly and the poor. It did not create jobs during times of economic depression. The capitalist system assembled the shacks in Hooverville and left cities of hungry people ravenous for change. For Elsie, the manifesto began to articulate the answers to all of her why's, but most of all, it presented a feeling of hope. I could imagine her sitting in the library that day where she lost track of time—immersed in reading as the windows blackened and a single light bulb hung from the ceiling and cast more shadow than light.

Elsie leaned over her book and read that with the demise of capitalism, a socialist system would follow and provide economic equality for all people. It started to make sense. She thought of her mother who struggled as a single parent on the ranch in Montana to provide for her young children. She thought of the ranch woman in need of health care, who risked her life to end a pregnancy. Elsie reflected on that day in the Seattle library eighty years later: "I saw everything falling apart around me in 1932. Hoover kept promising that things would get better, that big business success would 'trickle down' to the people. It's the same thing eighty years later. Like the houses in Hooverville—cardboard promises." Elsie knew FDR had a plan to aid the country in the thirties with his New Deal, but she wanted to be a part of a bigger change.

According to Karl Marx, the working class was the only force that could change the failure of the capitalist system. Elsie said, "I wanted to help bring about the transition from capitalism to socialism." Elsie checked out more books. She read *Mother* by Gorky and imagined herself as a heroine in the upheaval that was taking place in the world. She read *The Ten Days that Shook the World* by John Reed, where Lenin declared the establishment of the Soviet Union in 1917. "I read Dos Passos, a popular radical writer of the twenties. I read about

Mensheviks and Bolsheviks, Lenin and Trotsky, and the proletariat and the bourgeoisie. Pretty heady stuff for a ranch girl from Montana!" said Elsie. It may have been Natalie Notkin, the assistant librarian in charge of book collections in foreign languages, that directed Elsie to the economic section that wintry afternoon in 1932, but what Elsie didn't know was that on February 2, 1932, the Seattle Public Library fired Natalie Notkin for allowing Bolshevik literature in her department.[15]

Elsie continued her research. She determined that Communism was the chosen vehicle for the change toward socialism. While the United States was at the height of despair in the Depression, newspapers reported the Soviet Union expanding their industries through the construction of canal systems, new roads, and giant farms. They actually sought laborers to help build their country. A call sounded worldwide for workers to join the great socialist reformation. "Working men of all countries unite! The proletarians have nothing to lose but their chains."[16]

Elsie went to the newsstands to find newspapers that would tell her more about the Communist Party. She religiously bought the *Daily Worker*—the national Communist paper. She learned the Communist Party of the USA had a slogan, "the united front from below," which meant the party was working to organize the unemployed, attempting to found "red" unions, championing the rights of Negroes, and fighting the evictions of farmers and the working poor. "I was dying to meet a Communist!"

One day, an attractive young man with blond hair came into the office selling advertising in a local paper called the *Voice of Action*. Elsie glanced through the paper and realized it was radical. "I asked him, 'Do you know where I can find a Communist?' He laughed and told me he was one. I told him I would like to join the party."

"Lady, I can fix you up!" He arranged for Elsie to accompany him to a Communist meeting.

As was typical of Elsie, she wore a stylish, dark, gray suit, matching earrings, silk nylons, and high heeled shoes to the meeting. She noted their doubtful looks when she expressed interest in joining the party. This was a party devoted to the rise of the proletariat—the working class—and Elsie did not look the part. Someone most likely cast a glance at her shoes while telling her that marching in demonstrations and handing out pamphlets in boarding houses was part of the hard work the party demanded. She was asked, "Would you be able to do this?" Someone questioned her sincerity. Elsie would have to prove her worth. Sensing their hesitancy, even hostility, Elsie was adamant. "I want to join immediately!"

Dressed in style, she joined the Communist Party of the USA. (CP or CPUSA) that summer night in 1933.

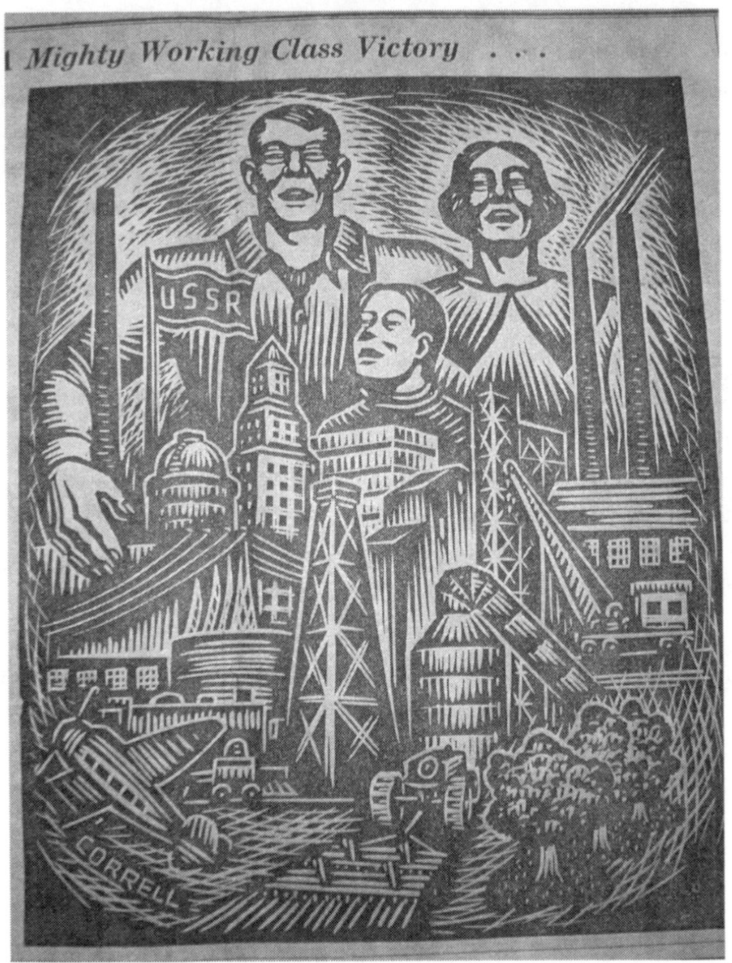

Voice of Action, August 30, 1935, Richard V. Correll, woodcut artist (University of Washington Libraries, Newspaper Collections)

CHAPTER 11:

Voice of Action

Meeting with Elsie

Elsie had told me about the *Voice of Action,* a progressive newspaper in Seattle, printed in the thirties, and I was able to obtain the microfilm containing three years of newspapers through an interlibrary loan. "It was fascinating, Elsie," I told her. "I read about Jesse Owens being insulted by Hitler, the Nazi's making it a crime for Jews to be German citizens, the KKK burning a fiery cross at a worker's house, and forced labor for grocery relief. I read articles by John Lewis and an interview with Stalin by H. G. Wells. In 1936, the newspaper's New Year's resolutions stated, "We will Fight for Peace, for Unemployment Insurance, for Jobs, for Unions." Elsie listened as I continued.

"And listen to this!" I read the 1935 article that reported a German man had moved to the United States when he was seven years old. The article, with journalistic flare, described his first sight of the Statue of Liberty. He was an eager immigrant boy who grew up in America, married, and had several children. Then twenty years later, he was arrested for "suspicious" activities as a result of his German ancestry. He was deported to Nazi Germany in 1935.

> Tugboats chugged and puffed. Whistles blew and bells clanged and roared a startling welcome to the incoming liner. A little boy of 7 years clutched tightly his father's hand and gazed upward with bewildered eyes. It was NY harbor 30 years ago and little Walter Baer enroute from Germany with his widowed father was seeing for the first time the Statue of Liberty. How was a child of seven to know her heart was made of stone. [17]

After immersing myself in the books, photos, and newspaper articles, I felt like I was living in the thirties. I wanted to join a cause, to sign up, to *do* something. The injustice, the unfairness, and the inequality—which decade was I living in? I told Elsie of my shock at different events, as if they had happened the day before. She just nodded knowingly. This was old news, remembered news, for Elsie. "And Elsie, I was struck with the correlation between then and now."

Again, she nodded. "Yes, dear. Now take the Fascists. I never would believe that there are so many of them today. You hear of the ones that get the press, like the Freeman up in Jordan (Montana) and a few other neo–Nazi organizations. But they (the Fascists) are right under our noses and we don't recognize that. That person that heads the House in our state legislature is a Fascist. That's what Fascism is: wanting it one way with no compromise and exerting total control." Elsie was referring to the March 2007 Montana headline news. With one hammer of the gavel, the speaker of the house at the state legislature killed the governor's proposed budget with no discussion or debate. The speaker's party then put their own budget plan into action. Elsie was furious. "We *have* to be vigilante." She repeated, "It's right under our noses, and we don't recognize it."

* * * * *

In 1933, Elsie told her friends and family that she had joined the Communist Party. Her mother disapproved. "I don't like you getting involved with those Bolsheviks." A Bolshevik was a term that originally denoted a member of the ruling proletariat Socialist Democratic Party in Russia in 1917—Mensheviks being the minority. In the United States, during the Red Scare of the early twenties, Bolshevik became a derogatory term that loosely referred to any radical, particularly a Communist. Her mother's disapproval didn't affect Elsie's decision. She began a pattern of continuing her day job, going to CP meetings, and volunteering for the party after hours and on the weekends.

In the first three years of the Depression, the CPUSA doubled its membership, and it doubled again in the first two years of FDR's New Deal. Communists had a reputation for their organizational expertise, something Elsie admired, and they had plenty of reasons for organizing. World and national events were lined up across the decade like dominoes—one push would trigger a collective fall. In Seattle, the chief tasks of the Communist Party included organizing the unemployed working class, fighting evictions, and championing the rights of African Americans, Filipinos, and the working poor.

> *Voice of Action* headlines: Monday April 17, 1933:
> FAMILY EVICTED-Sheriff Throws Furniture in Street
> Unemployed Lay Plans to Fight Cuts in Relief
> Salvation Army Aid Forced Labor
> 2 Jobs for Every Worker, 3 months Vacation with Pay in Russia Today

The Comintern—the Communist headquarters in Moscow, also known as the Third International—dictated the Communist Party line under direct control of Joseph Stalin. In the early thirties, the party line appealed to all Communists to overthrow capitalism by empowering workers throughout the world. The structure of the Communist Party in Moscow served as a model for Communists worldwide.

"I could go to a meeting at the North Pole, and it would be the same," said Elsie. Neighborhood units consisted of twelve to twenty members led by a chairman. Those units belonged to larger sections within a demographic area. Elsie's unit met once a week at someone's home. An agitprop, short for agitational propaganda director, would lead a discussion of current events. They might discuss the latest success story from the Soviet Union, but in the early thirties, the discussion topics focused on local and regional problems and how to apply Marxist theory to the issues. There were plenty of problems to address: unemployment, evictions, and racial discrimination against Filipinos and blacks. The prime commitment for Elsie and her fellow rank-and-file activists was to propagandize for socialism.

THE ENLARGED, IMPROVED

Voice of Action

SEATTLE, TUESDAY, MAY 1, 1934

Price, Five Cents

VOLUME II

Millions Fight Hunger, War, Fascism Today

MEET . . .

May Day in Moscow, USSR

May 1 Demonstrations Unite Toilers of All Countries in Struggle for fundamental Needs.

Our Answer . . .

Seamen Carry Strike on Vermar To Eastern Coast; Unemployed Aid

Silver Shirts Spreading Propaganda In Seattle

Drive Begins for 3000 New Readers by Aug. 1

Plans Progress for March on

Voice of Action, May 1, 1934
(University of Washington Libraries, Newspaper Collections)

The party required the members to educate themselves regarding Marxism, capitalism, and socialism and to attain a general knowledge of politics and culture. The high standards attracted intellectuals and gave them purpose. Elsie recalled, "I think the Seattle area had a higher concentration of intellectuals than other places I had lived. It was stimulating and exciting to be around them." The logistics of recruiting members, demonstrating for a cause, or distributing leaflets or newspapers were discussed and planned at the meetings.

The party partially drew membership from immigrants already familiar with socialist ideas. Most of the members in Elsie's unit were Finnish. The Finnish people had been revolutionists in Finland during World War I. After emigrating to America, they continued working for the cause of socialism in this country. Elsie remembered, "The only time I saw my Finnish friends hostile was when we were planning the refreshments for an evening meeting. Someone volunteered to bring canned milk, and the Finns gasped in horror insisting that we had to have real cream. How they could afford cream at the height of the Depression, I don't know, but they always managed to find some." The

Finns, recent immigrants in the Northwest and active in instigating change, were targeted by the police, and many were deported in the early thirties. Elsie became more resolved than ever to right those wrongs.

Elsie's first activity was Red Sunday—a day designated for recruitment and agitation. She and her comrades targeted the unemployed. She went to boarding houses to sell the *Daily Worker* or the *Voice of Action.* "Another gal and I would walk down the halls knocking on doors saying 'This is a worker's paper.'" They were met by men who were skeptical and beaten down and who begrudgingly took the paper, yet she never felt unsafe. She was simply trying to draw the worker into the cause.

Although the paper never promoted Communism directly, it certainly resounded with Communist sentiment. Elsie recalled, "If we couldn't sell the paper, we would give it away and invite that person to a party meeting or a social event. There was plenty going on in Seattle, all of which was advertised in the *Voice of Action,* but by in large, it was never a really successful way to bring in membership."

Elsie recalled very few quiet evenings at home with nothing to do. Belonging to the Communist Party was like belonging to a particular culture, even a close knit family. Every night of the week there were meetings, lectures, one-act plays, movies, and dances at halls all across Seattle with one thing in common—advocating social change.

> The Icor and Icor Forum are sponsoring an entertainment and dance in celebration of the recognition of the Soviet Union on Saturday, January 6th at the Rainier Masonic Temple. A musical program and speakers will precede the dancing. Refreshments will be served. Come all to celebrate the recognition of Soviet Russia! Come to the Finnish Hall tonight! The Red Front Players will perform "Eviction." Dance following.[18]

In 1933, Congress, under the encouragement of the Roosevelt administration, passed the Twenty-First Amendment to the Constitution, which repealed the Volstead Act or the Eighteenth Amendment. Prohibition was over. Elsie remembered, "It was a way to encourage better times in the country. That's where the song 'Roll out the Barrel' came from, and we did have a barrel of fun in the corner pubs. We'd meet and discuss the issues, drink, and dance."

The party organized evening classes to educate the workers and new members in the principles of Marxism. They encouraged working class people to sign up for the classes and needed teachers. Elsie was handed the material and assigned an evening class that ran for six to eight weeks. She had a lump in her throat and butterflies in her stomach before her first class. "I couldn't imagine myself a teacher, but that was what they expected of me so ..." Men and a few women drifted in until the room filled and buzzed with conversation. Most of the participants were from the Works Projects Administration—a New Deal program to put workers back to work.

Elsie glanced at the clock on the wall and took her place at the podium. "Thank you for coming tonight," she began. Then she explained the format—she would read a Marxist theory (e.g., "The distinguishing feature of Communism is not the abolition of property generally, but the abolition of bourgeois property."), and discussion would follow. Her nervousness dissolved with their enthusiastic participation. That first night, they discussed and debated the class struggle and present day issues. No one was shy. All were eager to talk. Everyone was looking for answers to the Depression and its consequences that wracked their world.

"If we get sick, that's it. There's no compensation if we lose a day of work. Hell, you're lucky if you have your job when you come back!"

"And if you get hurt on the job, that's just tough. Nobody to take care of the bills."

"They want us to work for our relief groceries. That way they don't have to hire for wages. Slave labor is what it is!"

Elsie spelled out the characteristics of a capitalist-based economy and compared it to an economy based on socialism. The evening sparked with intellectual dialogue. A young man approached Elsie after the class when the room had almost emptied. "Can I talk with you for a minute?"

"Of course." Elsie set her books down and looked at him intently.

"I wanted to tell you ... well, I won't be coming back to any of these classes," he said.

Elsie assumed he disagreed with the theories that she was espousing. "I'm sorry to hear that." She had noted that this particular young man had not joined in the discussion for the evening.

He continued, "After listening to everyone tonight, well, it all made sense. They're honest working stiffs just wanting some answers." Then he lowered his voice to almost a whisper. "The FBI hired me to get names, ya know. But I can't go through with it. See, I got in trouble with the law, just a minor offense. They promised to get it off my record if I got names of people at this meeting. And they were going to pay me money."

Elsie didn't know what to say. He continued as she looked at him dumbfounded.

"I'm leaving town. I'm not going to be their stool pigeon. You folks are trying to do something good. I'll straighten out my life somewhere else."

Elsie never forgot that incident and her first awareness of an informant for a governmental agency, typically the FBI. This would not be her last brush with stool pigeons.

The word "eviction" frequented the headlines in the *Voice of Action* during 1933. Entire families faced eviction after missing a payment on their mortgage. "I remember coming home, and the sheriff and his people were loading furniture out the front door of a neighbor's home onto a truck. Neighbors were taking the furniture off the other side and packing it in the back door of the house. That went on all over Seattle." Progressives and Communists founded the Unemployed Citizens League (UCL), which provided practical relief for the unemployed.

Evictions and unfair labor practices were the causes of demonstrations and street corner speeches. Sound wagons—Model A's or a flatbed truck with handmade signs hanging on the doors—would drive down the streets of Seattle honking their horns. Someone in the car or truck would yell into a megaphone, "Speech tonight, seven o'clock, in front of City Hall." Hundreds of people gathered to hear the street corner speakers. "I was amazed at how many people would come to those speeches. But what else was there to do? They were out of work and had no money for anything else. This was their entertainment," Elsie related. "The working class was incited to take action."

One of the causes the Communist Party in the Northwest took on was racial discrimination against African Americans, Filipinos, and other immigrants. At many of their meetings, they discussed the International Labor of Defense and the Communist Party defense of nine African American youths who were charged with the rape of two white women. "Those boys were unfairly charged. It was blatant racism. The Communists and their progressive trial lawyers fought for those boys," said Elsie. Above all, it gave the party national notoriety. Progressive trial lawyers like the ones that defended the Scottsboro case would come to play a major role in Elsie's life a decade down the road.

Ironically, despite Elsie's Southern Civil War roots, she met her first black person in Seattle. Elsie recalled, "I met Revels Cayton at a dance in the early thirties. He was the first black person I met, and I found him rather handsome. I would have pursued my instincts, but he was already dating my roommate's cousin Ethel Horowitz. Later, as I danced with him I remember thinking … what would my mother think?!" There are some things mothers are better off not knowing.

Elsie held Cayton in very high esteem. He played a major role in demanding equal rights for Negroes in the Northwest. Sarah Falconer wrote about Revels Cayton in the "Communism in Washington State History and Memory Project," a project conducted by the University of Washington directed by James N. Gregory:

> On February 19, 1934, a group of Communists involved in the League of Struggle for Negro Rights decided that discrimination toward African Americans and Filipinos in Seattle needed to come to an end. Led by a young, African American man, named Revels Cayton the group entered a Seattle City Council meeting demanding laws that would make discrimination based on race illegal. The group made such a strong case that the Council decided to have a mass meeting to discuss the conditions facing minorities in Seattle. Following the disruption of the council meeting another group of protestors went to a local bar called the Breakers Beer Parlor where they demanded that the "For Whites Only" sign be removed from the premises. The group chose to forcibly remove

> the sign from this business, and then went on to remove others in the area. [19]

Cayton wrote an article for the *Voice of Action* with a plea "to fight Uncle Tom Politics and to build the *Voice of Action*, the true voice of the militant white workers and of the Negro people."[20]

As the UCL enacted further change, Elsie signed up to gather signatures for petitions sponsored by the UCL, demanding unemployment insurance for the workers. FDR offered relief and food vouchers, but the profit seekers knew how to work the system. The bosses fired workers at industrial plants knowing that the long line of unemployed waiting for jobs would simply work for relief vouchers. The employers didn't have to pay prevailing wages or provide insurance or health care. They merely handed the worker their vouchers, a system that became known as slave labor. Elsie remembered standing at the labor union building during her lunch hour to gather signatures from unemployed workers on a hand written petition.

Elsie was quite possibly wearing a fashionable, gray hat and a knee-length, red skirt with a fitted jacket that accentuated her figure, and she boldly held her petition out to people as they passed by. Men dressed in work clothes with their shirtsleeves rolled up and hats pulled down over their foreheads slowed to notice this striking woman intent on getting their attention. One man listened, shrugged, and reluctantly signed. "Alright, but we'll never get benefits—the bosses will see to that." Another man listened to her stump, took a last drag on his cigarette, and dropped it on the ground. He blew the smoke out of his mouth in a quick burst as he mashed the butt into the sidewalk with his scuffed boot. Just before he strode away, he said, "It'll never happen. You're wastin' your time, girl." Elsie quickly turned and assailed the next man in the crowd. She held out her pen and petition and began her spiel.

"By the time it was all said and done, we *did* get our unemployment insurance," reflected Elsie. "President Roosevelt didn't dream those benefits up by himself. He heard the demands of the people. People today should realize those benefits didn't just fall out of the sky. A united front of people by sheer hard work and sacrifice won those benefits we have today! There is nothing so basic in democracy as writing up a petition and getting signatures."

In the thirties, Washington State had the fastest growing elderly population in the nation.[21] During the Depression, they were the most vulnerable with no place to go. Seattle area activists, Communists, and progressive labor unions formed the Washington Pension Union to advocate broader social policy issues for the elderly as well as the Aid to Dependent Children program. "The Pension Movement really took hold in the Seattle area. Everybody volunteered, of course. They would have demonstrations and raise money and do all the things that organizations do. There would be maybe one paid official in the Pension Union and maybe one paid office worker." By the end of the thirties, Washington State had one of the most successful welfare and pension policies in the nation.

Another movement swept the country in 1934 that the Communists embraced. A California man by the name of Townsend developed a plan for pensions and benefits for working people. Elsie went to the Townsend meetings in Seattle where petitions were formulated and circulated nationwide. Social Security benefits initiated by FDR grew out of the Townsend petitions. "The Townsend Plan petitions signed by ten million people led to the Social Security Act of 1935. Social reform does not come from the top down. It should be the reverse. That's how it worked in those days—a grass roots movement. *That* is where the power should be!"

By the midthirties, the Communist Party line changed. Capitalism was no longer the immediate foe. The Comintern declared Fascism—a rigid, one-party dictatorship that forcibly suppressed any opposition—the number one threat to Communism and the world. Democracy must be defended. Socialist and liberal forces must be united to oppose Fascism. The new mantra was "Communism is twentieth-century Americanism." The strategy partnered the Communist Party, albeit discreetly, with reformist organizations and progressive institutions. It became known as the Popular Front Strategy. It was also a way to continue recruiting within the labor unions and social organizations, in a sense, undercover, particularly amidst the hostile police and FBI environment. The Pension Union fell under the definition of a front organization. Many Communists in the Seattle area, particularly from the Pension Union and the Washington Commonwealth Federation, ran for political office under the guise of the Democratic Party.

The Communist Party had criticized FDR when he first assumed his presidency, but the Soviet foreign minister, Maxim Litvinov, negotiated the diplomatic recognition of the Soviet Union by the United States. As a result, the CPUSA supported Franklin D. Roosevelt's New Deal, which was well under way in 1934. The Communists backed FDR's New Deal reforms, which stacked up like alphabet blocks: CCC, NRA, WPA, CWA, PWA, NIRA.

In 1934, Elsie began volunteering during her noon hour at the office of the *Voice of Action.* It was another moment of her life she remembered with clarity. She stood at a desk watching a woman attach a stencil to a mimeograph machine. As the woman turned the handle with rhythmic motion, leaflets spewed out one at a time onto a tray. Elsie introduced herself over the ka-chunk of the machine. "Here," the woman, smiling, thrust a pile of leaflets at her. "You can start by folding these. That'll be a great help." Taking off her coat and draping it across the back of the chair, Elsie sat at the desk and started on the task. Men clustered at a desk on the far side of the room—shirtsleeves rolled up, cigarettes dangling from their mouths—discussing an article for the upcoming issue. Several women sat at desks typing stencils for the mimeograph machine. Elsie finished folding the first pile and was discussing the logistics of distributing them when the door opened. She looked up to see a handsome blond man with bright blue eyes striding toward her desk. Elsie noted his muscular build and felt drawn to his inquisitive eyes. As he approached, she stood up, thrust her hand out, and said, "Hello! I'm Elsie Gilland. I volunteer for the paper."

He smiled and firmly held her hand. "Nice to meet you, Miss Gilland. I've come to volunteer, too. My name is Ernest Fox."

CHAPTER 12:

A Man and a Cause

Meeting with Elsie

"Now, I'm going to tell you about Ernie," Elsie announced in her business voice after we were settled in the living room. She sat on the edge of the sofa, hands folded in her lap. "What I'm telling you is a complete fabrication, or at least part of it is. I've based this on some pieces of truth that I learned about Ernie long after we were married. I imagine it this way: Ernie, a young merchant marine—before I knew him—lying on the streets of New York City, near death. Sores have broken out all over his body, oozing and risking infection, but he has no money and is too weak to find help. Along comes a young man who, for some reason, feels sorry for him. This young man gives Ernie some food. Over the next couple of days, the young man sneaks food from his family's table to give to Ernie. He finds a shelter for him, and Ernie's sores begin to heal. This young man saves Ernie's life. The two friends keep in touch throughout the years. I met this young man many years later."

Elsie paused and set her jaw almost in a grimace. Her voice sounded cold, edged with bitterness. "Better that Ernie had died on those streets."

* * * * *

Ernest Fox, a merchant marine, landed in Seattle in the early thirties and was working as a port patrolman. He was a member of the Sailor's Union, which was part of the American Federation of Labor (AFL). The waterfront boiled with union activity among the longshoremen and the sailors. Competing unions vied for membership with the workers and made demands of the employers. Strikes were a picket sign away.

Ernie, attracted to a more radical element, joined the Marine Workers Industrial Union (MWIU) and became a leader along with Jimmy Archer, Blackie Cannelonga, and Walter Stack.[22] They distributed leaflets up and down the waterfront that proselytized for industrial union organization, higher wages, and better hiring procedures.

After Elsie met Ernie in the *Voice of Action* office, they started seeing each other regularly. Elsie was still living with her stepfather and mother, but on the weekends, she stayed with her friend Rose, who had an apartment in Seattle. Rose's boyfriend was Walter Stack.

The couples found plenty to do together—attending movies, dances, and street corner speeches. Ernie and Elsie were participating in a demonstration at Pioneer Square in Seattle when Ernie suddenly sat down on the curb, dropped his placard, and grabbed his chest. Elsie knelt next to him.

"What's wrong? What hurts? Should I call an ambulance?" Elsie recalled that a strange look came over Ernie's face. "No! I don't want any doctors! Just leave me be. I'll be fine in a minute!" He was very adamant. Then, in a short time, Ernie's chest pain passed, and they rejoined the demonstrators. Later, he never talked about the incident, and Elsie didn't ask.

The environment in Washington State was hostile for a card-carrying Communist and for union members agitating for change. Police harassment was common, and demonstrators and street corner orators were arrested and charged with vagrancy, which resulted in jail terms. Those of foreign birth, those "suspicious" immigrants, were threatened with deportation. Ernie had been born in Germany and had immigrated to the United States with his family when he was four years old. He was a German National. It's unknown if he was aware he risked deportation. There is reason to believe Ernie assumed he became a U.S. citizen when his father obtained citizenship shortly after the family immigrated. Whether it was naivety or fearlessness, Ernie joined the Communist Party, despite the risk for noncitizens.

Communist leaders were charged under criminal syndicalism laws, which made it a crime to defend, advocate, or set up an organization to bring about a change in the existing form of government. The criminal syndicalism laws directly threatened free speech and the First Amendment. Fear of a Red Scare in the thirties allowed the syndicalism statutes to aim their sights on the Communists. All Communist members were instructed by the party not to carry their cards or anything identifying them as Communist, but Ernie and Walter carried their cards—tempting fate.

Elsie admired Ernie's bold spirit. Easy to pick out in a crowd, he was first in line at a demonstration or rally, shouting and waving his handmade sign. Elsie learned that, before she had known him, he led a demonstration of thousands of people to Seattle City Hall asking for food.

Walter and Ernie became effective street corner speakers in the skid road area where they addressed the unemployed masses. The sound truck would drive through town and announce the evening rally, and hundreds of people would show up. Elsie described the scene: "Sometimes these speakers had megaphones, but mostly they just yelled to be heard. One time, when Ernie and Walter were speaking—the topic probably had to do with unemployment insurance or encouraging workers to join the union—a religious group set up a podium on the other side of the street. They told the workers that their particular brand of religion was the answer to their problems." The two groups yelled louder and louder, vying for the attention of the crowd. "Ernest and Walter were shouting so loudly for so long that they were actually spitting blood." Theater in the round. Jesus and unions advocating for the poor and agitating for change.

Ernie, Elsie, and many other people congregated like moths to the light of the radical movement during the dark years of the Depression. As a result, their lives became more entwined. One Saturday, the couple took part in a demonstration. They marched with placards down the streets of Seattle, protesting against discrimination of Filipinos and Negroes in hiring practices. Afterwards, they may have gone to see an art show displaying Diego Rivera's murals, which was advertised in the

Voice of Action, praising present-day Russia and questioning the future of capitalism in the United States. The evening culminated at a friend's house where beer and drinks mixed well with fluid conversation. Eventually, Ernie walked Elsie back to Rose's apartment. Elsie especially remembered the full moon that night, and her recollection painted the scene with vivid details.

The moon winked through wispy clouds as it scattered silver blue light on the sidewalk. A warm breeze played with Elsie's summer dress as they walked hand in hand. Their walk slowed, and they stopped. Ernie pulled Elsie around in front of him. She stood on tiptoe as they embraced, kissing long and passionately. They spent the night at Rose's apartment making love and talking about marriage.

There was a slight glitch to the wedding plans—Ernie was already married. It had been a very brief affair, and she lived elsewhere, but the marriage needed to be annulled. Elsie understood. In the meantime, they decided to find an apartment and live together—a bold move for a woman in those days. There was another slight glitch—Macie. After meeting Ernie, she instantly disliked him. "He's no good, Elsie," she told her daughter. Macie, always protective of Elsie, was wary. Perhaps she didn't want Elsie to repeat the pattern she had had with her choice of men. But twenty-six-year-old Elsie, with a mind of her own, disregarded her mother's warning.

Elsie held her mother in high esteem and did not want this to create a fissure in their relationship. One can imagine Elsie silently folding her stockings and dress suits with precise determination while her mother stood in the doorway, arms crossed as she delivered a series of protests. "It was a very uncomfortable scene," Elsie remembered. After Elsie snapped her suitcase shut, she called a cab. Just as the taxi pulled up, Elsie turned and hugged her mother. Macie's vitriolic attack dissolved with the realization of the finality of Elsie's decision. She returned the hug, squeezing herself to her daughter. As Elsie bent to pick up her suitcase, she said, "I'll call next week, Mother. Maybe we can go out for lunch." Eventually, Macie would accept her daughter's decision. The two maintained a lifelong, close relationship despite the disparity in their viewpoints of politics, men, and lifestyles.

Macie and Elsie shopping in Seattle

Ernie and Elsie rented a one-room apartment in a boarding house near the advertising agency where Elsie worked. Elsie was not going to waste her time worrying what other people thought about her living situation. Times were changing, and she wouldn't be caught in the snare of being a traditional housewife.

At that point, Elsie made a decision that would seal the promise she made to herself as a young girl—she would never rely on a man for money. Elsie kept her job—a job she loved—and paid the bills. She maintained her own financial security, which allowed Ernie to work full time for the party. The radical involvement in the Communist Party, the drive for socialism, and the anticipation of the fall of capitalism was the magnetism that drew Ernie and Elsie together—extending far beyond their mutual physical attraction for each other.

"I wanted nothing more than to work and make a living so that Ernest could become a full-time revolutionary, otherwise known in the Communist Party as a functionary." A functionary worked full time on the Communist Party payroll. But Ernie's pay, based on Elsie's income, was just fifteen dollars a week.

Ernie's fire and Elsie's commitment did not go unnoticed in the party. Morris Rappaport was the district organizer of the Washington and Oregon area. Elsie and Ernie became well acquainted with the Rappaports, and soon Morris Rappaport recommended that Ernie attend the National Training School in New York. This was a prestigious Marxist school set up to educate and train CP members as leaders. In addition to studying Marxist theory, the attendees also learned how to organize workers and speak at open-air meetings and what techniques to use, or not, at demonstrations. Elsie was thrilled for Ernie. This was a great honor. In celebration, she bought him a brand-new, navy blue suit.

While Ernie was in New York, Elsie received an invitation to live with the Rappaports rather than alone in the boarding house. Elsie recalled that the Rappaports were Russian Jews, and she was quite fond of them. As a young girl in high school, she had always longed for diversity. In her adult life, diversity was a daily experience. "I even adopted Russian style blouses—full, puffy sleeves with a mandarin collar. That was very popular in party circles at the time." According to an article in the *Voice of Action*, many progressive women in Seattle wore similar white blouses of crepe de chine with red buttons and long, checkered skirts—a proletariat badge supporting the rise of Communism.[23]

Ernie's intrepid courage once again tempted fate. While Ernie was in New York, a German Nazi ship had anchored at the waterfront. Hitler and Mussolini's Fascism was on the rise, directly threatening Communism and the Soviet Union in particular. Ernie and some of his fellow Marxist friends worked out a plan to sneak on the ship at night and replace the swastika flag with the Communist hammer and sickle flag. Elsie learned that it was Ernie who swapped the flags.

After Ernie returned from his six-week stint in Marxist leadership school, he continued his role as a Communist functionary. Upon Elsie's insistence, they moved to a better apartment made affordable by Elsie's full-time job. The desire to dress smartly and live in a fashionable home coursed through her veins as strongly as her desire to right the wrongs of the capitalist country in which she lived. Unusual and even contrasting genetic and past influences—Huguenot bloodline, Southern gentility ancestry, an isolated ranch upbringing, and her mother's struggle against poverty—all combined in Elsie's psyche to bolster her for what was to come.

CHAPTER 13:

Modern Times

Meeting with Elsie

"You've never seen Charlie Chaplin in *Modern Times?*" Elsie chuckled. "*That* movie was one of the greatest artistic accomplishments of the century, my dear. You mean to tell me you've never heard of it?" She wasn't making fun of me but was excited to advance my education. "I consider Charlie Chaplin the most creative genius of the twentieth century."

"And I grew up thinking Walt Disney had that distinction."

She laughed, and then continued, "If I remember right, Charlie Chaplin produced *and* directed *Modern Times*. I think he even wrote the music for it. What a contribution he made to society."

A few weeks later, I watched the vintage movie. I imagined myself sitting in a movie theater in 1936. My neighbor who had been evicted from her home sat on one side of me. She couldn't help smile at the scene when the little mustached man closed the door to his shack, and the roof fell down. In front of me sat a factory worker who threw his head back in a big guffaw when Chaplin's character lost control as the assembly line accelerated on command from the patriarchal master. The audience laughed at the silly antics of that comical man with the expressive eyebrows, baggy pants, and derby hat. We left the theater empowered by the somber truth beneath the slapstick humor.

I remembered a notation in Elsie's copy of the *Communist Manifesto* midway through the book where she had written Chaplin's name next to a starred paragraph. The paragraph began, "Modern industry has converted the little workshop of the patriarchal master into the great factory of the industrial capitalist. Masses of laborers, crowded into the factory, are organized like soldiers."

"That movie has a timely message even now," said Elsie.

* * * * *

While the Great Depression shattered peoples' lives, the conditions that were spawned as a result triggered the massive organization of the industrial unions. Elsie's story played out alongside the growth of the unions, particularly on the waterfront. The Communist Party and the unions—part of a powerful social movement—hissed like a pressure cooker on a hot stove. The working class was the force of ultimate social change, and organizing labor was the chief task of the party. Elsie and Ernie's lives became immersed in union activity.

While Elsie was gathering petitions for pensions in Seattle, workers on the west coast waterfronts in 1934 simmered with discontent. Harry Bridges, an Australian born sailor who rose up in the fray, led a charge demanding better working conditions. Bridges had worked as a longshoreman since 1922 at the San Francisco waterfront—loading and unloading the cargo from ships. He had belonged to the radical union the Industrial Workers of the World, otherwise known as the Wobblies, and he participated in strikes after World War I. He was a seasoned union man.

The unions that existed along the docks were company owned and operated. In order to get a job, a worker was required to join the company union under their terms. If the employer or company owner wanted a ship loaded and unloaded faster, the dock foreman was ordered to start a speed up. A speed up exacerbated the already dangerous conditions by adding long hours of hard physical labor that resulted in many injuries. A worker's injury cost the ship owner money. A longshoreman risked his job if he claimed an injury. Bridges related an injury he suffered during a speed up in a taped interview for the ILWU Oral History Collection by Harvey Schwartz and printed in the September 2000 issue of the *Dispatcher*, the International Longshoreman and Warehouse Union (ILWU) newspaper. "I broke my foot in '29 working in the hold. I was standing there on a pile, and we let a load go out, and my foot got jammed between two cases that came together. I worked for a couple days with it—couldn't afford to lay off, you see?"

Speed-up Kills Butte Miner

BUTTE, Mont.—Clarence Martin, 39-year-old iner, paid with ris life for the demand for increased production made by the Anaconda Mining company. Martin was a miner in the Belmont mine and was working Saturday night when he was caught in a fall of ground and killed instantly. He was a member of the International of Mine, Mill and Smelter Workers. He leaves behind him his wife and three children.

The practice of contract labor carried out in the Butte mines has been resulting in numerous injuries and deaths during the past months.

Voice of Action, May 13, 1936
(University of Washington Libraries, Newspaper Collection)

Experiencing firsthand the poor working conditions of the time radicalized more than one person. Elsie had a girlfriend in Seattle who worked at a grocery store near the docks. Rather than report an injury, the company foreman would send an injured dockworker to the grocery store for help. Elsie's friend scrambled around the store for first-aid supplies, and the worker would go back to his job. After a series of increasingly serious injuries involving workers, she saw the disparity between owners and workers and joined the Communist Party.

The shape-up system of hiring also increased the workers' rumblings on the docks. Each company hired steady, sixteen-men gangs. Every day, a gang boss would be on the dock to hire new gangs or replacements. The workers would gather at the docks or in front of the ships early in the morning and sometimes stand for hours waiting for a gang boss from the company union to assign work, if it was available.

As a sailor and merchant marine, Ernie spent time on the docks before making his way to Seattle in the early thirties. His ship had landed in San Francisco, and day jobs were at a premium. The workers knew a bribe to the gang boss would help their hiring prospects. Corruption was part of the game since being first in line did not assure you a job for the day. Any suspect behavior, like marching in a Labor Day Parade, might put a worker on the blacklist and cost him his job. Skin color was also a determining factor. "If you're white … alright, if you're brown … stick around, if you're black … step back." Once the hiring was done for the day, and before the unlucky unemployed workers went home or to the bootleg joint or pool hall down the street, the gang boss employed one more hiring tactic. Years later, Ernie described the scene to Elsie.

The men knew what was coming. They pushed and elbowed each other, trying to anticipate a strategic place to stand. One man in a visored, cloth cap pulled another man out of his way to get a better advantage. There wasn't room or time for a fistfight. The boss stood on the steps of the company union hiring hall, or the fink hall as the workers referred to it, the Ferry Building between Market and Mission Streets. He raised his arm high so the workers could see his clutched fist. The mob of men lifted their waving hands skyward like a flock of seething birds on the take-off, readying for the moment the boss released the metal tokens. A metal token meant a job for the day. A slight look of amusement flickered across the gang boss's face as he let the tokens fly. A man in the middle of the mob jumped and caught a token in mid air. The rest of the crowd dropped to the ground, scrambling on their hands and knees. "I got one!" a worker stood up and adjusted his hat, but the triumph in his face only masked the humiliation that shot through the core of his being.

The bosses knew that the workers found strength in unity. The risk of a strike, which meant loss of profits, would be less likely if the workers competed for desperately needed jobs. But desperation breeds discontent and nurtures the rumbling of change.

Stumping for workers to unite against the inequitable practices caused by the capitalist ventures of the owners aligned Ernie's socialist ideologies with the unions. Help for the workers came from an unlikely place—the executive office of the White House. After Franklin Roosevelt became president, rumors began to circulate that the National Recovery Act (NRA) in Washington DC included laws that would allow the worker to organize and not be forced to belong to the company unions.

Bridges, working on the San Francisco docks in 1933, did not wait for the government decree but began instigating change immediately. He helped resurrect the International Longshoreman Association (ILA) and rallied for support. Using the same tactic as the Communist Party, he used the mimeograph machine as a weapon. The workers cranked out a newspaper one stencil at a time, and, just like Elsie with the *Voice of Action,* they handed out the papers for a penny a piece during shape-ups and at fink halls. They left bundles of the leaflets in the hulls of ships that were bound for other ports. When the ships docked, people like Ernie Fox looked for the clandestine bundles and then distributed them to the Seattle longshoremen. The word spread. The workers were organizing. The *Waterfront Worker* played an important role in unifying the workers up and down the coastline.

It was hard work convincing laborers to risk their jobs and join the workers' union. Holding meetings, making leaflets, and "chewing the rag" with fellow workers were some of the techniques they employed. Bridges recalled, "At this point, I spent all my time working and at union meetings. I went home to sleep, and that was just about all. So home and family—they were just forgotten. I remember that. I'm saying it the way it was."[24]

Membership of the rank and file for the longshoremen union grew but only because of steady proselytizing by Bridges and company. They were on the move and headed north—stopping at all of the ports to gain more support, and a dance was organized in Seattle. Elsie danced with Harry, who, she remembered, was a fine dancer.

Elsie recalled, "Harry and I talked about how great it was that Ernie was a functionary in the party, and Harry mentioned Ernie's contribution to the union organization. He commented that I must be proud to have Ernie hold such good influence in the party and the marine union."

The ILA made demands for a six-hour day, thirty-hour week, a wage increase, and union hiring halls. The owners wanted to negotiate port by port instead of on an industry-wide basis. Unity was definitely threatening the bosses. Just like the shape-up token tactic, the owners wanted to pit one port against another, but no deals were made and a strike date was set. The White House sent a telegraph. "Don't strike—let us try to do something", and it was either refused or ignored. The ILA went on strike May 9, 1934 and as a result every seaport was closed from San Diego to Juneau. It was the first industry-wide strike on the west coast. "We had a hell of a time because picketing was illegal. One of the reasons is the waterfront was state property. We'd get out there with our flag, our union banner, and I think we had a couple of drums to march along. Then the cops would move in and beat the shit out of us."[25]

The owners hired the football team from Cal State as strikebreakers, and things got ugly. The owners offered an attractive offer but did not include any settlement for the other maritime unions that went on strike with the ILA, so the longshoreman refused the offer.

The police lobbed glass, tear gas bombs at the strikers, who returned the pitches with a broom. Some strikers carried buckets of water to throw on the glass bombs as they broke on the pavement, rendering the fumes harmless. Many of the policemen were mounted on horses and trampled their way through the strikers. "But we had a few tricks up our sleeves," said Bridges. "One of our maneuvers was that when we had enough dried peas or marbles, we'd scatter them around so that the horses would fall over. There were horses scattering in every direction." [26]

The workers carried sharp objects, like hatpins, in their pockets to poke the horses in the belly, unseating many a policeman. The press fed on the fervor and claimed it was the beginning of a Communist Revolution. It would not be the first time or the last that union strikes were equated with the rising of a red tide. In the meantime, fear fueled the fire of discontent on the waterfront. Bridges compared a strike to a mini-revolution. "A strike is a very serious thing. The strike weapon should never be used except as a last, desperate resort when there's no way out. It simply means a form of revolution because you take over an industry or a plant owned by the capitalists, and temporarily you seize it."[27]

In Seattle, there were 1,500 longshoremen that were out on strike and 12,500 maritime workers up and down the west coast making demands. Elsie remembered walking to the Seattle docks and watching the strikers in the picket line cook dinner over jerry-rigged stoves. She admired the tenacity and determination of the strikers. While she watched the action play out on the docks, she didn't know that her life would eventually center on the longshoremen's new union under Harry Bridges.

Bridges related, "We were all greenhorn amateurs. The one who had a little actual past union experience was me. One time we were marching, and the attitude of the guys was the cops would never shoot us. I couldn't convince them otherwise because they knew all the cops. Shots rang out. One of our guys falls right down, and he's squirting blood. And, of course, my partner, who was a real anti–Communist guy said, 'Hey, he's been shot!' I said, 'Of course he's been … shot! I've been trying to tell you that's what happens.'"[28]

According to the article, Bridges and his friend took off on foot, rounded a corner, and missed a bullet by six inches. The day was deemed Bloody Thursday, July 5, 1934. Two strikers were shot dead by the police. Then, the unheard of happened—a general strike ensued. The city streetcar operators, warehouse workers, grocery store owners, restaurants … everyone empathized with the longshoremen, and the city was paralyzed for four days.

In Seattle, shipping companies hired men desperate for work as strikebreakers and housed them in ships to avoid confronting the picket line. Police used tear gas and clubs. A longshoreman was shot to death, and a deputy sheriff was killed. Several strike-breakers were killed in accidents on the docks, probably due to inexperience. Elsie remembers going to the docks to see "what was doin.'" She recalled men cooking dinner in a make-shift kitchen and admired their stamina and courage.

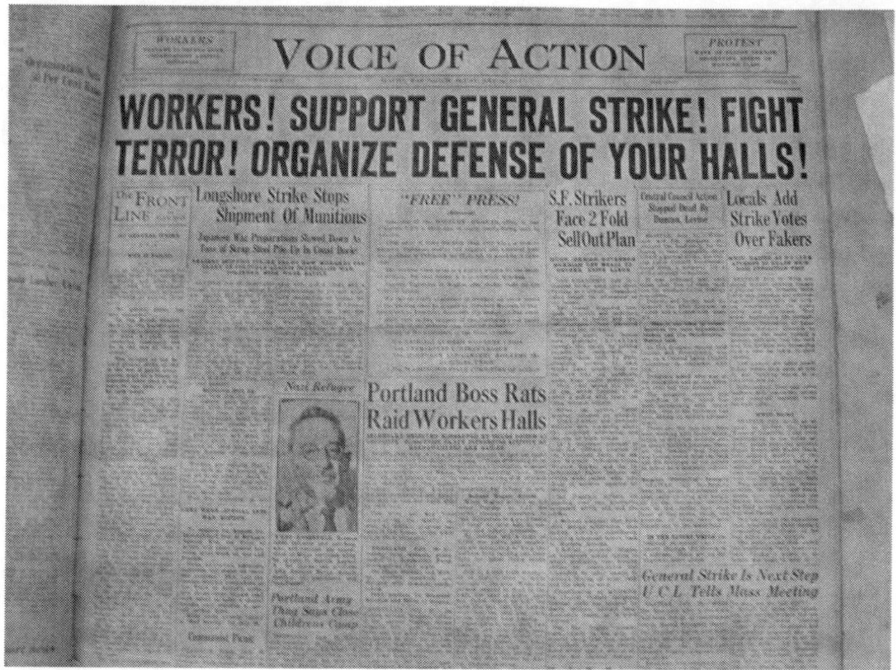
VOICE OF ACTION

WORKERS! SUPPORT GENERAL STRIKE! FIGHT TERROR! ORGANIZE DEFENSE OF YOUR HALLS!

Longshore Strike Stops Shipment Of Munitions

"FREE" PRESS!

S.F. Strikers Face 2 Fold Sell Out Plan

Locals Add Strike Votes Over Fakers

Portland Boss Rats Raid Workers Halls

General Strike Is Next Step U C L Tells Mass Meeting

Voice of Action, July 20, 1934
(University of Washington, Newspaper Collections)

By the end of July, the strike was settled by arbitration. The IWA got what they wanted in San Francisco—a hiring hall near Mission Street and the Embarcadero. The shape-up hiring system was over, and the industrial unions were gaining strength. The rank and file—the workers—were being heard.

The longshoreman strike won collective bargaining rights for unions under the National Recovery Act (NRA). Under the NRA, the Wagner Act, which gave all workers the right to form and join unions, was passed and enforced by the National Labor Relations Board (NLRB). According to Elsie, the NLRB was the Magna Carta of American labor. Under the NLRB, several unions could represent different groups of workers. The new system meant that the union who won the majority of the worker's votes would represent the employees. Employers could no longer blacklist, company unions were banned, and workers won the right to organize. The industrial unions, which represented the unskilled workers, were on the rise and gaining momentum throughout the nation. Workers of the world were uniting.

Industries no longer relied on the artisans and craft unions of previous decades—the assembly line and the influx of hard working immigrants changed all of that. Unskilled workers needed representation in unions. Now was the time to get rid of the craft unions—carpenters, plumbers, masons, etc.—where only skilled workers were represented under the guise of the American Federation of Labor. One man led the charge.

John L. Lewis, the powerful leader of the United Mine Workers of America, demanded that the AFL charter the industrial unions at a convention in September of 1935. Someone called Lewis a bastard, and Lewis threw a punch at the jaw of the belligerent. The deed was done, and by November, the split was made. Leaders of the clothing, steel, automobile, and rubber industries split from the AFL and formed the Congress for Industrial Organization (CIO). "Formation of the CIO was a new, popular movement that excited an almost unexampled enthusiasm and support from all radical and liberal forces. It brought to terms for the first time in American history most of the industrial and monopolistic giants who had, until then, kept the big fortresses of open shopism unbreeched."[29] Elsie remembered Lewis speaking on the west coast at a union gathering. She recalled, "He was a powerful speaker, dynamic, and he knew how to work the crowd. It was inspiring to hear him talk."

There were many more industries to woo into the CIO camp and hundreds of thousands of workers to organize. The masters of organizational skills were the Communists—a known fact. They had earned a reputation for being a dedicated, tenacious bunch willing to work night and day despite occasional threats of physical violence. The Communists won the workers' trust.[30] John Lewis recognized the tenacity of the members of the CPUSA. Despite his opposition to Communism, he specifically hired Communists to recruit members for the CIO. "Who gets the bird? The hunter or the dog?" he answered when questioned about hiring "reds."[31] In Seattle, Ernie was hired as a CIO organizer.

This was a time before red-baiters, loyalty oaths, and a suspicious fear, which infected the nation in decades to come. The mid thirties were a time of a united front against the capitalist, profit-seeking bosses of the big companies. During the parallel rise of the industrial unions and the Communist Party, Elsie and Ernie rode the crest of the progressive wave into the decade of the forties.

CHAPTER 14:

Fear, Hatred, Marriage

Meeting with Elsie

"What's doin'?" Elsie greeted me with a smile.

"What's happenin'?" I countered. She chuckled, and then we chitchatted about news around town. Elsie had recovered from her stint in the Fourth of July Parade where she rode in the sidecar of a 1947 Harley Davidson. She still beamed from the fun of it. Of course, it was her own idea for which I assisted as best I could—making the sign she wanted and taking her to and from the parade. Someone else found the motorcycle and driver.

A new blouse inspired the whole thing. "Don't you think it needs a parade?" she had asked me. The western style blouse shimmered silver with primary colored threads streaking through the yoke like the trail of fireworks. She set it off with a silver straw hat and sat in the sidecar throwing candy to the children in the crowd that lined Main Street of Miles City. The sign that she had instructed me to make was placed on the sidecar. It read "Being politically active is the secret to longevity. Elsie Fox is proof!" I speculated that shopping for new clothes also played a role in her longevity.

2007 Fourth of July Parade, Miles City, Montana

"I'm going to the Hanson's tonight for a party. We're going to celebrate Bastille Day," she swept her hands in front of her, and her voice rang out, "Liberte! Egalite! Fraternite! Which reminds me, I thought of something else I want in the book."

"What's that?"

"I want you to stress my ancestral heritage—the fact that I'm descended from French Huguenots. And include some history on the Huguenots. I think it's important to my story, dear."

Another history assignment from Elsie. At home, while Elsie partied with friends, I pondered her life. So often in the course of our meetings, Elsie left her story (or did she?) and delivered a lecture on historical events—the Bonus March, Prohibition, union organization. Then she instructed me to "look it up, dear" or "make sure you put that in the book." Sometimes, I lost Elsie in the reference books and information overload that was piled on my desk and referenced on papers stuck to my walls in the room I now called "The Elsie Room." I constructed a time line of Elsie's life, drawn on heavy brown paper with a dark blue magic marker and taped to the wall above my computer. The events of her life, the ones she remembered, intermingled with the political and economical milestones of this country. It was clear that she defined her life by the politics of the time. But lives don't always follow a tidy straight line—they twist and turn in their forward motion to that ultimate date with destiny. I stared at the sepia photograph on my desk of a young woman with short, curly, auburn hair—her cheeks tinted a light pink. She wore an easy, confident smile and gazed at me with a self-assured, eager look in her eyes as if saying, "What's doin'?"

* * * * *

Elsie and Ernie rarely spent an evening at home together; there was no time for family life. Ernie was learning the ropes of organizing the unorganized for the CIO, which, in part, meant hanging out in the pool and dance halls of Seattle.

One evening, Elsie went to a meeting at the Finnish Hall on Ninth and Yesler by herself, which was not unusual for Elsie. As she approached the hall, there was a group of men hanging out on the stairs—leaning on the stoop, smoking cigarettes, and eyeing Elsie as she approached. She started up the stairs when one said with a sneer, "Dirty Jew." The others laughed, and more anti–Semitic remarks followed. Elsie paused slightly but fought back the impulse to deny their assumption she was Jewish. She realized by simply doing that, she would play into their hands, validating their hateful opinions of Jews. She hurried into the hall. "They were obviously Nazi sympathizers. My god, anti–Semitism is a scary thing," Elsie related after recalling the incident. Elsie's sharp facial features and prominent nose set her up for racial slurs. While workers were making gains for better working conditions on the home turf, Fascism had gained a foothold overseas, and anti–Semitism spread slowly like dark undercurrents that lapped against the docks worldwide.

Shortly after this incident, Elsie volunteered for a special job with the *Voice of Action*. Elsie's party unit directed her to contact Lowell Wakefield, the publisher of the newspaper, to offer her services as a writer. Lowell asked her to do undercover reporting on the rising popularity of a Fascist group called the Silver Shirts, which had been meeting in the Seattle area and to submit her findings to the *Voice of Action* editorial staff. So Elsie developed her own plan of action.

Voice of Action, Sept. 14, 1934, Richard V. Correll, woodcut artist (University of Washington Libraries, Newspaper collections)

During her lunch hour, Elsie walked to a particular newsstand where she knew Silver Shirt literature was displayed. She picked up and flipped through various journals but made sure she returned to the Fascist propaganda so the newsstand owner could see her. After several days of this, the owner finally approached her.

While looking at the leaflet she told him, "This country sure is in a lot of trouble." She made other patriotic remarks knowing that one of the Silver Shirt mantras was "100 percent Americans."

"I've noticed your interest in this," he motioned with his head at the leaflets. "You've been comin' all week. So … d'ya wanna do something about this terrible fix our country's in?"

"Well, sure, if I could." He told her about the next Silver Shirt meeting and extended an invitation.

"Strength is in numbers," he said. Elsie didn't have to be told that!

During hard times, new ideologies take root. Some appear like noxious weeds—innocent on the surface but entangled and deeply rooted, choking out the competition. Fascism fed on fear of anything or anyone different—immigrants, races, religions, and Communists, to name a few. Extreme patriotism mixed with extreme Christianity and a good douse of fear made for a volatile mixture.

The Silver Shirts were followers of the Silver Legion—a Fascist organization formed by William Dudley Pelley in 1933. He read *Mein Kampf*, admired Hitler, and hated Communists and Jews—he believed, along with Henry Ford, that the Jews were going to take over the world. An out-of-body experience and seven minutes in eternity led Pelley to mix Christianity into his ideology, forming the foundation of the movement. Hitler's Nazis wore brown shirts with their uniforms and inspired Pelley to outfit his Fascists in silver shirts

The call was upon him (Pelley) to join Hitler in the work of liberating the world from the grip of the Jews. According to the writings of Pelley, The Depression, unemployment, bank failures, repealing prohibition, Roosevelt, the brain trust, and recognition of Russia was all brought about by the Jews. According to the same source, our problems are all a matter of race, and Germany is the only nation that is attaining that racial purity.

By attempting to arouse hatred against the Jews, the Silver Shirts substitute race hatred for class consciousness to break down the solidarity of the working class, divide it, and wear off its resentment. This is one of the oldest political stratagems known—to make a scapegoat, center hatred against it, and thus gain power. In his autobiography, Hitler says, "*The people must be misled in order to gain the adherence of the masses*" (Author's emphasis).[32]

Elsie went to her first meeting and witnessed anti–Semitic and antiracial talk of blacks, Filipinos, and immigrants. Their extreme patriotism conveyed a self-righteous tone. The Ku Klux Klan, whom

Hitler admired, rubbed shoulders with this group. After each meeting, Elsie returned to the safety of her home and wrote what had occurred. She submitted her articles to the *Voice of Action,* using a pseudonym because of fear of repercussions if she was discovered.

At Silver Shirt meetings, Elsie listened to sensational stories about Communists with machine guns and armored cars who were hell-bent on taking over the country. The Shirts stressed the U.S. Constitution in their discussions: "All we need to do is enforce the Constitution." The American Vigilantes were an offshoot of this group, possibly the "enforcers." The Vigilantes frequented the waterfront, particularly during strikes, spotting leaders and reporting names to the authorities. They acted as guards for the scabs, and it was rumored that several Seattle policemen were members of the Vigilantes. At meetings, they practiced drills regarding the finer techniques of clubbing, boxing, and wrestling. A rattlesnake was their emblem. They had a bouncer or sergeant of arms at every Silver Shirt meeting. Elsie could feel his eyes scrutinizing her as soon as she walked in the door and took her place at that first meeting.

At the second or third meeting Elsie attended, she handed the bouncer her coat and sat down just in time for the meeting to begin. She nodded in agreement now and then, trying to act composed. Inwardly, she was terrified, and cold chills ran up and down her spine. People were milling around during a coffee break when someone tapped her on the shoulder. Elsie looked up into the bouncer's face. He was holding her coat. "I want you to leave right now. We know who you are." She slipped on her coat as she ran down the front steps. Her heels beat out a rapid staccato retreat as she made her way to the interurban stop and the electric train that took her home. "I don't think I imagined this.... I know I was followed. There weren't many people on the street. It was raining a fine mist, and I heard someone behind me. I turned around and there was somebody in a long coat trying to hide behind a telephone pole. I was terrified they would follow me home and attack me in the middle of the night." Elsie spent a sleepless night. She finished writing the article and told Wakefield she would no longer be doing undercover work.

On May 22, 1934, the *Voice of Action* continued its series on Fascism with an article "What Fascism Means to Women." The reporter was

Mary Jordan. Was that Elsie's pseudonym? She doesn't remember. The article began:

> Northwest women know that Fascism means the rule of capitalists by terror and force, the grinding down of workers to slavery and starvation; that it means war surely and inescapably—that it kills intellectual advancement. But do you realize what Fascism means to you (women) as a sex? ... Hitler came to power and issued an edict that "the employment field is to be relieved of women, who in accordance with the National Socialist program, are to be led back into their own domain." He has revived the phrase coined by the Kaiser that women should return to the Kinder, Kirche, Kuche (children, church, kitchen). Another reason why Fascism finds it necessary to end women's independence is because women oppose war. Government and law are closed to women in Germany.... Contrast this to the Soviet Union, the only country in the world where there is no discrimination because of sex. The highest role of women according to the Nazis is to be the "handmaid and servant of man." Lenin (Russian revolutionary leader) said: "We must free woman from her prison—the kitchen. We must win over to our side the millions of toiling women in towns and villages. Win them for our struggles and in particular for the Communist transformation of society. There can be no real mass movement without women." If Fascism engulfs America it has a worse fate for you than for men. When women join the struggle against Fascism they are not only fighting war and hunger, they are fighting the forces of decaying capitalism that would degrade them to the level of animals.

If Elsie didn't write those words, she most certainly agreed with them. She didn't know that just two years earlier on August 23, 1932, the Seattle Public Library Board of Trustees voted not to hire married women. The married women on staff were asked to resign. They had to cut costs because economic conditions had drastically cut their funding. The resolution read:

> "It shall be the policy of the Seattle Library Board not to employ a married woman whose husband is able to provide her a living. Any library employee marrying a husband able to provide a reasonable income will be required to tender her resignation."[33]

The economic and political dominos of world events began to teeter—Fascism vs. Communism, the call to war vs. pacifism, workers vs. owners, AFL vs. CIO, rich vs. poor, immigrants, Filipinos, Mexican-Americans, Jews, Negroes vs. job opportunities. Fascist Mussolini invaded the democratic country of Ethiopia under Haille Selassie in 1935. In Spain, the Spanish Civil War erupted in 1936. In the United States the same year, the autoworkers staged a sit-down strike at the Ford factory.

In this cauldron of fomenting issues, Ernie's divorce was granted, and Ernie and Elsie married on April 8, 1936. "We went to the courthouse. It was a civil ceremony with a justice of the peace and a couple standing up for us. It was short and not much to-do. I suppose we went out for drinks afterwards." No pictures were taken. No black and white photograph with a happy couple smiling back at the camera that would be saved for decades. The only preserved image of that day is faded in the back of Elsie's memory.

CHAPTER 15:

A Stage Set for Change

Meeting with Elsie

"Not to change the subject, dear ..." I took that as a signal that we were done for the afternoon, "... but I'm very depressed." Elsie looked at me intensely. "You may not agree with me, but I believe our government is behind the invasion of Lebanon, and I have been to that train station in India that was blown up. It is a very busy place where all the trains come together. These terrorists are brilliant. How do you fight that?" I stuffed the rest of my things in my bag. "The world situation is a mess." Her voice rose, and her eyes burned like hot coals. Then I jumped at the sound of her hand slapping the table. "And that son-of-a-bitch in the UN isn't helping matters. He's just a warmonger." She paused. "It's going to escalate into a nuclear event. I've never felt this sense of hopelessness before. I'm glad I won't be around to see where this is going."

This rare moment of pessimism, something I had not seen in Elsie, possessed her and left an oppressive feeling in the room. "Elsie, how can you say that? After all you've been through ... the Depression, WWII? Didn't you feel hopeless then?"

"No. Never. People took a stand in the thirties, and during WWII, our government had a plan, but this present administration is taking us all down. And people are so apathetic. I don't see any commitment to stand up and make a difference. And …" her voice sounded tired as she finished the conversation, "I don't see anyone rising up to lead the way." Elsie followed me onto the deck. I was almost surprised to see the sun still shining and the birds in a nearby tree still chirping. Potted tomatoes, orange marigolds, blue petunias, and aromatic herbs lined her deck.

Then Elsie walked to her potted plants and said, "Here, dear." She bent over, picked two tomatoes, and handed them to me. "Aren't they lovely?" I took that hope home with me.

* * * * *

The bitterness of the January 1937 air edged the retreating day into darkness by the time Elsie got off work. She hurried to Washington Hall for a benefit to raise money for Tom Mooney's release from prison—a labor leader from San Francisco who had been in prison since 1916 for a crime that could not be proven he committed. As Elsie entered the warmth of the building, she was met with the rousing sounds of Papery's orchestra. Ernie planned to meet her as soon as his meeting with the Filipino union leaders was over. She ducked into the ladies' room to refresh her makeup and hoist up her orange, cotton stockings, which insisted on bagging toward her ankles. All the radical women were boycotting silk stockings after Japan had invaded Manchuria and threatened continued, aggressive action in China. As Elsie tried to smooth out the wrinkles, she smiled to herself, remembering the first time her mother saw her wearing those stockings. "Honey, now I'm convinced you're committed to the Communists, otherwise you wouldn't be caught dead in such ugly stockings!"

As Elsie left the ladies' room, a woman dressed in black brushed by her, and they exchanged a brief greeting. The woman wore a black, floor-length skirt with a tight bodice buttoned to her neck. She did not wear makeup and had pulled her hair into a tight bun, which gave her an old fashioned look. As the woman made her way to the bar, a few men approached her with cocky swaggers. One man offered her a cigarette. She held the cigarette in her mouth and leaned toward him for a light while she placed her hand over his. The bartender winked when a customer at the end of the bar motioned for another drink and said, "She's got a mattress on her back, that one." Elsie was familiar with this cult of women within radical circles. The dress was the reverse of the hippie culture of the sixties, but the effect, rebellion of the status quo, was the same. A social and political movement attracted a diversity of people no matter what decade.

Elsie scanned the crowd for Ernie and spotted him in a circle of men just as he took a fast gulp of whiskey. The men's conversation, punctuated with gesticulations and bursts of laughter, grew louder while the drinks flowed. At one point, she noticed the men lean toward Ernie, drinks in hand, nodding their heads in agreement as he spoke. Elsie wound her way through the mix of men and women. The hall buzzed with talk and laughter amidst the sounds of the orchestra warming up. She caught bits and pieces of conversation as she crossed the floor. A man with a drink in his hand, his voice edged with agitation, said to his friend, "We need our civil liberties protected I'm telling you. Our freedom of speech and assembly—we have to preserve them. And that's what the vigilantes are trying to do—take all that away."

Another man replied, "Heard the vigilantes raided a unit meeting last night. One of these days the mayor's goons are gonna go too far. They're after the union guys, too. Guess they arrested nine people. Damn it all! That criminal syndicalism stuff has got to go, speaking of civil rights!"

Voice of Action, March 1, 1935, Richard V. Correll, woodcut artist (University of Washington Libraries, Newspaper collections)

Elsie skirted a cluster of men and women as they engaged in lively conversation. "Can you believe the Nazis? How can we have the Olympics in that Fascist state?"

A woman remarked, "Damn right they should boycott the Olympic games."

Ernie and Elsie drifted between the dance floor and conversation at the bar. The more Ernie chewed the rag, the more he drank. As the evening wore on, Ernie became soused. He stumbled unsteadily toward Elsie and motioned for another dance, but Elsie thought otherwise.

"Ernie, we're going home." He leaned on her as she struggled to keep him upright. "Come on, Ernest. Let's go. I have a cab waiting." Someone offered to help, and she defiantly shook her head. She saw people's looks of embarrassment for her as they turned to avoid eye contact. The crowd moved to make way for them. Elsie, half the size of Ernie, strained under his weight as he leaned on her and tripped and stumbled across the floor, down the stairs, and outside to the waiting cab.

This scene repeated itself on a regular basis. In telling the story, Elsie said, "Why he was never brought before the Review Commission—the disciplinary part of the Communist Party—I'll never know. Other people were disciplined for drunkenness in public places. Ernie was not. Maybe his drinking was a result of resenting my steady job, my independence. I didn't want a conventional marriage of being a homemaker and having children and neither did Ernie. But I also wanted companionship in our marriage, yet when we were home alone, Ernie spent his time reading and studying the issues. We didn't talk. I was disappointed we didn't share more intellectually. I suppose he was my alter ego. When he was stumping for the party or the CIO—that was me up on the soapbox, working to bring socialism to the people. And yet, I sensed there was something always eating at Ernie, something he couldn't tell me. At that point my life, my independence, began to fall into a mire." Ernie and Elsie spent less time together, and threw their entire energies into the organization of industrial unions, for which the Communist Party was in full support. Workers of the world unite.

As a CIO organizer, Ernie was assigned to organize the cannery workers, who were generally Filipinos who worked in Seattle and Alaska. The Philippines was a U.S. Territory, and as a result, its citizens were educated about the "land of opportunity" and the great American dream.

Immigration was tightening up for Asians, but the Filipino nationals were able to move to the states. Many of them enrolled in the University of Washington so they could return home to the Philippines and educate their people or remain in the United States and earn a decent living. "We often times commented that the Cannery Workers Union had more PhD's than any other union," said Elsie.

The Filipinos experienced the graft that came with the job. They worked summer cannery jobs, taking the unskilled positions that no one else wanted—cutting and canning the salmon. The companies learned how to navigate around the governance of the NLRB. A hiring contractor charged the immigrants a fee just to work in a cannery. The Filipino workers knew they were being taken advantage of and used the rights guaranteed by the NRA to establish their own union. In 1933, the AFL issued a charter for the local cannery union. Membership grew, but the labor contractors were not happy. A union for the Filipinos was a threat to the hiring contractors' job security. Trouble brewed, and in 1936, the president of the cannery union was murdered, and the blame fell on a labor contractor. Ernie started to recruit the Filipinos in Seattle for the CIO, trying to convince them not to sign up with the AFL. He promised the CIO would halt the racial discrimination and stop the contract hiring. With CIO recruitment in mind, Ernie and Elsie spent many nights socializing with the Filipinos at pool and dance halls.

Dancing and socializing nearly eclipsed the potency of the mimeograph machine when it came to recruitment for the party and the CIO. Due to the lack of women at the dance halls— many of the Filipinos had left their wives and sweethearts in the Philippines to come to America—Elsie did not sit out a dance. Ernie thought she was making a great sacrifice in helping the cause, but she wasn't. She loved to dance, and she enjoyed the company of these men. Elsie recalled, "They had a wonderful quality that was new to me—a singleness of purpose, a unity that was beautiful, and purity I had never seen." Many planned to return after they were educated to improve their homeland.

The vote—CIO or AFL—was put to the cannery union in 1937. Ernie had worked day and night to recruit their votes. There was one final push, one final dance, before the day of the vote. The dance hall was packed, and the talk circulated around the union vote. The memory of the murder of their popular union president stirred emotions. Groups of men throughout the hall formed huddles of heated discussions. Some were afraid of retaliation by the labor contractors if they left the AFL. Some questioned the authenticity of the CIO. Ernie was in the middle of one of the huddles. Elsie was dancing when she noticed the huddle grew into a mob, and a man was down. Ernie had been stabbed in the groin. "I'm sure it was a goon working for the labor contractors. It happened so quickly that no one saw it. Fortunately, it was a superficial wound." But Elsie didn't know it at the time. She rushed over to Ernie, and told him she would call for an ambulance. Someone offered to take him to the hospital. "No! I'll be okay!" By the harsh sound of his voice, no one argued. Elsie credited it to being "merchant marine tough."

The vote that ensued had to be held at the fire stations throughout Seattle because there were so many workers voting. "If I remember correctly, there were as many as ten thousand." The vote overwhelmingly favored the CIO. Ernie and the other organizers had gained the trust and following of the workers, and the CIO was growing in strength and numbers. As a result of his leadership skills, Ernie was sent to Alaska for several months to oversee the CIO union contract and make sure it was observed. While small victories were won on the home front, major world events were lining up and threatening freedom and democracy all over the globe.

The headline news of the *Voice of Action* in the spring of 1935 cautioned about the escalation of war and Fascism. The political winds warned of war. Elsie remembered the shock of hearing the news that Mussolini had attacked Ethiopia, a burgeoning, democratic government run by Hailie Salasie.

That evening, Elsie and Ernie were at a social event at one of the meeting halls. The buzz of conversation focused on the invasion—evidence of Fascism on the march, which meant an immediate threat to the USSR and the world. Elsie, drink in hand, joined a small group that included Revels Cayton. She was alarmed by the invasion and voiced her concern: "Mussolini's move on Ethiopia is proof of Fascism spreading in the region. It's terrible, and I can't imagine where it's going to lead." Heads nodded but no one really seemed clear as to what they should think. She asked Revels, "What do you think? What's your opinion on this invasion?"

Revels replied, "I'll wait and see what the *Daily Worker* says about it." That was the end of the conversation. Elsie was disappointed. It was obvious to Elsie what this invasion meant, yet an opinion should not be proffered until the party line was determined. The party's opinion was the only opinion. Period.

At times, Elsie's independent, discerning nature reached an impasse with the Communist Party line. She could be described as being headstrong—maybe it was her Huguenot ancestors whispering warnings through some genetic transmission, but Elsie always made up her own mind after weighing the odds. "I had a firm footing in Marxism before I ever became a Communist Party member. My economic and political beliefs were based on my own experience and not someone propagandizing me. I came to those beliefs *entirely* on my own, so I had a somewhat different attitude than many of the Communists I associated with. And that included Ernie. Ernie accepted the party mandates hook, line, and sinker. A Communist party member was expected to endorse the party line dictated from Moscow whether or not you agreed—no questions asked. And you were subject to discipline if you disagreed."

A rumor started circulating within the party regarding a fellow comrade. The rumor spotlighted this woman's disloyalty to the party because she questioned some leadership decisions. Discipline was in order. As a result, Winifred suffered character assassination, and her career was destroyed. Elsie, terribly upset with what had transpired, tried to confide in Ernie on a rare evening when they were home together. "These rumors they're spreading about Winnie are a hatchet job! Ernie, she's a good, sincere person. We can't let this happen!"

"She deserves it. You have to support the leaders' decisions. That's just how it is. Otherwise there's no unity!" Ernie's words sizzled with anger. Elsie threw her opinions back at him, and the argument escalated. Then Elsie realized where it was going and let it drop. She knew that if she persisted and went to party officials to complain about Winifred's case, she not only risked being expelled from the party, but she knew it could lead to serious consequences for her marriage. She kept her probing questions to herself, and Ernie and Elsie never discussed the issues in the privacy of their home after that.

"So, to my everlasting *dis*credit," ninety-eight-year-old Elsie stated, "I kept my mouth shut. If there are any regrets that I have in my life, it's that I didn't stand up for Winifred." The party and Ernie were bringing Elsie's independence into check.

The Communist Party used democratic centralism—a political principle of resolving any disagreement of policy regarding the party line handed down from the Comintern in Moscow. Elsie realized later that it was also a way of circumventing democracy. According to Elsie, the party had become heavy on centralism and weak on democracy. Winnie experienced democratic centralism at work.

Independence on the world stage was also being threatened. In 1937, when Fascism reared its ugly head, the ILA up and down the west coast refused to load scrap iron onto Japanese ships. Bridges warned, "It'll just come back to us in the form of bullets." The union workers also refused to unload ships from Hitler's Germany. "Interfere with the foreign policy of the country? Sure as hell! That's our job, that's our privilege, that's our right, and that's our duty!"[34]

The crash of 1929 that led to faltering economic conditions worldwide tilted the dominoes of global issues. Fascist leaders like Hitler and Mussolini gave the final collective push. In 1937, the same year Ernie helped organize the Filipino workers, the Spanish Civil War raised an alarm with progressives, radicals, and the CPUSA. Elsie's anti–Semitic incident of mistaken identity and the Silver Shirts ideology were being played out on the world stage. Elsie's unit meetings began to take on urgency when discussing world events.

The internal struggle in Spain had been brewing for some time, as most conflicts do. The tension involved the Nationalists, headed by General Franco, and the Loyalists, made up of socialists and Communists, also called the National Front. They were battling for control of the democratically elected government of Spain. Fascist Italy and Nazi Germany sent troops and military to aid the Nationalists. The USSR, feeling the squeeze from its Fascist neighbors, sent military equipment and advisors to aid in the struggle for the Loyalists and a democratic socialist government. The governments of the United States, Britain, and France remained neutral. The Comintern in Moscow sent out a call for volunteers from Europe and the United States to form the International Brigades to fight for the Loyalists. In 1937, Ernest Hemingway went to Spain as a newspaper correspondent, and Picasso painted the horrors of the bombing of Guernica, where Germany's Air Force honed their skills for a future conflict.

In 1937, Ernest Fox became a recruiter for the Abraham Lincoln Brigade, which was composed of young American men ready to defeat Fascism and protect democracy. The Lincoln Brigade was the first American military force to include blacks and whites integrated on an equal basis. The waterfront and the Communist Party were likely places to find recruits. The median age and attitude involved single, young men anxious for adventure and ready to fight for a righteous cause. Morris Rappaport's only son went to Spain, and never returned.

Elsie befriended many of the recruits before they shipped out. She remembered one boy in particular. "He was a very sweet boy. Ernie and I decided to buy him a new suit to wear on the ship to Spain. We went to a men's clothing store with him. Before we bought the suit, he checked to make sure there was a union label on it. He looked so handsome in that new suit and so proud ... and so very young."

The losses were great. The war ended on April 1, 1939, when Madrid fell, and General Franco took control. In the next four years, under Franco's authoritarian rule, the Loyalists were dubbed "reds," hundreds of thousands were imprisoned, and as many as thirty-seven thousand anti–Spain suspects were executed. However, the Spanish Civil War portended a much bigger conflict.

The United States government tried to appear neutral when it came to world politics yet began taking measures to rein in the radicals at home. The success of the progressive changes in the industrial unions, namely the Communist Party, caught the attention of corporations, capitalists, and congressmen, and Congress started enacting laws. The Voorhis Act, passed in 1938, stated that the U.S. Government had the right to prosecute anyone advocating the overthrow of the government. The Dies Committee was formed to investigate subversives, and Communists were suspect.

Finally, the precarious line-up of conflicting ideologies came crashing down. Stalin, who had called for help in protecting the motherland from the Fascist scourge, did an about-face and signed a pact with Hitler in August of 1939. The Hitler-Stalin Pact was a nonaggression pact between the USSR and Germany. The two leaders secretly divided Poland. In

Hitler's mind, the USSR was neutralized, so he kept up the pace. He invaded and occupied his share of Poland.

In America, the news of the pact was like an unexpected tsunami to the CPUSA. Hitler, driven by his desire for more land for agricultural and industrial purposes, hated Communists, and Communists hated Hitler and his Fascist intentions. How could Stalin reach across the border and shake Hitler's hand? While the party was reeling and trying to make sense of what they viewed as a betrayal, Elsie was trying to make sense of her marriage. The strain of staying in the party while questioning its motives and Ernie's alienation became too great for Elsie. She was on the verge of a nervous breakdown.

The morning alarm went off—a typical workday—and as Elsie stood up and walked to the bathroom, she lost her balance. She grabbed the wall for support, but her legs continued to weave and buckle. She knew the imbalance was not her physical but mental state. It made her angry that she let herself get to this state. She reasoned that she needed time to gather herself and get back on track. She called Mr. Parry and took the day off from work. Then she called her mother. "I'm going to spend the day at the peninsula. Would you come with me?" Elsie reached out to the security she remembered as a child—her mother and the outdoors. She was looking for an anchor in a world spinning out of control.

Elsie rented fishing equipment from a lodge. Sitting on a boulder beside a clear river, she concentrated on the mechanics of fishing.

1939 - Elsie, fishing on the Washington peninsula

The line whirred as she cast and then clicked as it set. The current pulled on her line as she reeled and stopped, reeled and stopped, waiting patiently for a nibble or bite. She repeated the motion over and over, moving every so often farther upstream while her mother sat on a blanket reading a book under the cover of towering pine trees. Birds chattered in the boughs, and an occasional swallow skimmed above the water. Elsie must have felt herself return to a center of calm and security—a feeling that drew Macie back to the haven of the Powder River ranch as a single mother, the peaceful feeling of a young ranch girl on the plains of Eastern Montana. Elsie never caught a fish but it didn't matter. She felt renewed and back in charge of herself in a world of uncertainty.

Elsie had befriended a woman who lived on a dude ranch in Eastern Washington near Ellensburg. She spent weekends at the ranch renewing her love for horseback riding and met new friends. Her present social circle did not include Ernie.

1939 - Dude ranch, Eastern Washington

The party, as a result of the Stalin-Hitler Pact, was losing membership, but Ernie hung on to his core beliefs. "It's just capitalist propaganda; there's a bigger reason Stalin did this," he reasoned. In the meantime,

Britain and France declared war on Germany but did not come to the aid of Poland. In the spring of 1940, Hitler overpowered Denmark, Norway, the Netherlands, Belgium, and finally France. Then in June of 1941, Hitler invaded the Soviet Union. The nonaggression pact that Stalin had signed became null and void. The lines of war were drawn.

The European Allies declared support of the Soviet Union in their defense. The Communist Party was now allied with the United States, and the party was vindicated, at least overtly. However, J. Edgar Hoover, the director of the FBI, was still persistent and on guard, looking for reds wherever he could find them, and he worked with Congress to tighten the noose. The Voorhis Act morphed into the Smith Act and made it a crime to advocate the overthrow of the United States Government. The escalation of the war in Europe fueled fear on the home front, encouraging Hoover and team to sniff out the subversives.

Routing out Communists became a popular sport. When the party was working in a popular front strategy within other organizations, Ernie wasn't afraid to make his political affiliation known. It wasn't difficult for the FBI to track Ernie, and criminal syndicalism charges were a threat away. Elsie and Ernie took a direct hit when a radio announcer pointed out their lifestyle on the air. "And there are people working out there, espousing around the city that they are working to improve conditions of the working class. Like Ernest and Elsie Fox—Communists who live in a luxurious apartment and apparently are not wanting ..." He tried to make them out as frauds. But like Elsie's comrades found out after that first meeting when she arrived in her high heels—looks are deceiving.

Between 1939 and 1941, the FBI, under the blessings of the Department of Justice, compiled lists of dangerous "enemy aliens" and citizens—a list called the Custodial Detention Index (the CDI).[35] Unknown to Elsie or Ernie, Ernie's name was on the list. In 1940, the census identified people based on their ethnicity. Under the 1940 Alien Registration Act, later known as the Smith Act, all aliens were ordered to register with the U.S. Government. Ernie, although he had been born in Germany, believed he obtained derivative citizenship when his father, Otto Fuchs (Fox), filed for citizenship in 1910. When Ernie discovered in the late thirties that his father never completed the paperwork, he did not try to apply for citizenship because of his involvement in the radical unions and the Communist Party. A lawyer advised him to wait and apply for citizenship after things quieted down politically. German immigrants, just like in World War I, were viewed with suspicion. Since Ernie did not register in 1940 as an enemy alien, the FBI took notice.

In the meantime, Elsie came to the conclusion that her marriage reflected the chaos and uncertainty of national and world events. Elsie's good friend Irene had moved to San Francisco and found a job with the Harry Bridges' ILWU (International Longshoremen & Warehouse Union) as a secretary, and Elsie decided to join her.

In September of 1941, Elsie told Ernie she wanted a divorce. "When I told him, he had this look on his face as if he was relieved. I wondered to myself, why? But I just filed that thought away. It was a mutual agreement, and we divided what little we had. It was all quite friendly." Soon after, Elsie boarded a train for San Francisco.

TOM JONES PARRY, INC.

Advertising

HOGE BUILDING - SEATTLE

TELEPHONE SENECA 0989

October 9, 1941

To whom it may concern:

This letter is written to set forth the qualifications and character of Miss Elsie Gilland, who has been in our company since 1927 until the present -- during the last ten years holding the office of secretary.

During these fourteen years Miss Gilland has proven herself to be a woman of unusual ability, energy, and unfailing devotion to the duties of her work.

This work, in addition to that of taking dictation, typing, filing, etc., has been varied and difficult.

She has kept books faultlessly, made out accurately and correctly all the various government tax statements, kept track of the finances, negotiated loans and put through trade acceptances with our bank, and, in general, handled every phase of accounting and business management in addition to her secretarial duties.

In addition, she has been an excellent office receptionist, dealt with clients and salesmen alike in a manner to win respect and goodwill, and, on several occasions when illness or long trips have necessitated my absence from the business, she has handled all its affairs competently and intelligently.

In the fourteen years she has been with our company we have had periods of prosperity and of adversity. During the dark days of '32 and '33 she worked courageously and intelligently to keep the business on an even keel.

I can think of no office or secretarial work for which I cannot recommend her without qualification. In addition to her business experience, she has had high school and some university education, is well read, and is in every way a young woman of character, intelligence, and culture.

The individual or firm which employs her will be fortunate, I am sure, and will find that I have in no way exaggerated her abilities and character.

Yours very truly,

TOM JONES PARRY, Inc.

By Tom Jones Parry

TJP:EG

CHAPTER 16:

A Woman with Independent Means

Meeting with Elsie

Elsie and I had talked for several hours. We passionately addressed issues of the thirties as if they were current events instead of chapters in a U.S. History book—or not, as Elsie believed. "They take a lot out of history before it's printed into textbooks and taught in schools. Students these days only learn half of the story."

After awhile, Elsie sat back against the sofa cushions. She said softly, "You should have been born back then, dear. You would have enjoyed those times. You would have fit right in." The decades that separated us dissolved in that moment. I saw Elsie as my contemporary, my girlfriend, as we walked arm in arm down the Seattle streets on our way to a lecture, dance, or movie. We went shopping for clothes, and she advised me on what looked best for my figure. We stopped off at a corner pub, ordered a frothy beer, and flirted with some handsome men while we discussed the headlines in the *Voice* or the *Seattle Post-Intelligencer.*

I looked at my ninety-nine-year-old friend and said wistfully, "I love big-band music, and Nat King Cole has always been my favorite singer of all time!"

She rolled her eyes in an imitation swoon and in mutual agreement. Then she started singing "Imagination."

* * * * *

Elsie secured a secretarial job at an advertising agency in San Francisco during the fall of 1941. She and Irene settled into an apartment on Green Street. "It had a balcony that overlooked the bay and Oakland Bay Bridge. There was a fireplace. It was perfect. And it had rosemary bushes along the steps to the apartment. You could smell the rosemary as you walked up the steps." The change of environment suited Elsie. She wrote her mother and told her the shopping was fantastic. She may not have told her the nightclubs were even more fantastic. Smoky bars and nightclubs were a haven to jazz musicians on Market Street. Elsie remembered one small nondescript joint where she spent an evening drinking with friends and listening to Louis Armstrong singing. One of the songs was "A Kiss to Build a Dream On."

According to Elsie, the Top of the Mark was another popular place. "I heard Tony Bennett perform there. Oh, honey, there was such terrific music at the clubs." And so was the dancing. Elsie attracted several suitors but found that they lacked a certain spark and fire. She wrote Ernie and gave him her address and phone number.

Irene, her roommate, had nine siblings and had grown up on a farm in Washington. When Elsie discovered Irene had never had a birthday party, she went to work on planning a party. They would make it a double birthday celebration since Elsie's birthday was a few days earlier. The morning of December 7, 1941, Elsie and Irene were cleaning their apartment and cooking for their guests that would arrive in the late afternoon. The radio's volume was turned up high, sounding throughout the apartment. Glenn Miller's rendition of "Chattanooga Choo Choo" may have been playing when a frantic news bulletin interrupted the upbeat song: "Pearl Harbor has been attacked! Japanese bombers have targeted ships in the harbor!" Elsie and Irene turned the radio up and stood in shock as they listened. Elsie's brother, Frank, was stationed at Pearl Harbor.

As the day progressed, news reports escalated from shock to terror that the west coast might be the next target. The scrap iron that the progressive unions and Communist Party warned about in the thirties did indeed come back in the form of bullets. The surprise element, Elsie knew, wasn't *if* they would attack, but when. The birthday festivities turned into a somber gathering of friends with an ear to the radio for news bulletins.

Elsie later found out that her brother, who had been on a ship collecting garbage from the naval cruisers, encouraged his crew not to panic. Once Frank had helped restore order, he and his crew began pulling sailors from sinking ships or plucking them out of the water. His valiant spirit won him a medal for valor.

Elsie, Macie, and Frank Jr.

The next day, December 8th, the United States Congress declared war on Japan. Three days later, Hitler declared war on the United States, and the United States declared war on Germany and Italy. Overnight, the country went from a somewhat neutral player in the world conflict to fighting a war on both the Pacific and European fronts.

Patriotism was the fever of the day and knew no class or social boundaries. Everyone backed the war, from the bosses to laborers, unions and employers, rich and poor. Boys walked out of high school classes to enlist. The Allies, now strengthened by the might of the United States military, pledged to help defend the Soviet Union. The American Communist Party joined the cause with the mantra, "We must subordinate the class struggle for the national interest."

The country spun into a frantic motion of military preparedness. San Francisco was a naval hub on the west coast, with ships being built and sailors shipping out to the Pacific arena. Ernie came to San Francisco and signed up for duty, probably as a merchant marine on a liberty ship.

Elsie quit her advertising job out of principle. The ad agency she worked for put a full-page advertisement in the major newspapers from Alaska to Arizona claiming there was no connection between Standard Oil of California, the ad agency, and IG Farben—the leading industrial giant in Germany. IG Farben had backed Hitler's rise to power and was a chief supplier of war material for Germany "You don't have to be very smart to know that if there was no connection you wouldn't have to deny any of those claims by putting ads in the papers!" Elsie explained. It was repugnant to her to be part, however slight, of any institution that even suggested a connection to Hitler's Fascist state.

Elsie immediately found work at the Labor's Unity for Victory Committee—an organization made up of the AFL, CIO, Railroad Brotherhoods, and Independent Unions. It was one of many committees that sprung up nationwide and worked toward avoiding strikes and concentrated on the war effort. During this maelstrom of activity, Ernie and Elsie were reunited.

Once again, their relationship was ignited by the passions of the times. They talked about how, finally, the Soviet Union would get help and recognition from America. Ernie felt the Communist Party was vindicated from the Hitler-Stalin Pact. The country, it seemed, was on the cusp of a new world where Fascism would be defeated and socialism would take hold. While waiting for Ernie to be assigned to a ship, they attended party council meetings, went to social events, and made acquaintances with progressives. Once again, Elsie felt a forward momentum in her political convictions, driven in part by Ernie's incessant energy and drive. They decided to have their divorce annulled. Elsie can still see Market Street with the Ferry Building on one end and the bustle and excitement of wartime activity.

Elsie's high heels clicked lightly as they turned the corner onto the brick sidewalks of Market Street and made their way to a lawyer's office. They walked past the Ferry Building with the giant clock at its center. Elsie put her arm through Ernie's while clutching her handbag in the other hand. "We must be closer together this time, Ernest. We need to be honest and forthright. Don't you agree?" Ernest squeezed her hand and nodded, smiling at her. A boisterous bunch of sailors strode toward the embarcadero where ships awaited them. Bouquets of flowers wrapped with red, white, and blue ribbons filled a street vendor's cart, and tugboat horns sounded in the distance. A yellow streetcar clattered by, electricity sparking from the cables. Ernie and Elsie dashed up the stairs to the lawyer's office and signed the necessary papers to cancel the interlocutory divorce decree.

Ernie was due to sail sometime in April. They would stay the next month at 273 Green Street. Then, Elsie planned to continue rooming with Irene until Ernie returned from war.

While the United States staged their battle on two fronts, plans to secure the home turf swung into motion. Wartime breeds suspicion, and Germans, Italians, and Japanese were now the enemy, even if they lived in the United States. A law buried in the depths of congressional records since 1798, called the Alien and Sedition Acts (or Enemy Aliens Act), was resurrected with renewed importance. Congress had passed the act a century and a half ago to give presidents executive control over resident enemy nationals during time of war. It enabled a president to apprehend, restrain, secure, and remove enemy aliens.[36] President Roosevelt decided to dust off the act and enforce its statutes. The FBI, the Immigration and Naturalization Service (INS), and even the United States Army joined in the effort of rounding up and securing enemy aliens.

Japanese Americans were arrested and relocated to inland concentration camps away from the west coast. They could be released and find new homes in the interior under certain conditions: (1) they signed a loyalty oath to the government; (2) they obtained a sponsor to vouch for them; or (3) they joined a branch of military service. Many of them opted to stay in the barbed wire containment camps scattered throughout the West.

Selected internment was chosen for the Germans and Italians with care in order not to induce the hysteria caused by the sedition laws during WWI. The hysteria of that time simply went underground, where it simmered in the undercover work of the FBI and the Department of Justice. Selected Germans and Italians, many referred by the FBI based on information collected by informants, were designated "potentially dangerous." Unlike the Japanese, they were not given options. They were simply interned, oftentimes without being charged. Ernie had several strikes against him: he was German without U.S. citizenship, he was on the Custodial Index List, and he had an extensive FBI file documenting his Communist and union activity.

In September of 1941, an FBI agent interviewed a murderer scheduled for execution at San Quentin penitentiary. The convict, who had probably been an informant for the FBI, told the agent, "Yes, I know Ernest Fox." The agent took notes while the man described being at a meeting where Ernest and other party leaders gave instructions on how to sabotage a ship and bring it down. One could speculate the inmate produced juicy information for the FBI in hopes that his sentence might be commuted. It didn't help. He was executed the next day, and the agent filed the interview with no evidence to prove otherwise. The 1798 law provided the ammunition, and the FBI provided the targets.

In April of 1942, Elsie went to Fisherman's Wharf with Ernie, who was reporting for duty on a liberty ship due to sail soon. The scene was repeated over and over again on docks, harbors, railway stations, and airports throughout the country. Crying families and girlfriends sent the soldiers off and watched as the ships disappeared over the curvature of the horizon, headed for a world in chaos. Elsie may have shed a few tears; certainly, they shared a long kiss and one last hug. Ernie marched onto the ship with confidence and pride, ready to defend democracy. Elsie, unlike many women standing on the dock that day, was a woman of independent means, and despite her husband's forthcoming departure and extended absence, she was secure and confident about her future.

The next day, the phone rang at the Victory Committee's office, and Elsie answered. It was Ernie. FBI agents had boarded his ship and arrested him the day he was supposed to sail. He was charged with being a dangerous enemy alien and taken to Sharp Park, a detention camp near San Francisco. He asked Elsie to send him a change of clothes and told her it seemed he would be there indefinitely. Elsie wasted no time. She sent the clothes and immediately secured the help of a progressive lawyer, George Anderson. A letter from Ernie soon followed:

> Detained Enemy Alien Mail—Sharp Park, Calif.—April 1942
>
> My Darling Elsie
>
> It's rather difficult to write a letter under the present circumstances, because my main concern is over you. My detention at this camp will be tremendously easier if I know you have the patience and fortitude to wait.
>
> Mr. Anderson was out to see me Tuesday and assured me everything would be done to find a hasty solution to my particular problem. Elsie, if I've caused you any unnecessary hardship or sorrow, I'm dreadfully sorry. I had some difficulty in getting my clothes but they finally arrived and [I] feel considerably better.
>
> Visiting hours at this camp are limited from 9 A.M. to 9 P.M. except Monday. Mr. Anderson will give you detailed instructions on how to get here. Try and get someone to drive you out if possible. Please tell my friends to write.
>
> With deepest love, Ernie

A total of 292 people were held in this camp waiting to be sent to more permanent camps. The detainees received prisoner of war stationery, were allowed three letters a week, and were informed of visiting hours. Most of the detainees were Japanese. Forty-one of them were Germans with a mix of loyalties—German Jews, German Communists, and Germans with pro–Nazi leanings.[37] Some of the Germans arrested had direct ties to Germany or membership in a pro–German organization. Others, like Ernie, were either ignorant or defiant of alien enemy regulations. A few detainees opposed the American involvement in the war.

Before the German aliens could be interned, paroled, or released, the Justice Department granted hearings. A U.S. attorney for each judicial district heard the cases and then made recommendations to U.S. attorney general, Francis Biddle. A board consisted of FBI and INS representatives and three civilians appointed by Mr. Biddle. The board would decide if the internee was dangerous, not so dangerous, or harmless. The Alien Enemy Control Unit (AECU) under the Justice Department reviewed the board's recommendations before sending the case to Biddle, and he would make the final determination. An internee could apply for a second hearing.

Ernie sat in the internment camp thinking of his fellow mates sailing to war. He asked Elsie to send books. His ire grew. Being idle did not suit him, and he exchanged heated words with FBI agents; the incident added yet another page to his already bulging file. Now he was labeled as having a violent temperament. In May, he was taken to the San Francisco Post Office for a hearing. He was charged with failing to register as an enemy alien in 1940 and accused of lying about his citizenship, yet the AECU recommended parole. In May, Biddle denied parole and ruled that Ernie would remain interned. Biddle reasoned Ernest Fox was potentially dangerous, taught sabotage, and had a violent temperament. At the end of July, Biddle ordered Ernie sent to Ft. McDowell on Angel Island—an island on the way to Alcatraz—before being sent to Camp Forrest, Tennessee, the end of August.[38]

Ernie and the other German internees ultimately faced deportation to Nazi Germany—it was just a matter of when. All of the Germans were held in one area, which added to the stress. There were German Jews with Nazi sympathizers and Communists. The volatile mix made everyone edgy.

Elsie traveled weekly to Sharp Park. She would not be able to visit Ernie once he went to Angel Island, since the only transportation to get there was an army transport ship. Elsie brought him some food, clothes, the *Daily News,* and books of political interest.

A young man arrived to visit Ernie and offer support. This was someone Elsie had never seen or heard of before. "We met in New York," he explained. "I was just a kid. Ernest was a merchant marine, and he ate at our house a few times. We got to be friends. Guess we've always stayed in touch." Elsie remembered the puzzled, questioning look he gave her when they were introduced. It made her slightly uncomfortable, but, like a pesky fly, the feeling eventually went away. There were more immediate matters to deal with. On her last visit before he was transferred to Angel Island, Elsie couldn't give Ernie a reassuring hug as they said good-bye—a wire fence separated them.

Elsie started job hunting again after the Victory Committee folded due to lack of funds.[39] She had established a reputation for being a hard worker and soon found a temporary, secretarial job in the Machinists Union at the Labor Temple in the Mission Area.[40] When that job ended, Elsie went to work as a dispatcher for the National Maritime Union—a job she held throughout most of the war years.

Elsie and three other women were the first female dispatchers ever hired on the west coast and they were under the gun to get the job done with little or no training. It was either figure it out now or look for another job. Elsie saved a 1943 newspaper article that reported on the women dispatchers featuring a picture of Elsie at the dispatcher's window and a sailor peering through the bars at her. According to the article these four women—Elsie, Mrs. Jennifer Polk, Miss Evelyn Levin, and Mrs. Mary Lee—handled hundreds of men in the course of a day. "Their task is difficult—they're the first woman group to perform it on the west coast and it consists of serving in liaison capacity between ship operators and the men who wait for merchant marine assignments. The four speedily and accurately assemble the crews for the ever increasing armada of tankers, freighters and troop ships that stream from this port."[41] Elsie and other dispatchers filled the jobs for deck engineers, pumpmen, oilers, galleymen, and utility men when a ship operator requested a crew and at the same time tried to fill the job preferences of the men.

IDENTIFICATION ONLY—NOT A PASS
CAPTAIN OF PORT
San Francisco, Calif.
FOX, Elsie Mary
NAME
Dispatcher
OCCUPATION
Nat'l. Maritime Un.
SPONSOR
P.E.CRONK, COMDR.
VALIDATED - UNITED STATES COAST GUARD

It was a job Elsie never forgot. The dispatch room in the National Maritime Union building filled with cigarette smoke as the men sat around and played cards, waiting for a ship assignment. Elsie handed a job order to a young man and said, "Good luck." He hardly looked old enough to be a merchant marine as he reached for the envelope, just tall enough to look at Elsie and nod a thank you. There were white-headed old salts, talking among themselves, proudly wearing NMU pins that signified their ship had been torpedoed. One man stood at the window and presented his union card and passport to Elsie. "Hey, am I going to have to ship out with them?" he asked as he jerked his head toward a group of black union members.

Elsie shoved his papers back at him and retorted, "Listen, Buster, you don't have much choice. It's either this or the army. Now what's it gonna be?" He fired a look of surprise at her. He wasn't used to a woman behind the window, especially a woman who retorted with an authoritative challenge. Without further conversation, he slipped his papers back under the bars, and she added his name to her list.

After work, Elsie was ready to put her feet up in her Green Street apartment, but there was little time for relaxing. Ernie was on his way to Tennessee, and she knew this was a longer separation than if he had been on the liberty ship. She also felt the urgency of his situation. Deportation to Germany meant certain death at the hands of the Fascist Nazis. Elsie geared up to fight a war in her own country, and she needed reinforcements. Like an army general, she began to organize. Impatient with the hearing process, she called Harry Bridges and made arrangements to meet him. Maybe, she reasoned, his influence could affect Ernie's chances of landing a parole.

1940's - Elsie in San Francisco

The internees, including Ernie and the other Germans, took the ferry from Angel Island to Oakland where they boarded a prison train with barred windows. They had no idea where they were going. The heat was suffocating. Two days into the trip, the train stopped, and a long line of Japanese men, women, and children disembarked from the train. The New Mexico heat glistened along the horizon as the train pulled out for six more days of travel with the remaining Germans and Italians before reaching its destination. Elsie received a telegram on September 7, 1942.

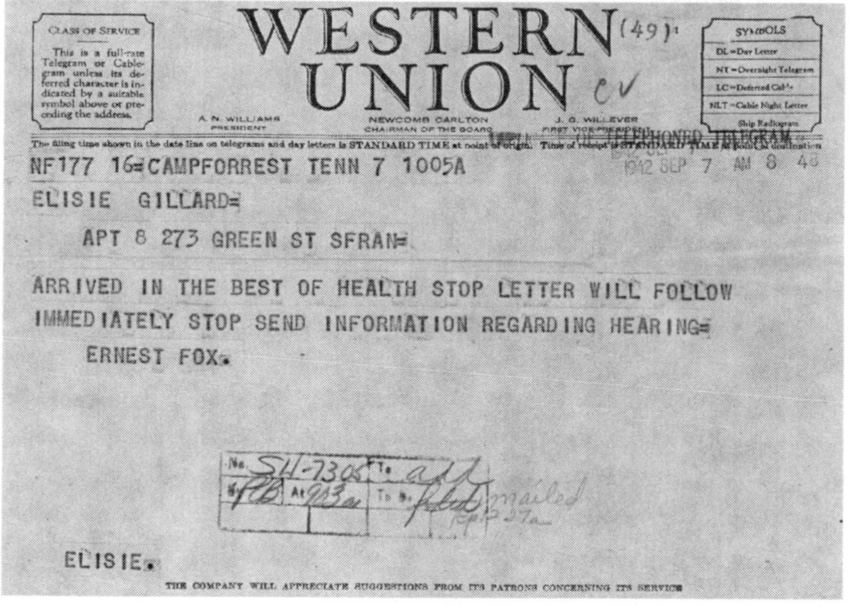

CLASS OF SERVICE

This is a full-rate Telegram or Cablegram unless its deferred character is indicated by a suitable symbol above or preceding the address.

WESTERN UNION

A. N. WILLIAMS PRESIDENT — NEWCOMB CARLTON CHAIRMAN OF THE BOARD — J. C. WILLEVER FIRST VICE-PRESIDENT

SYMBOLS
DL = Day Letter
NT = Overnight Telegram
LC = Deferred Cable
NLT = Cable Night Letter
Ship Radiogram

The filing time shown in the date line on telegrams and day letters is STANDARD TIME at point of origin. Time of receipt is STANDARD TIME at point of destination

TELEPHONED TELEGRAM

NF177 16=CAMPFORREST TENN 7 1005A   1942 SEP 7 AM 8 43

ELISIE GILLARD=

APT 8 273 GREEN ST SFRAN=

ARRIVED IN THE BEST OF HEALTH STOP LETTER WILL FOLLOW IMMEDIATELY STOP SEND INFORMATION REGARDING HEARING=

ERNEST FOX.

ELISIE.

THE COMPANY WILL APPRECIATE SUGGESTIONS FROM ITS PATRONS CONCERNING ITS SERVICE

Part of Camp Forrest, a National Guard compound located in Tullahoma, Tennessee, functioned as a civilian internment camp during the war. Guard towers overlooked the internment compound, which was enclosed with a barbed wire stockade. There was a mess hall, a recreation hall, latrines, and shower and laundry facilities. Wooden huts slept five men. The camp was equipped to handle three thousand internees. The men were allowed two letters a week and two, half-hour visits per month. Ernie told Elsie not to plan a trip to visit. It wasn't worth it.

Camp 4—Camp Forrest, Tennessee, September, 1942

Darling Elsie,

I've written Six letters and one telegram and haven't rec'd a reply. I can't understand the delay. Well, darling, how are you? Well, I sincerely hope. As to myself, well, I finally recovered from the train trip and am feeling normal again. Gee, Elsie, I miss you tremendously, and believe you me, I'll be tickled pink to get back to the coast again. God, this climate is miserably hot during the summer months. Honey, I'd certainly appreciate an occasional letter from some of my friends. Our visits are restricted to two, half-hours per month. Well, darling, keep your chin up and hope for the best. Ernie

Meanwhile, Elsie arranged a meeting with Harry Bridges in the coffee shop of the ILWU offices. Bridges knew Ernie as a hard-working, dedicated organizer for the CIO, a labor union organizer, and a member of sailor unions. He was also aware of Ernie's arrest.

Elsie explained the situation as the coffee cooled in her cup. Bridges listened intently, stirred sugar into his coffee, and nodded his head occasionally. Ernie's second hearing was coming up in January of 1943, and she needed Bridges' support. "Maybe with the backing of the ILWU, we could pressure the Department of Justice to release Ernie," she said. Then Bridges set his jaw and swirled his coffee. Elsie began to feel uncomfortable. That's when he lit into her.

"You sure have a lot of nerve to think that labor should be diverted from the war effort at this critical time. All our energy has to be the war! What are you thinking?" He shoved his coffee cup away and stood. "The important thing now is winning the war. Ernie should divorce you for asking the union for support." That was that. Elsie was stunned and deeply hurt. Instead of taking a bus, she walked back to her apartment on Telegraph Hill, and by the time she reached the front steps, she was all cried out.

"I felt like a fish swimming upstream while everyone was going downstream. I realized I had to do something, and it had to be all by myself." Maybe she went to the library to find direction or maybe one of her progressive friends recommended she contact this specific national organization. Either way, she wrote to The American Committee for the Protection of Foreign-Born and solicited their help. She also typed letters to the Communist Party newspapers—the *New World* and the *Daily Worker.* She contacted the crews of liberty ships, friends in Seattle, and unions that Ernie had belonged. Her campaign for Ernie's release was underway.

Ernie's "dull routine" contrasted drastically with Elsie's life in San Francisco. Irene became engaged and moved out of the apartment she shared with Elsie when she married in January of 1943. Wives of soldiers and sailors were constantly looking for places to stay while they waited for their husbands' ships to come in, so Elsie easily found roommates to help with rent payments.

In the evenings after work, Elsie would sit alone with her typewriter, tapping out letters for support of Ernie's case. Ernie's second hearing was scheduled for January of 1943 in San Francisco, where the AECU would determine Ernie's immigration status. George Anderson kept Elsie informed and Ernie kept writing letters.[42]

Elsie attended the hearing. Her lawyer tried to make the appeal that Ernie's case should be heard in a federal court with a trial, not by the AECU under the jurisdiction of the Justice Department and Attorney General Biddle. The news was not good. Ernie was now branded a "subversive" because he represented himself falsely as a citizen. Continued internment was recommended. By March of 1943, the government launched deportation proceedings against Ernest Fox.

CHAPTER 17:

Internment

Meeting with Elsie

I sat at my writing desk studying the yellow sticky notes that haphazardly framed the screen of my computer. Ernie's letters, handwritten on internee of war stationery, each one stamped in red ink by a censor, lay underneath a pile of history books. The confusion of papers and reference books matched my state of mind. I tried to untangle and sort through the conflicting messages of Elsie's story. When she talked of Ernie, her voice was steely and bitter. Yet she had saved his letters and telegrams for sixty years. Then there was the question of German internment.

I did not recall learning about the U.S. German internment in any history book I read in high school or college. I flipped through one of the history books in search of information on the Japanese internment during the war. I knew *that* was in the history textbooks. I didn't live far from an historic Japanese internment camp in Wyoming. But what about the Germans?

In an effort to refresh my memory, I read an article on the Japanese relocation camps from one of the books. I came across these words in parenthesis as if an afterthought: "Americans of German and Italian heritage were not similarly interned." However, Elsie's story told me something very different. Upon further digging in other sources, I discovered that at least eleven thousand German Americans were interned in the United States from 1941 through 1945. Some Germans endured internment at Ellis Island as late as 1949. "That's part of our problem, dear," Elsie said when I told her my findings. "The school textbooks, the publishing houses, and whoever is behind them are controlling what we are taught. The truth isn't being told!" And what about Ernie, I thought to myself. What is the truth in his story?

* * * * *

Ernie befriended a young German Jew while living at Camp Forrest. Eric told Ernie his story, which Ernie later retold to Elsie. As the situation became desperate for Jews in Germany in the midthirties, Eric's parents tried to get passage on a freighter that was scheduled to leave the country. The family could only afford passage for one person. Eric, the older of two sons, had training as a dental technician. They decided he, more than anyone else in the family, had skills to make a livelihood overseas. Eric boarded the freighter filled with other Jewish families and never saw his family again. It turned out to be the last ship to leave Germany with Jewish evacuees.

The United States refused entry to the castaways. The ship was running out of fuel and food when the South American country of British Guiana, now called Guyana, accepted them. Eric began to rebuild his life along with the other refugees who found jobs, married, and started families. Eric was working as a dental technician in 1942 when the Latin American military, under the direction of the United States military, captured Germans living in Latin America. Approximately four thousand German Latin Americans huddled in dank holds of ships, not knowing where they were going and were transported to the United States. Families were interned in Crystal City, Texas, while single men were shipped to Camp Forrest.[43]

The U.S. military operated an exchange program with Germany where German internees held in the United States could be exchanged for U.S. prisoners held in Germany. In all, two thousand prisoners were exchanged. People were accused of being spies by the Gestapo, the German state police, and sent back to war-torn Germany—including families with American-born children. Many of the exchanged prisoners were Jewish. One can only imagine their fate. After WWII, the families at Crystal City were transferred to Ellis Island. The Statue of Liberty, the lady whose heart was made of stone, could be seen from their barbed wire exercise cages.[44]

Ernie understood the problem of mixing the different German factions—Nazis, Jews, and Communists—into one camp. The stress of internment mixed with such diverse and conflicting ideologies was potentially dangerous. Ernie wrote letters to authorities advocating the separation of the German Jews and the pro–Nazis. His campaign was successful. Eric and the other Jewish men were transferred. Before leaving, Ernie gave Eric Elsie's address, "In case you need help getting a job when they let you out." In the meantime, Elsie kept up the drive for Ernie's release.[45]

The American Committee for Protection of Foreign Born (ACPFB), based in New York City, was founded in 1933 for the purpose of defending the rights of the foreign born, especially radicals and Communist Party members. The committee aimed to protect civil rights through litigation, legislation, and public education. In its early years, the ACPFB focused on campaigning for asylum rights for those refugees who had fled European Fascism in the 1930s and were facing deportation, particularly European Jews. Toward the end of the thirties, the committee formed a group to protect immigrants who had gone to Spain to fight against Franco and who had reentered the United States illegally. With the outbreak of World War II, the committee's attentions turned toward promoting national unity against Fascism. The ACPFB aided Japanese Americans who were being relocated by the U.S. Government. After Elsie informed them about Ernie's case, the committee began working for his release.

Although most of her free time was devoted to fighting Ernie's deportation, Elsie was not wont for entertainment. While the city buzzed with wartime activities, Elsie and her roommates entertained friends at their apartment. San Francisco had a plethora of new tastes to discover, and Elsie began to learn gourmet cooking. Concerts at a variety of venues played all over San Francisco. If Elsie couldn't find friends to accompany her to concerts, she would go by herself.

She saw Paul Robeson perform *Othello*. "And I'm proud to say I talked to him at a party following the performance," Elsie said. "After

I was introduced to him, he expressed his appreciation for the efforts of the progressives during the thirties and their continuing fight for equal rights for the working class. He was such a commanding figure, not only because of his physical stature. He knew twenty languages and carried himself with great dignity." Sadly, Paul Robeson—a goodwill ambassador throughout the world and famous for his resonant voice and solid character—became a direct target of the McCarthy Persecutions in the fifties.[46]

Elsie maintained a dizzying schedule at her job and, on the off hours, working to obtain Ernie's release. Ernie was sent to Ft. Lincoln, North Dakota, in May of 1943 to a Civilian Conservation Corps (CCC) camp five miles south of Bismarck. While deportation proceedings were under way, George Anderson applied for another hearing. Ernie filled out an application for release before he left Camp Forrest, but the Justice Department continued with deportation procedures.[47]

Elsie began to make arrangements to travel to Bismarck. Attorney General Biddle would not grant Ernie a rehearing and pursued deportation charges. Elsie would have to strengthen the front lines of her defense. While Elsie continued the fight, Ernie started working on the railroad as a gandy dancer, repairing and maintaining railroad tracks, which took him away from the camp.

In a September 1943 letter, Ernie wrote Elsie:

> Last Sunday, Elsie, dear, I was very fortunate in having a lovely pheasant dinner, shot by a local acquaintance. Honey, the surrounding country is teeming with wild bird life. Last week we were invited to a local church social, [with] stewed chickens and all the trimmings ($.35 per head). Wednesday we're leaving for the eastern part of the state to complete a repair job. Rumors are that we may be working in the vicinity of Bismarck during the winter months. As I stated in my previous letter slowly but surely I'm reading my current literature. I sincerely hope the Second front is established before winter, the immediate calling of a Three Power Conference would also solve many important problems.

In an October letter, he expressed gratitude at receiving a radio sent by Elsie. "Honey, you have no idea how happy it made me. Everyone in my sleeping car is very grateful. Sunday [night] I turned in on our old favorite station, all girl orchestra, Manhattan Merry Go Round. God, it made me mighty homesick." He continued by expressing his frustration at not hearing any more news on the conference with Senator Coffee and Biddle. Then he added, "Since my departure from the internment camp, I feel considerably better. Elsie, dear, I wish I could express in words what your continued devotion and loyalty means to me, suffice it to say that your steadfast love really makes life worthwhile." Reading between the lines, Elsie knew that sleeping in a boxcar on the plains of North Dakota was a relief from camp life. Ernie had to maintain a low profile in camp, fearing retaliation from the proactive, Nazi element that clashed with his ideology. But Ernie could not write about the details; his letters were still being censured. Elsie tapped away at her typewriter and organized a list of potential supporters to contact for a second hearing.[48]

Ernie's widespread reputation as a CIO organizer and union member allowed Elsie to gather an impressive coterie of support: the Maritime Union, the Fishermen's Union, Seattle congressman Hugh DeLacy, and California congressman Senator Coffee. Even the once reticent Harry Bridges was now willing to write letters on Ernie's behalf. She wrote to newspaper editors, intent on publicizing Ernie's case. She sent letters to Ernie's merchant marine friends, many of who were serving on various liberty ships. Two liberty ship crews signed a letter to President Roosevelt requesting intervention in Ernie's case. Congressman Coffee received a reply from Attorney General Biddle stating that Ernie's "lawless conduct and terrorism threatened the 'internal peace' of the country."[49] Apparently, the sabotage charge was holding.

While Elsie contacted individuals and unions, the ACPFB drew up petitions and gathered thousands of signatures to present to Congress and the president. Ernest received notification from Biddle that a rehearing would be granted in April of 1944. Elsie felt it was nothing short of a miracle helped along by a little elbow grease. Deportation and prisoner exchanges shifted into motion for the Bismarck Camp internees. George Anderson and Elsie planned to attend the rehearing and pull out all the stops, and she arranged to travel to Bismarck. Sixty years later, Elsie remembered that trip in vivid detail.

Elsie handed the conductor her ticket as she stepped into the passenger car. The soldiers and their families, who had boarding precedence, packed the booths with their luggage and conversation. Elsie carried her suitcase and handbag as she made her way down the aisle of first one, then another car. The conductor approached her, "You'll have to find a place to sit, ma'am. We're ready to roll." She used her suitcase as a makeshift chair and settled near the door of the car, trying not to block the aisle. A sailor offered his seat, and she politely refused. They had made enough sacrifices, she reasoned to herself. She changed trains in Seattle, and this one was even more crowded. At one point, the only place to sit was the space in between the cars. The couplings visibly shifted and clattered under her feet. Cold wind whipped through her hair and permeated her skin, causing her to take frequent walks through the cars before returning to her perch. She arrived in Bismarck exhausted.

After checking into her hotel, she left a note for George Anderson that she had arrived, and then she took a taxi to Ft. Lincoln. The wide-open landscape reminded her of eastern Montana, and despite the frigid situation, she warmed with the thought of her childhood and the excitement of seeing Ernie. It had been over two years since she had said good-bye to him through the wire fences at Sharp Park. She tipped the taxi driver and hurried toward the desolate-looking camp. She was allowed thirty minutes, and two guards were stationed outside the open door to a small concrete room. They informed her that the door would remain open. Elsie rushed in but paused for a breathless moment to look at Ernie. He was clean shaven, which sharpened his square jaw line but did not hide his wide smile. He had replaced any ounce of body fat with muscle. They pressed into each other's arms for a long, familiar kiss before exchanging a speedy discussion about Ernie's upcoming hearing. Elsie left the room awash with a renewed passion for Ernie's release.

George and Elsie had enlisted the help of a Seattle union leader and the international vice president of the Building Service Employees Union, who was willing to travel from Seattle to Bismarck and appear before the board on Ernie's behalf. They met in Elsie's hotel room and discussed their strategy and the charges of sabotage and false citizenship against Ernie.

The next morning, Ernie, Elsie, George, and the union leader appeared at the courthouse for the hearing before the assembled board. The union leader testified that Ernie was a respected labor leader and most definitely not a terrorist. Then Ernie was called to the stand. He faced the courtroom with a confident posture and charisma that reminded Elsie of his days as a CIO organizer.

"In regards to my citizenship, I assumed my father had obtained U.S. citizenship in 1920. I had no reason to believe he did not. I thought I had obtained derivative citizenship for that reason. My enlistment is proof of …" The officer conducting the meeting cut him off.

"That's enough. I don't want a speech." He moved on to the sabotage charge. George Anderson asked to see the evidence against Ernie. He was denied. He asked the name of Ernie's accuser. He was denied. George demanded Ernie be able to face his accuser. Of course, he was denied; his accuser had been electrocuted. Ernie tried to explain that he would never sabotage a ship. He was a merchant marine and had high regard and respect for his fellow sailors. Again, he was told to be quiet. The hearing was contentious, and the officer running the hearing seemed more than irritated.

Anderson tried another tactic. "Mrs. Fox is an accomplished secretary. I want her to take the record." He was denied, but Elsie continued to record all verbal exchanges in shorthand. Later, Anderson tried to submit her notes as the record but … he was denied.

One of the board members started questioning the appropriateness of the "potentially dangerous" classification. He suggested there was no real proof that Ernie advocated violence to overthrow the government. He also made note that, according to the multitude of letters that were in Ernie's file, eighteen informants in Seattle told the FBI that though Ernie was an active Communist, none of them said he had advocated violence. He went further to state that maybe, just maybe, the FBI files were not accurate. He suggested that if Fox did indeed teach sabotage by putting emery dust in the bearings of ship engines, others would certainly have heard about him, not just one man. The accusations woven into the fabric of Ernie's case were beginning to appear like moth eaten holes that could not be ignored. Considering his loyalty, the board member noted that Fox showed no hostility to the U.S. Armed Forces and had in fact been signed up for duty before he was arrested. The large number of persons from the labor movement who attested to Fox's patriotic loyalty could not be ignored.

The board member noted that Ralph Rogers of the National Maritime Union, which represented ninety thousand members, had spoken on behalf of the union when speaking of Ernie's patriotism. Rogers also represented one hundred thousand members of California's CIO. Rogers told the board that "Fox valued democratic values … highly," and he fought against anti–Fascism by protesting the scrap shipment to Japan when it wasn't a popular thing to do.[50] Then the hearing abruptly ended. Elsie went back to San Francisco, and they awaited a decision.[51]

The *SS Gripsholm*, meanwhile, awaited orders at its home port in Germany. It began steaming to the United States by the end of the winter in 1945, destined for Ellis Island. Its cargo for the return trip to Germany was to be 180 Germans presently interned at Ft. Lincoln, North Dakota.

The orders arrived at Ft. Lincoln in late May of 1945, but Ernest was transferred to Sharp Park in San Francisco. There were no more letters written on POW stationery, and Elsie could visit every week. She looked for changes in Ernie after two years of internment and noted he was in good physical condition and seemed anxious to continue his life of activism. He reiterated his appreciation for Elsie's persistence in fighting for his release.

Attorney General Biddle ruled for continued internment under the safeguards of the Immigration Service. The sabotage charges were dropped, but Biddle told Louis Goldblatt, the secretary of the ILWU, that he still considered Ernest Fox potentially dangerous as long as the war was being fought. Goldblatt, a friend of Elsie's, quickly notified her of his conversation with Biddle. The executive board of the ILWU, under Goldblatt's decision, appealed Biddle's ruling to President Roosevelt and the Justice Department, but there was no response.

The *SS Gripsholm* was in port on the Eastern seaboard, waiting for the deportees from Ft. Lincoln. Elsie, still rattling away on her typewriter, kept her supporters informed. In the winter of 1945, Hugh DeLacy—a Washington State congressman from Seattle, a secret Communist Democrat, and a good friend of Elsie and Ernie's—wrote to Biddle questioning his decision. In the meantime, the FBI was bugging the headquarters of the CIO Maritime Committee, to which DeLacy belonged. The FBI had begun a file that recorded all of Ernest Fox's supporters.

Then it happened. At a conference between DeLacy and the AECU, a Justice Department official admitted to DeLacy that Ernie was being held because of his Communist activities. Period. His exact words were, "Fox would be a threat if this country ever gets into trouble with the Soviet Union." Ernie was being held on pure speculation. The same man also admitted, "If we let him go, it would cause unfavorable publicity for the department." DeLacy responded, "Let the man go now, and pick him up again later if he ever does become a menace." Biddle turned to DeLacy and tried to refute what the official had said. He denied holding Fox just because he was a Communist. He was holding him based on the findings of the FBI, which had documentation regarding Ernie's Communist and labor activities.[52]

Delacy then threatened to go to President Roosevelt with the official's admission about possible "trouble" with the USSR. That wasn't exactly something the government would want made public when the United States was presently an ally with the USSR in a world war! Finally, in April of 1945, George Anderson filed a habeas corpus action using the premise that Ernie was being held not because he was presently dangerous, but because he *might* be dangerous *if* hostilities broke out with the USSR. In June of 1945, Attorney General Biddle paroled Ernie with no explanation. In July, the remaining Germans at Ft. Lincoln were deported to Germany via the *Gripsholm* without Ernie. Unknown to Elsie and Ernie, deportation proceedings remained on the books for Ernest Fox.

CHAPTER 18:

The Bolsheviks Are Coming … Again!

Meeting with Elsie

We sat in Elsie's living room where an electric heater, made to look like a wood burning stove, warmed the space. Elsie told me that it gave her a great deal of comfort in the evening to feel the heat and see the orange glow of the fake logs through the glass door of the stove. It was a reminder of the fireplace at the Green Street apartment in San Francisco—a time she called her "golden years." As we talked into the afternoon, we didn't notice the dry leaves pelting the window with each gust of wind. Daylight lingered and cast long shadows before giving way to the lengthening darkness of late autumn.

We had both been immersed in the fifties—the decade of my birth and Elsie's middle age. Elsie's politics wove itself into every aspect of her story, then and now. I was amazed at the strength in her voice as she expressed her opinions. "My understanding of the basic workings of the capitalist system and the corruption that comes with it remains untouched. Democratic socialism is the only answer to the problems of our society. But it *must* be based on democracy, not democratic centralism or dictatorship or totalitarianism. Lenin and Stalin's so-called "socialism" was not built on Marxism, but instead, as we know

now, it was simply a dictatorship of the proletariat ruled by a group of gangsters. Capitalist economies are based on warfare, not peace. Despite the failure of Communism, I am more convinced than ever, that a true, just society evolves from the collapse of capitalism." She stood up and took her purse off the counter, as I noted the time. She had a hair appointment at four and would catch a ride with me on my way home.

"So, dear, I didn't lose hope; I believed in my convictions."

"And what about Ernie? Did he share in your hope?"

She looked at me while processing my question, then sat down with her purse sitting on her lap. "Let me tell you something, dear," she took in a deep breath. "I was loved and respected by the people I worked for in the ILWU. My bosses could have fired me for being a radical, but they didn't." Tears welled up in her eyes. "That is a tremendous feeling to have that love and respect among such a large organization." There was a pause. "I don't mean to sound like I'm bragging, but I want you to know I was loved by a great many people." Another pause. "Maybe the name of the book could be *Elsie, One Who Was Loved*."

I smiled at her and held out her walking stick. She rose from the sofa, took her stick, and I followed her out the door. What she didn't say spoke louder than words.

* * * * *

> **FBI REPORT**—Date: 7/5/45
> File #:100-20596
> Title: Elsie Mary Fox, nee Elsie Gilland
> Synopsis of Facts: Subject continues membership in the CPA Club in San Francisco. However, no activity on the part of the subject has been noted during the past three months. Subject has recently sought the advice and counsel of BILL SCHNEIDERMAN regarding the release of her husband ERNEST FOX, an interned Alien enemy. Subject continues to reside at 273 Green Street and is presently on leave from her occupation as dispatcher at the National Maritime Union, 91 Drumm Street.

Ernie's internment only emphasized Elsie's independence and self-sufficiency. Never one to back down from a party, there was a reason Elsie referred to those years on Green Street as her golden years—years with glittering excitement and days filled with activities. Her new roommate, another Irene, was a striking woman with auburn hair, which attracted men like a magnet. Elsie did not refuse the constant male companionship in their apartment. After Elsie and Irene's dinner parties, they more than likely pushed the furniture aside and danced to the latest be-bop jazz music by Dizzy Gillespie that was playing on the radio.

Social events, a strong work ethic, and a cause—this time Ernie's cause—filled her days and nights. Although she maintained membership with a local Communist club, her priorities and extra time were spent in obtaining Ernie's release. She quit going to unit meetings, but informants still kept track of her whereabouts and activities and filed their reports with the FBI.

The world stage continued to shift with a succession of changes. On April 12, 1945, Franklin D. Roosevelt died, and Harry Truman was sworn in as president the same day. On April 25th, the U.S. Army met the Russian Army at the Elbe River in Germany. April 30, 1945, Hitler committed suicide. In May, U.S. troops liberated the Buchenwald concentration camp, Germany surrendered, and Soviet troops reached Berlin. The war was over in Europe.

When the soldiers returned stateside, the two hundred thousand women who were employed during the war typically went home to continue their traditional roles as homemakers. Not so for Elsie. Now that her dispatch job was over, she found a job with the ILWU—the union that Harry Bridges built. The union was organized into local divisions representing the dock and warehouse workers. Elsie went to work as office manager for Local 6 located in San Francisco. In 1945, the ILWU had a membership of fifteen thousand men, and by 1949, its membership swelled to nineteen thousand.

She had worked at Local 6 for several months when Ernie finally came home. Elsie vaguely remembered the party she planned upon his release. "We had a big party with lots of food and drinking at the Whitcomb Hotel. We invited all our friends—the labor people and other progressives that had helped us through Ernie's internment. I remember it as a big celebration. And then, life just went on. I went to work, and Ernie took up where he left off."

In August of 1945, two months after Ernie was released, the atomic bomb was dropped on Nagasaki and Hiroshima, ending WWII. The war, on all fronts, was over. Elsie recalled, "Much to the discredit of the human race, we were jubilant when the bomb was dropped. There were a lot of hard feelings about the Japanese because of Pearl Harbor."

Ernie, James Drury (Port Agent for Natl. Maritime Union), Elsie, June 6, 1945. (Courtesy Labor Archives and Research Center, San Francisco State University)

Elsie, a half century later, remembered the celebration in bits and pieces. Ernie had probably already joined in the celebration by the time she got off work. She decided to walk to Market Street to take in the festivities. Hoots and hollers, sirens and spontaneous singing added to the din that could be heard blocks away. As Elsie approached, she saw sailors, soldiers, and working class men drinking straight from whiskey bottles, pushing and shoving with occasional fistfights breaking out. The celebration had escalated to mania. She sized up the situation and determined it wasn't safe for a woman to be in the middle of the fray. As much as she wanted to celebrate, her instincts won out, and she went back to her apartment. She mixed herself a drink and stood on the balcony overlooking the bay where, for four years, the shipyards had bustled with the activity of war, carrying men to and from the Pacific arena. Now it was over. Little did she know that another war was brewing and was about to settle like a winter sky over the world for the next forty years—otherwise known as the Cold War, which pitted Communists against capitalists.

A brief period of optimism and unity graced the United States after the war. The Bolshoi Ballet from Russia was welcomed warmly in San Francisco. Many people, including Elsie, went to see the Russian performance and were intrigued by the foreign flair of the United States' most recent ally. The United Nations had officially formed in San Francisco and with the emergence of two world powers—the United States and the Soviet Union—a promise for world peace and international cooperation prevailed … but not for long.

Post-war economy and conditions were less than ideal. The cost of food in 1946 rose 30 percent. There were housing shortages and high inflation. Wages had no cost-of-living allowance to make up for the inflation. Women had become accustomed to working outside the home during wartime and fought for equal wages. The black population struggled for equal rights and, along with women, were the first to lose their jobs when the soldiers came home. The working class needed help, once again, to maintain their strength in numbers and make their demands to the corporate powers.

Corporate America emerged from the war in fine shape. Wages were frozen during the war but prices were not, and profits swelled. The only thing standing in the way of corporate domination of the United States was the CIO. Union membership was on the rise nationwide in the forties.[53] Eight million workers went on strike in 1945 and 1946 to demand equitable wages and fair work hours.[54] The revolutionary undercurrents made the corporate world nervous. They began to lay plans to disrupt the growing solidarity of the unions. Capitalism was embraced at home while, at the same time, the Communist Soviet Union declared war on it. Elsie continued her support for the working class in her capacity as office manager of Local 6 of the ILWU.

The ILWU was a democratic union. It was distinctively different from the standard union protocol. The officers, the people Elsie worked for, were elected by the rank and file. The officers' salaries were equitable with the workers' wages. There was little class disparity among the workers and administrators within this union. The ILWU practiced fair hiring practices long before the equal rights movement in the sixties gained momentum. It banned discrimination based on race, color, creed, or political choice before most other industrial unions. It allowed Communists and republicans and Catholics and Baptists as long as they were "good union workers." As a result, Harry Bridges' democratized union gained a deep trust of the working people. Elsie and Ernie's ideologies were a perfect fit in the ILWU.

The ILWU stood out among unions for its progressive political and social vision for the world, and its constitution verified its stance. The ILWU, because of its nondiscriminatory policies, became a left-wing haven for radicals. The Communist Party had clubs within the union on an industry–by-industry basis. The clubs had their own officers and took on political issues. Because of the union's sense of equality, anyone could develop a resolution and present it before a general union meeting or the executive board, where it would be voted on. As a result, the Communist clubs within the union were influencing policy, and Ernie was in the middle of the action. When Ernie was not working in the Hills Brothers warehouse or unloading the banana boats as a longshoreman, he taught Marxist classes and handed out leaflets.

> **FBI REPORT: 5/23/47** ELSIE FOX attended a meeting of the Professional Workers Club April 11, 1946 at ——. FOX read a report of a County meeting concerning the expulsion of TROTSKYITES from the CP. —— reported on Dec. 8, 1945 that ELSIE FOX attended a meeting of the North Side Club on Dec. 6, 1945 at ——, and on April 11, 1946 attended a meeting of the Miscellaneous Branch of the Professional Section at ——.
>
> ——advised on July 14, 1945 that ELSIE FOX is a delegate to the CP State Convention. This same informant on Feb. 20, 1946 advised that he learned that ELSIE FOX was President of the Columbus

Branch and chairman of the THEODORE DREISER
Branch and handles finances for that club.

Sixty years later, Elsie's loyalty to the ILWU was still rock solid. "The longshoremen especially brought new ideas from all over the world to the union. They saw other countries with different forms of government and economic systems. They saw that capitalism was not the only answer to profit gain. They were hard working people with worldly ideas." Maybe Elsie recognized in the union what she had seen in the Filipino workers in Seattle throughout the thirties—a singleness of purpose, a unity that was beautiful to see. Through her job as office manager, Elsie rubbed shoulders with the "working stiffs" who played as hard as they worked. It was a man's world in the ILWU Local 6 in the forties, and Elsie fit in with ease. She stayed there for twenty-six-and-a-half years.

As office manager, Elsie facilitated the operation of Local 6 by attending all board meetings with the officers and taking minutes by shorthand. She was responsible for the Local's expenditures and payroll, and she did so efficiently. She saw to it that procedures and general operations of Local 6 were followed. Elsie called to task a woman that claimed a phony travel expense and used the money to buy gasoline for her family and friends. "I called her into the office and told her I knew what she was doing. She denied it but I had proof. I didn't tell my bosses so she didn't lose her job. She never liked me after that but she never tried that little scheme again either."

Corruption at any level could undermine the organization of the union, and Elsie knew it. One day, she was taking dictation from an officer. He closed the door to his office as soon as she was seated. A cigarette dangled out of the corner of her mouth as she readied her notepad in her lap. "I need you to book a flight for next week. I have a union meeting in L.A." Her boss had to go through Elsie, since she approved all purchase orders and kept track of expenses. But Elsie knew the score. His wife kept a tight rein on him by controlling the purse strings, knowing his propensity for an overnight fling and drinking habits. He had to devise secretive schemes to circumnavigate her suspicions of his trysts and to find money to pull them off. Just before the flight, he would cancel his bogus trip and the airline would send Elsie the refund, which he expected in cash on his desk. This had happened a time or two before Elsie caught on to his game. It wouldn't happen again. Local 6 could lose its union charter if theft, bribery, and corruption of any kind were involved.

Elsie took the last drag of her cigarette, blew the smoke at the ceiling, then looked at him directly, and said, "No, I can't approve that, and you know why." Leaning forward, she reached for the ashtray on his desk and snuffed out her cigarette. He began yelling expletives and slammed his fist on his desk, but he did not sway her decision.

"I could just throw you down those stairs!" he yelled, but he knew he was caught, and Elsie would not be his confidante. The rank and file were the raison d'être, and their dues were not going to be spent on the secret indulgences of an officer.

Elsie's professionalism worked on both sides of the fence. She handled the employers with respect and firmness, and, in fact, the ILWU was one of the few unions that had a reasonable relationship with the employers, ship owners, and companies like Folgers Coffee, whose products were stored in the warehouses. The officers and the employers grew to trust Elsie in her decision making.

On occasion, one of the officers missed several days of work unannounced. Elsie recalled that he had probably been out late the night before at the bars or nightclubs, an occupational hazard of those postwar years. In his absence, an employer came to the office with a problem that needed immediate attention. Elsie maintained her professional demeanor and after a few phone calls resolved the problem, much to the satisfaction of the employer and with no compromise to the union. She called the hung-over officer at home that evening and told him of the situation and how she had handled the employer. The absent officer approved and was grateful for her adeptness in averting a problem. Hanging up the phone, she relaxed by reading the *San Francisco Chronicle* before rushing off to a club meeting somewhere in the city, where she was scheduled to present a program. Elsie's dignified approach spawned trust and respect.

Elsie's job intensified when the ILWU called for a strike. Multiple committees within the union contributed to the efficiency of the organization while Elsie's logistical skills played a significant role in the strike's effectiveness. Each committee had thirty to forty members with elected officers. The Strike Committee oversaw the logistics of a strike. The Publicity Committee wrote and printed pamphlets and bulletins to distribute to the members. During a strike, the Health and Welfare Committee helped members who could not make their rent or house payments or needed help with medical bills. Theatrical groups, sports teams, and social activities helped to uplift the workers' moral. Elsie organized all their needs—pencils, paper, mimeograph machines, meeting rooms, and even the sticks for the picket signs.

The strike swung into action like a well-greased machine. The committees moved into the building, and Elsie's office was dubbed the war room where the mimeograph machine was essential in their arsenal of weapons. Elsie had to dodge people to get out of the room. She had her arms filled with pickets to deliver to the Strike Committee set up in a conference room downstairs. After dropping them off, she made sure they had enough pens and paper and then made a mental note to bring more coffee cups to the room on a return trip.

Back at her office, she turned her head away from the din of voices to talk into the phone. "Yes, send any donations to my office." She was notifying the other locals in the ILWU that the strike may be longer than expected. Donations to support the union members on the picket line were beginning to pour in. She set up a special fund and put ads in the newspapers, soliciting donations from the public. Requests for assistance to buy groceries or help with medical bills were already coming in from striking workers. A worker came into the office and stood at Elsie's desk until she was off the phone. "How can I help you?"

"No matter how I figure it, I can't pay next month's rent. What can I do?" Elsie put him in touch with someone on the Welfare Committee, who would take him to the bank the next day.

She picked up the phone and called her contact at a jail bond company to notify him of the strike and remind him of their previous arrangement. She probably had met him at a party or in a bar and recognized that his acquaintance would come in handy. It was understood between Elsie and the jail bond officer that if a striker was hauled to jail in the middle of the night, his release would be immediate. The bailiff would inform Elsie during office hours the next day, and she would take care of the bail. The workers came to rely on her expertise in getting the job done, and they came to love and respect her.

Elsie spent little time at home during these strikes. Ernie and Elsie met each other coming and going. She remembers the hard work of the strikes with fondness. "Looking back, it truly was such an exciting time that I view it as the highlight of my career." Her job wasn't the only thing that kept her busy.

> **FBI REPORT** – 6/21/47
>
> ELSIE FOX continues to reside at 273 Green Street, San Francisco, and to be employed at the Warehouse Union, Local #6, ILWU. Subject active in local Communist Party affairs, formerly serving as Dues Director and currently Educational Director of the North Beach Section. Subject subscribes to the *Daily People's World.*

In 1946, the Hawaiian sugar and pineapple strike was in high gear. Lou Goldblatt, the Secretary-Treasurer of the ILWU, worked hard to organize the thousands of workers on the islands that worked for the Big Five—the five biggest corporate owners of the pineapple and sugar companies. The Big Five dominated the island before it became a state in 1959. "The Asian workers suffered brutal exploitation until the ILWU organized them," explained Elsie. "The ILWU had people like Jack Hall and Frank Thompson, an old-time wobbly, as organizers. They'd tramp the fields and plantations where the workers lived in separate camps. Everyone lived in separate camps—Japanese, Filipinos, Chinese, and Portuguese. But the organizers got them to sign on to the union, and they had to all work together to be effective." There wasn't room in the union for racial separation. Under the ILWU, the Japanese, Filipino, and Chinese workers voted to go on strike.

The employers had a ship coming from the Philippines loaded with Filipinos to take the place of the striking workers. But one of the Filipino cooks on the ship belonged to the Marine Cooks and Stewards Union. He signed up all the workers on the ship as ILWU members so that by the time they got to the island, the strikers had six thousand more pickets on their line.

After seventy-two days, the strike was over. Elsie had made hotel reservations and arranged for rental cars to bring the leaders of the strike to San Francisco for a meeting. All day meetings culminated, as usual, in a bar or nightclub. Elsie tipped her glass and listened to the war stories of the strike. She was the only woman at the table, and the men were as comfortable with her as she was with them. The talk, which covered politics in and out of the union, flowed as easily as the drinks, and Elsie was not shy to join in with questions and her own opinions. Hall had passed out after a few drinks, which Elsie attributed to his diabetes. Elsie made sure everyone's accommodations were in order before taking a taxi home, looking forward to a long night's rest. "No one would be getting up too early after a night out on the town," she had reasoned. Early the next morning, the phone rang. It was Jack Hall. Elsie remembered his voice sounding "as bright as a silver dollar," and he informed her she was late for breakfast.

Despite the strike's success, corporate and union tensions persisted. The strength of the industrial unions sent chills through corporate America. In the spring of 1946, Tom Clark, attorney general of the United States, addressed the American Bar Association and told them there was a "plot" afoot by "Communists … and small groups of radicals" who were trying to seize the country by destroying its unity through strikes and civil rights protests. He claimed the Communists were gaining a foothold in industries by putting officers in the labor unions.[55] Fear of Communism, once again, fueled the hunt for the Bolsheviks. Hoover must have sat in his office and smiled as the hounds were released. Any problem—economic, racial, or otherwise—was blamed on the Communists, and demands were made on the CIO to get rid of them. The CIO members argued about their course of action. Solidarity within the ranks was weakening.

At the 1946 CIO Convention, the CIO adopted a resolution to strengthen their stance. The resolution directed the CIO to fight against anti–Semitism, racial discrimination, war preparations, and reactionary, anti-labor laws and to fight for higher wages and unity between the United States, England, and the Soviet Union.[56] But it was too late; the opposing teams were forming their strategy before coming to the line of confrontation.

The Taft-Hartley Act (formally called the Labor-Management Relations Act, informally called the Union Busting Law), if passed, would nullify the National Labor Relations Act of 1935. The National Association of Manufacturers backed the bill sentence by sentence, paragraph by paragraph, and page by page and used their money to assure the passage of the Taft-Hartley Act.[57] John Lewis, president of the United Mine Workers, told the 1947 AFL Convention that the act was the "first ugly, savage thrust of Fascism in America. It symbolizes and parallels historically what happened in Italy before the coming of Fascism … and what happened in Germany before the coming of Nazism."[58] Everything the unions had gained in the thirties was being undermined by this act—minimum wage, social security, pensions, child labor, restrictions on organizing, and strikes were threatened. Vito Marcantonio, a congressman from East Harlem, New York, testified before the House on April 15, 1947, regarding the Taft-Hartley Act. "You are going to do this to get rid of the Communists in the unions.… [U]nder the guise of fighting Communism, you are with this legislation advancing Fascism on American labor."[59] But Congress passed the measure, despite Truman's veto.

Tacked on to the Taft-Hartley Act was the Loyalty Oath for unions. It required labor union officers to deny under oath any Communist affiliation. The noose tightened. If the unions did not file an annual affidavit saying their officers were not members or had never been affiliated with the Communist Party they would be denied the right to use the National Labor Relations Board which oversaw the legal rights of the unions to exist. Every union officer had to sign the oath, but no corporate officer was required to sign.

The attorney general issued a subversive list on November 24, 1947, in response to Executive Order 9835 by President Truman, which called for loyalty investigations of two million federal employees. It included "organizations, groups, and movements which had significance in connection with the National Security. Membership in or affiliation with any of these organizations led to investigation of government workers." Members or sympathizers of these groups could be fired.[60]

Elsie did not have to sign a loyalty oath. As office manager, she was not a member of the union; she was "just a hired hand for the union." Ernie was not an officer, either, but he did not try to hide his affiliation with the party. Once again, he was tempting fate. Within the unions, grumbling grew and could be heard in bars, restaurants, and union boardrooms.

"Route out the Communists now before big brother takes our bargaining rights. Without those rights, why pay dues to a union?"

"I hear some of the employers aren't going to do business with any union they think is red. No work, no pay. I say we don't have a choice."

"But because of the CIO, I got hired, ya see. I couldn't get hired nowhere else 'cause of the color of my skin!"

"They're just making trouble for us. I say get 'em out."

Union solidarity was crumbling. Red baiting was just one of the tactics to break the union's unity. Landlords willing to let the FBI line their pockets allowed agents into apartments to plant bugs. "Oh, honey," recalled Elsie, "it was just a given that our phones were bugged. And they checked our mail, too." Sixty years later Elsie's FBI file testified to that fact. It read like a diary regarding Elsie's comings and goings. During the Cold War, Ernie was on the front lines, and Elsie kept the time clock punched. The FBI tracked them both.[61]

The year 1949 was the test for the ILWU and Elsie's office skills. The Hawaiian Dock Strike lasted 171 days and tested the endurance of the workers and the threat of the Taft-Hartley Act. The Asian longshoremen in Hawaii were paid considerably less than their mainland counterparts. A strike ensued, demanding wage parity. But the Big Five promptly responded via media and stubborn control. They likened the strike to a Communist takeover ordered straight from Moscow. Now was the time to break the strength of organized labor. According to them, they fought Communists, not workers who wanted better wages. Unions and Communism were synonymous to the press and public.

Elsie worked to raise money for the beleaguered workers who planted gardens for food because produce and other food stuffs rotted on ships during the strike. A flurry of organizers and directors came to San Francisco. Elsie arranged hotels, meals, and transportation and provided directions. She recorded minutes at union meetings and socialized with the same men in the evenings.

The smoke in the bar was likely as thick as the talk around the table. "Yeah, the Big Five's got their wives marching now. They carry brooms and claim they're gonna clean out the union, get rid of the reds. Call themselves the Broom Brigade. Bet some of 'em don't even know how to use a broom, marching around in high heels and clothes they didn't get at no discount department store."

Hall ordered another round of drinks. "Course, the hunt is on for the reds. Gotta be careful in meetings, what you say and all, or somebody'll accuse you of getting your check from Moscow."

"Did you see the editorials they put in the Honolulu paper? Even the media is putting on the heat. Those Joe Stalin letters …" he turned to Elsie to explain. "It's an editorial that's in the form of a letter, supposedly from Stalin, telling how to Sovietize Hawaii. Yeah, it's propaganda, but you know, it affects people. People believe what they read in the paper."

Elsie asked Lou Goldblatt about the Hilo Unity Conference—the one they organized to address the threat of unions separating from the ILWU because of its left leanings.

"Well, I'll tell you what I told 'em there. I said we are unionists. But we're the kind of union that lets people believe what they please. I told 'em we can be Democrats or Republicans, Communists or Catholics, as long as we are good union people, we're not gonna tell 'em what to believe. This union is run by its members and no one else." [62]

"It's gotta be pretty tough for the workers right now. We're ninety days or more into it. How are they getting on?" asked Elsie.

Goldblatt responded, "They're getting on okay if we can keep helping them. The economy is pretty much paralyzed—you get that many people out of work and the longshoremen refusing to load or unload. I heard shelves in the grocery stores are empty. The union said they would unload if it were a union ship. A ship came in loaded with food but we wouldn't touch it. Word reached us ahead of time. It was a hot cargo. No union guy's gonna unload a ship that's been loaded by scabs."

"Hey, ya hear? They picked Bridges up again. Accused him of being red. Guess he tried to apply for citizenship, and they pulled out the goods on him. Trial's coming up. He's denying it, of course."

"Yeah, well the talk on the dock is the same. Bridges has never sold us out or double-dealed us. He's never finked on us. Don't give a damn if he's a commie or not, he comes through for the rank and file. He puts his pants on one leg at a time, just like the rest of us."

The ILWU ultimately won the Hawaiian Dock Strike but not without a cost. The glorious organizing days of the CIO in the thirties was seeing its demise by the end of the forties. Owners threatened to take their business away from unions suspected of hiring Communists. Unions all over the country buckled under pressure to sign the loyalty oath. The loyalty oath threatened the unions that had prided themselves in their democratic elections. Red-baiters in the guise of rank and file workers, postal workers, even Catholic priests were rooting out the Communists.[63] The ILWU was under attack to submit to the loyalty oath as mandated by the Taft-Hartley Act. Under the direction of Ray Beck of the AFL, a raid ensued that targeted Local 6 and enticed workers to join their side and expose Communists. The ILWU resisted the attack and survived the raid intact. Then pressure was directed by the CIO, to which the ILWU belonged. Bridges was removed from his position as California's CIO regional director in 1948. At the 1949 CIO Convention, a vote banned Communists or people even suspect of being Communist as members. As a result, ten progressive unions that did not comply with the loyalty oath were kicked out of the CIO, which affected a million workers. Those unions were denied collective bargaining rights under the NLRB. By 1950m the CIO expelled the ILWU due to Communist leadership within its ranks.[64] Yet, despite the attacks, the ILWU under Bridges' leadership continued to thrive. Anywhere else, Elsie's job would have been at risk because she actively participated in Communist Club activities, but her job was intact. The ILWU remained a safe haven for radicals and progressive intellectuals because of its democratic principles.

The FBI continued their vigilance in tracking Elsie. They verified her high school education in Miles City, her marital status, and employment records. They periodically checked files at the San Francisco Police Department for criminal records to no avail. They made a list of places she had lived for the last two decades and checked retailer credit records and phone books. Elsie's Communist activities were easy to track. She was a delegate to the Communist Party State Convention in 1945 and held different posts at several different clubs. She subscribed to the *Daily People's World*—a west coast radical newspaper. The FBI made note of her connection with the front groups the Civil Rights Congress and the Committee for the Protection of the Foreign Born. Informants fed the information to the Bureau, and her file grew.

> FBI REPORT Sept. 2, 1953, Period for which made:
> 8/3/49 – 8/25/53

> SF T-13 on August 18, 1950, advised that at that time the subject's husband ERNEST FOX stated that the subject at that time was a Section Educational Director which requires her going out nearly every night.

Ernie would not be intimidated by the fear of informants and growing animosity toward the political left. He was the Waterfront Organizer for the Communist Party and taught Marxist classes at meetings. But the Cold War was escalating. Even the Vatican joined the ranks of the reactionaries. In 1949, a decree announced that any Roman Catholic practicing or preaching Communism would be excommunicated. At the same time, the Ku Klux Klan in the United States increased membership and burned crosses on Catholic lawns. Fear found a foothold in hatred and suspicion of change in the United States at the end of the forties.

Two more world events rounded out the eventful year of 1949: the USSR detonated a nuclear bomb and Mao Tse-tung seized Communist power in China, forcing President Chiang Kai-Shek to withdraw to Taiwan. The People's Republic of China was formed. As a result, five hundred million more Communists were added to the world. Then Russia and China formed an alliance, and the Cold War took shape due to the threat of a growing Communist world. The United States, vying for ultimate, superpower status, refused to acknowledge the new regime in China.

Elsie recalled, "We were so excited. China was such a big country, and the hope for socialism was growing." Eight Chinese Party representatives came to San Francisco, and Elsie and Ernie received invitations to attend the festivities. "There was no braggadocio atmosphere. These men were very humble, and yet there was a feeling of great accomplishment. I felt such a sense of camaraderie." Men with similar backgrounds to these visitors had lived in large caves deep inside China when Japan had invaded. It was in these caves that Mao Tse-tung developed his philosophy and plan for a new government. Now that their liberation had arrived, the American Communists welcomed them. Ernest had his picture taken with the group. Flanked by two Chinese men in suits, Ernie stood in front of an American flag hung next to the Chinese flag blazoned with a hammer and sickle. His face captured the solemnity of the moment. Or maybe his serious gaze glimpsed the future storm despite the brief silver lining after WWII.

1949 - Chinese vice premier and Ernest Fox

CHAPTER 19:

Determined and Challenged

Meeting with Elsie

Elsie listened intently as I read from articles regarding Communism in Seattle during the thirties. She recognized names and latent memories surfaced as she added comments such as, "Oh, he was a terrific speaker," or "He didn't let fame go to his head," or "Oh, baby, could he dance!" I saw the black and white photographs of young, idealistic faces come alive with Elsie's running commentary.

"There were so many wonderful intellectuals involved in the movement in Seattle," she nearly bubbled with enthusiasm. "I wish I could remember the name of the young man that was the head of the pension movement. Everyone knew him. He was very well liked and very self-sacrificing, dedicated, and capable." Elsie sat still for a moment, basking in the pleasant memory of a man she had not thought of in over half a century. Then she laughed. "I cannot believe my memory! His name was Bill Pennock. He was the main reason the Pension Union was so successful."

The coincidence seemed too much as I looked at the black and white photograph before me. "Here's a picture of him, Elsie, taken in the thirties!"

A man with round, wire-rimmed glasses and a receding hairline with a Mona Lisa smile looked at the camera. She took out her magnifying glass and smiled as her eyes focused on his picture. "Yes, that's him. He was one of the sweetest men I have ever known and so intelligent and mannerly. I wonder what became of him?" Under his photograph was the following subscript:

> William Pennock became President of the WPU and presided over it during its years of greatest influence. One of a number of secret Communists to gain prominence in Washington state, he also served in the state legislature. A chief target of the red hunters, he was indicted in 1952 under the Smith Act but took his own life before the trial concluded.[65]

Elsie sat in shocked silence. "Oh, god." The words dropped onto her lap. Her shoulders slumped, and she shook her head. Then, after a minute or so, she reached over to pet Mia and said, "Unfortunately, that was more common than people think." It startled me to feel the impact of this man's death fifty years later—a man who took his own life the year I was born, at the height of the McCarthy Period. "And if we aren't careful, that same kind of fear can happen again!" On the way home, I thought of my widowed mother's Social Security benefits that put my brother and me through college and the GI Bill that gave my brother—a Vietnam veteran—a college education. Elsie's words echoed in my mind. "Those benefits didn't just fall out of the sky. They were won by sheer hard work and sacrifice by the people!"

* * * * *

The First Amendment to the United States Constitution states that "Congress shall make no law respecting an establishment of religion, or prohibiting the free exercise thereof; or abridging the freedom of speech or of the press; or the right of the people peaceably to assemble and to petition the Government for a redress of grievances." The following quote is Supreme Court Justice Hugo Black's dissent regarding *ACA v. Douds*,[66] which was a challenge to the Taft-Hartley oath using the First Amendment:

> Beliefs are inviolate under the First Amendment to the U.S. Constitution. We need the First Amendment to avoid thought control. Test oaths have been used time

> and again to identify and outlaw opponents, as the French did against the Huguenots. It helped English rulers identify and outlaw Catholics, Quakers, Baptists, and Congregationalists—groups considered dangerous for political as well as religious reasons. And wherever the test oath was in vogue, spies and informers found rewards far more tempting than truth. What is to prevent Congress from keeping members of other political parties out of union office?[67]

The decade of the fifties fired Elsie's determination to actively engage in defending those rights. It was more of a challenge than she anticipated. An incident that occurred one day when she walked back to work from a luncheon meeting was an omen of things to come.

Elsie walked briskly through the crowded streets. She had attended a meeting at the California Labor School on Market Street, where she gave a speech praising Oleta Yates and Dorothy Healy for their dedication to the party. She saw him coming a half a block away. The trademark trench coat and hat made him easy to spot. Elsie kept her head down as she walked but he fell in step beside her. "Ma'am, I'd like to talk with you."

"I don't talk to strangers," said Elsie without pausing. She picked up her pace and wove through the noontime rush of people. The hunt was getting closer to home. The following article is taken from the *Dispatcher* (ILWU Newspaper) January 10, 1947:

> The *New Republic* stated March 11, 1946, that during the days of the Palmer raids, Hoover compiled a list of some half million persons suspected as dangerous because of their economic or political beliefs. That catalog has since been added to and is now the basis for the FBI's reported plans for "thought control" being readied for use at the proper moment.
>
> Naturally, the FBI records are not limited to radicals but include the most effective labor leaders and hence those most dangerous to the big industrialists. Hoover and the FBI are the guardians of private monopoly. Attorney General Harlan Stone—later Chief Justice of the Supreme Court disbanded Hoover's General

> Intelligence Division of the FBI in 1924 and wrote.... "When a police system passes beyond these limits, it is dangerous to the proper administration of justice and to human liberty which it should be our first concern to cherish."

Despite Attorney General Stone's clear-cut warning, the FBI continued investigations with Hoover in command. Worse yet, when the General Intelligence section was reestablished in 1939, it gave unrestricted power to the FBI, directed by J. Edgar Hoover, to hunt for subversives that might threaten the security of the United States. Fear and suspicion fueled the direct assault on the First Amendment. Honing his skills, Hoover began the full assault in the fifties. Just like the thirties, Elsie found plenty of issues to protest or reasons to circulate petitions. Her evenings were as scheduled as her work day.

Uncle Bud, Girlie, Macie, Elsie on the Gay Ranch, Southeastern Montana

Somehow, despite her responsibilities at work and progressive causes to champion on her off hours, Elsie found the time to return to Montana once a year in the fifties to visit her aging mother and sister. Riding horse, fishing the Powder River, and visiting Uncle Bud at the Gay Ranch grounded Elsie, and she never failed to return to San Francisco without renewed vigor.

Elsie - Gay Ranch, Powder River country, Montana

In October of 1950, Ernie was arrested and held for deportation under the McCarran Internal Security Act. Ernie was not a citizen.[68] "I don't remember much about that arrest," said Elsie. "He wasn't imprisoned long. Somehow bail was met. I guess in my memory it was overshadowed by the next arrest." The McCarran Act required Communist Party members to register with the Attorney General. It also targeted immigrants with a rigid immigration quota system. President Truman vetoed the act saying, "The error of this bill is that it moves in the direction of suppressing opinion and belief ... that would make a mockery of the Bill of Rights and of our claims to stand for freedom in the world."[69] The Republican Congress overrode Truman's veto, claiming the president was soft on Communism, which ultimately led to his defeat in the next election.

On the west coast, it began in Hollywood. Actors, actresses, and writers, dubbed as subversives, were suspect for their left-wing ideas that played out on the big screen. Subpoenas were issued under the Smith Act. The House of Un–American Activities Committee (HUAC) began to investigate potential Communist subversives. The same scene played out in government buildings all over the country. "Are you now or have you ever been a member of the Communist Party? Have you ever been affiliated with the CP? Do you know X? Was X ever a member of the CP?"[70]

If an answer was not forthcoming, the defendant was charged with contempt of Congress. Ten Hollywood personalities were arrested and refused to answer the interrogation based on the First Amendment. They were given a choice: name names or go to prison and be blacklisted. The ten were found guilty and sentenced to six months, but the longer sentence was the blacklist, which affected hundreds of people associated with the arts and entertainment field—Charlie Chaplin, Leonard Bernstein, Dashiell Hammett, Burl Ives, Arthur Miller, Pete Seeger, Orson Welles, Paul Robeson, to name a few. Alvah Bessie, a screen writer, was lucky to find a job after being blacklisted. His office was near Elsie's, where he wrote for the ILWU newspaper, the *Dispatcher*.

Next on the FBI's hit list were the Communists, and everyone was suspect. Twelve Communist leaders were picked up on the east coast and convicted. Elsie circulated a petition protesting their arrests.[71] Hugo Black's dissenting statement on June 4, 1951, on the conviction of the leaders of the Communist Party defended the attack on the First Amendment:

> The charge against the petitioners (the Communist leaders) was that they agreed to assemble and to talk and publish certain ideas at a later date. The indictment is that they conspired to organize the Communist Party and to use speech or newspapers and other publications in the future to teach and advocate the forcible overthrow of the Government. No matter how it is worded, this is a virulent form of prior censorship of speech and press,

> which I believe the First Amendment forbids.
>
> I have always believed that the First Amendment is the keystone of our Government, that the freedoms it guarantees provide the best insurance against destruction of all freedom. The Amendment as so construed is not likely to protect any but those "safe" or orthodox views which rarely need its protection.
>
> Public opinion being what it now is, few will protest the conviction of these Communist petitioners. There is hope, however, that in calmer times, when present pressures, passions, and fears subside, this or some later Court will restore the First Amendment liberties to the high preferred place where they belong in a free society.[72]

Calmer times seemed far away in 1951. The criminal convictions of the Communist leadership made the party even more suspect in the eyes of the public. Hoover convinced Congress and McCarthy to enact laws that would root out sympathizers and supporters of the party. The anti–Communist virus spread like a red tidal wave from the east to the west coast. Another raid on the Communists was in the making—this time in California.

Elsie was cautious about talking politics during working hours due to the attacks from the AFL and the pressure on the CIO to cleanse the union of Communists. Red baiters, informants, and FBI special agents infiltrated most organizations, meetings, and suspect's homes. But while other unions succumbed to the pressure, Elsie's job at Local 6 was still secure. "We're the kind of union that lets people believe what they please … as long as they are good union people."

Looking forward to a rare, quiet evening at home after work, Elsie opened the door to their apartment and was stunned at what she saw. Most of their furniture was gone. If Ernie hadn't been sitting in one of the remaining chairs, she would have guessed they had been robbed. "My god, Ernie! What happened?"

"We have to move to a safe house. The party said things are heating up and suggested we try to be more discreet."

"What! When did you know this? Why didn't you consult with me first?" Elsie was furious. She had lived and paid the rent at Green Street for almost ten years. She had accumulated good memories along with the comfortable décor that made it feel like home, her home. "The party tells you to jump and you jump?"

Ernie sounded tired. "It's a done deal. The party found a place for us, but it won't be ready for a couple weeks. We're staying at Joe and Carol's until we can move in to our own place. They have a spare bedroom." He looked at her, the fight draining from his face. "As long as my health holds, well … we can handle the move." What did he mean by that? Elsie remembered thinking that statement was rather strange. They were in good health and in their midforties, but the shock of the moment overrode his odd comment.

She spent the weekend packing. They would be out of Green Street by Wednesday. The phone rang the night before their last day, and Elsie answered.

"I can't hear. Would you please speak up?" Elsie could hear voices in the background, and the laughter and dishes clattering suggested the call was coming from a crowded restaurant.

"I just wanted you to know," the voice—a woman's voice—was hurried and sounded as if she was talking into a wall. "Your husband is going to be arrested in a few days. I just wanted you to know."

"Who are …" Click. The woman hung up. Elsie realized the necessity of moving from Green Street after that phone call.

Their bedroom at their friends' house was on the second floor. The doorbell rang at six thirty in the morning, waking both of them. No need to jump up—their friends would answer the door. Elsie got up and pulled her bathrobe on when voices sounded, followed by the clomping of feet running up the stairs. As she looked at Ernie with alarm, the bedroom door burst open. Agents, four or five of them in their telltale trench coats and hats firmly set on their heads, pointed revolvers at Ernie while another motioned Elsie to stand where she was. Half a century later, Elsie remembers Ernie sitting on the bed, pulling on his trousers one pant leg at a time, with guns aimed at him. "I remember being scared to death, of course. But I didn't shed any tears. Instead, I was livid!"

Fifteen members of the California CP had been arrested in a well-coordinated effort. The California Fifteen, as they became known, were sent to Los Angeles to await a bail hearing. The charge was conspiring to teach and advocate the overthrow of the United States government by force and violence and organizing the Communist Party as a vehicle for such teachings.[73] The strategy was simple: arrest the party leaders, set the bail high, making it difficult to meet, which would keep the "subversives" in jail and out of commission. Communist Party activities in California would be effectively disrupted. The plan worked. "The bail was ridiculous; if I can remember correctly it was eighty thousand dollars or maybe more." During this time, Elsie moved, and the FBI, once again, made note in an office memorandum to Director Hoover:

> The Security Index Card on the captioned individual should be changed as follows: Residence Address—1116 Montgomery Street, San Francisco, California. SF T-7 on July 25, 1952, advised that at that time the subject was residing at 765 O'Farrell Street, Apartment 47, San Francisco.

Fear was spreading and not only through the working class. It was difficult to find lawyers that would take the case of the Communists. Simply becoming a defense attorney for them would be self-incrimination under the Smith Act. Any association with the defense of the Communists would subject a lawyer to persecutions by the bar association and an attack on their legal career. By this time, Senator McCarthy was conducting hearings calling forth government employees and even targeting government agencies based on FBI data collected by informants. "The arrests were splashed all over the news, and I am eternally grateful that my name was not included. I could very well have been next on the list," speculated Elsie fifty years later, "and even though my job was secure, I didn't want the notoriety to be trouble for Local 6." That did not stop Elsie from actively raising funds for the defendants. She also organized and marched in a picket line demanding reasonable bail for the California Fifteen on September 20, 1952, in front of the San Francisco Post Office.[74]

Shortly after Ernie was arrested, Elsie was doing union business, preparing for the monthly trustees meeting. Elsie described details of the incident as if it happened yesterday. "I was in the union hall, and there was this really 'lumpen proletariat'—it's a Marxist expression referring to unprincipled workers that are low down. They're for sale for anybody that has a dime. This worker, Owen Proviso, was a lumpen proletariat. Proviso was in the hall along with all the board members and officers. As I walked across the room, he shouted, 'Elsie, where's Ernie?' He knew Ernie was in jail in L.A. He was trying to bait me. I knew I had to handle this, so I walked on past the switchboard and went half way upstairs, and then I turned and said in a really loud voice, shouting practically, 'Proviso! If you have union business, you can come up to my office. Otherwise, knock it off!' Of course, there was dead silence in the hall. Frank Maxine, who was chairman of the board of trustees at the time and had some basic disagreements with the Communist party even though he was a very progressive man, knew what the score was. He came into my office, and I didn't know what to expect. He came up to my desk and said, 'Elsie, I want to compliment you on the way you handled Proviso.' And he dug a candy bar out of his pocket and gave it to me." Proviso never did come to her office. Elsie proved her worth that day in the union hall, and you can bet she savored that candy bar.

CHAPTER 20:

Trials and Tribulations

Meeting with Elsie

Elsie was in the mood to talk politics of the past and, as always, threaded the conversation into the present. "Charlie was a friend and a lover of mine." I raised my eyebrows, but she kept going. "He wrote for the *San Francisco Chronicle* and was the main reporter when the United Nations was being formed. You remember, all the meetings took place in San Francisco. That's where the United Nations was born." She continued in an instructional tone, "There was great opposition to this idea, but the progressives prevailed. The upsurge of independent nations after WWII in South America helped to form the UN, and the UN plays a tremendous role in the world … peace keeping forces result in the great growth of democracy. The reactionary forces tried to kill the UN idea." She leaned forward on the orange-cushioned sofa, "You see, the formation of independent nations is not good for corporate profit. They need to keep those countries in a state of underdevelopment so they can be exploited. It all comes back to Marxism, dear. I endorse and agree with Howard Zinn. History is just glossed over." Her jaw was set and she emphasized the next sentence. "They can say Marxism is outdated but not so, baby, not so." Then, after a moment of silence, like the breath of space before the punch line is delivered, she said, "The title for my book could be *Elsie Fox: Telling It Like It Is.*"

* * * * *

For Elsie and Ernie, the fifties were like the thirties turned inside out. The unions, the party, and ultimately their marriage were taking a direct hit. By now, she was approaching middle age and faced two major health complications—the early onset of menopause and a stomach problem that eventually was diagnosed as ulcers. Elsie had settled into the "safe" apartment—a place she later associated with the ten "dark" years of living in San Francisco. Yet, this was no time to weaken.

Elsie met with their lawyer, Norman Leonard, the progressive lawyer who tirelessly defended Harry Bridges and other rank and file members of the union and courageously risked his career and worked with other lawyers to defend the group. "The intellectuals and attorneys played a big role in the fight for democracy during that period," Elsie reflected. "They suffered financial loss by supporting the working class movement. I shall be forever indebted to them." Elsie could not remember how long Ernie was held in prison, or how the bail was met.

In July of 1952, the CP legal team developed a strategy for the forthcoming trial of the California Fifteen. In efforts to avoid a confrontational atmosphere, the lawyers decided the CP members would have little participation in the courtroom. However, they opted to put each of the defendants on the stand to testify about their beliefs and interpretations of Marxism and that they did not advocate violence. After the first defendant, Oleta O'Connor Yates, took the stand, she was found in contempt of court because, under cross-examination, she refused to name more people who were Communist members. Subsequently, the defense decided not to let any other defendants testify.

Elsie explained, "I would fly to Los Angeles on the weekends to visit Ernie and attend bail hearings. I stayed with progressive friends. The party was very strong in L.A. and there was a lot of support." Elsie also found time to shop for clothes. Shopping for new clothes had always been a curative tonic for Elsie.

Witnesses for the prosecution were called to the stand. "It was shocking," Elsie remembered. "You never knew which one of your friends or acquaintances was going to come through the courthouse door and take the stand against you. They were paid! I wish I had all the money the stool pigeons made in those years!" On August 6, 1952, Judge William C. Mathes pronounced the verdict—guilty. And the sentence was one to five years in prison plus a ten thousand dollar fine.[75] Appeals were immediately filed.

The Smith Act Trials effectively stymied the party and influenced public opinion. Hoover supplied McCarthy with information, however inaccurate, whetting his appetite for power that he exercised in the HUAC. Journalists, doctors, postal workers, government employees, next-door neighbors—all were suspect. Eventually, the Ninth Circuit Court of Appeals upheld the California Fifteen's conviction in 1955. It was then appealed to the Supreme Court.

With Ernie and the other defendants' case in the capable hands of lawyers, Elsie actively supported other progressive causes. She was a busy lady, and the FBI thoroughly documented her activity.[76]

Elsie maintained a full schedule at Local 6 as well. The red scare and McCarthyism targeted the CIO, and all unions were losing ground they had made in the thirties as a result of the enforcement of the NLRB. More control was going back to the companies, and the workers were losing ground. The AFL and the CIO were now vying more than ever for membership. Lou Goldblatt, an officer in the ILWU, began urging the AFL and CIO to merge rather than fight among themselves. Meeting after meeting was held to accomplish this task, and Elsie organized the essentials necessary for those meetings to occur.

After one such meeting, Elsie bustled around on the stage, clearing off the tables and gathering supplies. Goldblatt motioned her over to where he was standing. "Elsie, I want you to meet someone." He stood next to a short man, nicely dressed, who listened to Lou explain Elsie's role as office manager in Local 6. "Elsie Fox, I'd like you to meet Jimmy Hoffa."

Elsie distinctly remembered meeting the infamous union leader of the International Brotherhood of Teamsters, who mysteriously disappeared in 1975. "My impression of him was that he was a devoted family man, very polite, and almost shy. Of course, his big mistake was getting mixed up with the Mafia."

During this union turmoil, the ILWU was held intact, and, indeed, it was thriving thanks to the loyalty of the workers and commitment of the officers to the union. In 1955, the merger of the two industrial unions was complete and became known as the AFL-CIO.

The American Communist Party, on the other hand, faltered. Rumors of horrible abuse by Stalin and his cronies filtered into the States. The combined effect of the McCarthy Trials, the FBI surveillance, and the rumors from the Soviet Union—later proven true—tested Ernie and Elsie's convictions like never before. Ernie became increasingly depressed and bitter as membership in the party spiraled downward.

It was about that time that Elsie heard from friends in Seattle about their mutual friends. Elsie recalled the incident: "Grace and Jean were very good, Finnish friends of mine when I lived in Seattle. Their parents were very dedicated Communists when they lived in Finland before coming to Minnesota to work in the Misaba Mines and later moved to Seattle. In the thirties, the Soviet Union sent out a call to Communists around the world that they needed skilled workers to work in the industries to build the Soviet Union. Grace and Jean's parents went back to a village near the Soviet-Finland border to work. They exchanged letters for a number of years with their daughters. Then Grace and Jean lost contact with their parents. They wrote letters but got no response. After the war was over, Jean went to the Soviet Union to try to find her parents and made a horrific discovery. Jean found out her parents were victims of the terrible crimes that Stalin had committed. If just one person in a town spoke out against Stalin, the whole town was ordered killed. Their parents were among the victims. Not only was it a crime against those affected, but it continues to set back the workers' struggles and the cause of socialism throughout the world. Yet, when asked if she still believed in socialism, Jean answered, "Yes." She knew that "absolute power corrupts absolutely." Communism upheld the Marxist theory that Elsie embraced in the thirties. Now, in the fifties, it became an illusion with the revelations of the Stalin atrocities. However, Jean's unwavering faith that socialism would prevail fueled Elsie's activism for a better world.

In 1956, Nikita Khrushchev shocked the world with an address to the Russian Party Congress. He confessed to crimes of murder and deportation to work camps under Joseph Stalin's rule. It wasn't revealed until decades later that millions of people simply disappeared under the gulag system. Stalin died in 1953, but Khrushchev's revelation, along with the McCarthy hunts in America, proved to be the death knoll for the American Communist Party.

Ernie was devastated. Elsie felt betrayed by the party and Stalin, yet, like Grace and Jean, her core beliefs held true. Ernie's beliefs collapsed but Elsie's stayed rooted in Marxism.

On October 24, 1955, an FBI report documented that "individuals were selected from various sections of the CP for a special cadre training program in Marxism, the purpose of which was to train future leaders in the CP in San Francisco. T-15 stated that ELSIE FOX attended meetings of the special training class on the following dates at the listed addresses." The same report also documented that "Subject was contacted by Special Agents of the San Francisco Office regarding the investigation of the ILWU, and she refused to be interviewed." In the meantime, the California Fifteen's case was scheduled to be heard before the Supreme Court.

By the time the California Fifteen's case, *Yates, et al. v. United States*, was heard in 1957, McCarthyism was waning. Senator McCarthy had pushed the limits of credibility with Congress and the president, especially when he began to target the military and government employees. Edward Murrow's investigative reporting played a vital role in spotlighting McCarthy's tirade, headlining the issues in newspaper and radio programs, which revealed a government gone amuck.

The court, under Chief Justice Earl Warren, overturned the convictions of the California Fifteen. The court ruled that there had been no proof the defendants had conspired to promote illegal conduct. They merely promoted *beliefs* and *ideas* that, under the first amendment, are one of the freedoms of democracy. There was no proof that violent acts had taken place. Five of the men and women were acquitted while others, including Ernie, were ordered new trials. Hidden secrets lay in the archived files for the case.

Ernie's deportation proceedings still existed. After his California conviction and before the Supreme Court case, the State Department tried to convince Germany to take back the expatriate, Ernest Fox. Germany wanted proof that he was not a U.S. citizen. The State Department did not want to delay the trial and, as a result, did not push the matter. Neither Elsie nor Ernie were aware of these proceedings. In the meantime, the Justice Department decided not to retry the remaining defendants after the Supreme Court hearing, but the deportation charges stayed on the books for Ernest Fox.

The Yates decision ended the McCarthy hearings of the fifties. The Smith Act was no longer used to prosecute Communists. The Supreme Court ruling in *Yates v. United States* was not only a victory for the California Communists, but a victory for the civil rights of every U.S. citizen. An overzealous FBI Director Hoover and a power hungry congressman had chipped away at First Amendment rights for decades. Justice Hugo Black commented,

> The interest of the people lies in being able to join organizations, advocate causes, and make political "mistakes" without being subjected to governmental penalties. Without deviation, without exception, without any ifs, buts, or whereases, freedom of speech means that you shall not do something to people either for the views they express, or the words they speak or write.[77]

The Smith Act still remains on the books while the collective memory of a country's history fades, waiting for a people to become complacent. It waits like a leviathan biding its time, waiting for a time when fear replaces reason.

Despite the success of the Supreme Court hearing, Ernie started to lose his resolve. Elsie remembered, "I don't remember when I first realized he was not well. He seemed to have an obstruction in his upper respiratory system. We gradually stopped doing things together like walking along the waterfront, although we still went to bars occasionally. He continued to read radical literature, although our activity had greatly lessened. The party had been shaken by the Soviet Union invasion of Czechoslovakia and the increasing evidence of repression in the Soviet Union. This was something we, as loyal party members, had vehemently denied all these years. We referred to such reports as 'capitalists' rumors.' In my heart, I was not so shaken by all this. My understanding of the basic workings of the capitalist system and the corruption it inspires remained untouched and, incidentally, remains so today. I was depressed by such reports coming out of Russia, of course, but not shaken. I felt Ernest was shaken, although he never denounced the party, but I knew he was disillusioned and had lost the fervor of his beliefs. We no longer had the rudder of the ship of socialism to bind us together and guide us, and his increasingly declining health contributed to our failing marriage."

Late 1950's - Elsie and Ernie boating on the Bay

Stalin's deceptive practices forever changed the world's view of Communism. Deception ultimately destroys, and marriages are no exception.

> FBI REPORT: 4/3/58
>
> Place of Meeting and Remarks: The subject ELSIE FOX stated that the CP should take a strong position in a move to block the present economic recession. She stated that the situation is very much like that which existed in the 1930s and that the people are in the mood to listen to a good program of Socialism which would ultimately solve the "ills" of the American economic system. She said that the party line should be a fight against capitalism and for socialism.

CHAPTER 21:

Betrayal

Meeting with Elsie

Elsie's recollections came in fits and starts. I found myself either having to race to keep up with her or sit back and be quiet while she sifted through time where pieces of the past surfaced in the foggy sea of memory. One day Elsie puzzled about her mother's relationship with her father. "My mother discovered that Father was illiterate. I think this must have been a terrible blow to her to realize her husband couldn't read or write. I think she was ashamed of him for that reason, and I am sure it colored their entire relationship. I'm convinced he tried to make it up to her by running off to the gold fields, thinking he would strike it rich and prove himself to her. Guilt is a powerful force in relationships!" She seemed to speak from her own experience.

Elsie had retained only a few memories of her father, but one moment surfaced with surprising clarity. "I remember my father squatting down at one end of the room. He was holding his arms out to me. I ran the length of the room and into his arms." She continued, "Oh, and there's one more memory I have of him: The whole family was in the wagon. My father stopped the horses and jumped out of the wagon. He picked a big bouquet of bright yellow prairie daisies—

arrowleaf balsamroot—and presented them to Mother." She sat still for a moment, letting that image form in both of our imaginations. "I guess he really did love her."

I listened to this gentle outline of Elsie's father and recognized that select characters of our past only emerge when coaxed into the light for communion, understanding, and sometimes forgiveness.

* * * * *

It was a warm autumn day in 1962 when a group of Ernie's comrades came to see Elsie at the union office. They were concerned about Ernie's health and made it clear that, in their opinion, she was not a good wife because she did not make him go to a doctor. Ernie's persistent cough had lasted months. Elsie told them she had suggested every now and then that he go see a doctor. Cost was not an issue, since they had an excellent health care plan through Kaiser Health Insurance that was offered by the ILWU. "Ernie won't go to the doctor! I've tried!" she told them, but she could tell they blamed her.

As Elsie walked home from work, she could hear the accusing words of Ernie's friends echo in each step. She began to walk faster and caught herself clenching her fists as she nearly stomped up the stairs to their apartment. Later that evening, Ernie and Elsie sat in the living room reading when she put down her book and cleared her throat. He coughed, then noticed her gaze aimed at him. "What is it?" he asked.

Elsie leaned forward. "Ernest, you need medical attention! You must see a doctor!"

The suggestion quickly devolved into a heated discussion. "Elsie, don't push me too far," he snarled, clenching his fists and facing her with a grimness she had not seen before. Cold fear raced through Elsie's body. She was certain that if she pushed him any further, he would hit her. The next day, before she left for work, Elsie sat at her typewriter, sandwiched a piece of carbon paper between two blank sheets, and tapped out a letter:

> October 11, 1962
>
> Dear Ernest:
>
> I have moved out as I think that is the best thing for both of us. I agree with you that there is no hope for our relationship, and perhaps you are right that I should never have married. I am doing this like this

> because I think it will save feelings all the way around. You can say that it was your decision that we separate because this is really true. Also, I think it best for me to move because of the Immigration (issue).
>
> Regarding business things, I am taking half of the money out of the savings account and leaving your part in it and the pass book is herewith. The rent here is paid until Nov. 1st and I have paid the phone bill up to date. I will pay the income taxes for this year when they become due next year as in the past. I have taken only the record player and cabinet and a few books and pictures.
>
> I do not harbor ill will—I am sorry it turned out badly and I hope you feel the same. I think that maybe you are right when you said that maybe voluntary departure would be the best thing, but I know that it is up to you to make up your mind.
>
> Elsie

Elsie laid the original letter on the kitchen table and put the carbon copy with Ernie's POW letters in a box. She packed what she could carry with her. Communism, socialism, the battle waged during Ernie's internment, the McCarthy Trials—circumstances, events, and causes no longer cemented their marriage. She made arrangements to move temporarily into a downtown hotel before finding an apartment of her own. She ended their marriage like closing a checking account.

Ernie phoned her the next day. He asked if they could meet at a restaurant nearby. She agreed. She glanced in the mirror on the way out and was startled at her stern expression—one she remembered seeing on her mother's face when confronted with the struggles of being a single mother. Elsie straightened her shoulders, picked up a tube of red lipstick, and smiled confidently at herself in the mirror before leaving to meet Ernie.

"Elsie, I'm sorry about the other night. I have to know … is there someone else?" Elsie assured him there wasn't, and they agreed to be friends. She could sense his relief, just like the first time they ended their marriage. Then the following week, she took a day off work and secured an apartment at Jackson and Leavenworth on the edge of Chinatown and Pacific Heights. An FBI report filed in November of 1962 made note of the change of address: "Subject: ELSIE FOX resides at Apt. 17, 1312 Jackson Street, San Francisco, CA." Enlisting the help of her friend who was an interior decorator, she bought some new furniture, and among the items was an Oriental-style sofa with orange cushions in a dark, bamboo frame.

About that time, Elsie made another trip to Miles City to visit her mother, who was supportive of Elsie's separation from Ernie. Macie's words from almost thirty years earlier must have echoed in Elsie's mind: "He's no good, Elsie." Before returning to San Francisco, Elsie found time to fish on the Tongue River, a tributary of the Yellowstone River that flowed by Miles City. Elsie never told her mother the real reason for her separation from Ernie. Elsie never told anyone.

Fishing on the Tongue River, near Miles City, Montana

Upon her return, Ernie and Elsie made dates for lunch and occasionally went out to dinner in the evenings at friends' homes. Afterwards, they went home to their separate apartments. Ernie made a joke one evening that living apart had brought them closer together. As the year progressed, however, his physical condition deteriorated.

In December of 1962, Elsie answered the phone in her office. "This is Dr. Garfield, from Kaiser Health."

"Yes? How can I help you?" said Elsie.

"I would like to talk to you. Is there someplace you can go where you might have some privacy and call me back?" Elsie jotted down his number, went into a nearby office, then closed the door. She dialed Dr. Garfield's number.

"It's about your husband, Ernest Fox. He came for an examination. I'm sure you are aware of his health issues of the past. I felt you needed to know this, since you are his nearest family." Elsie held the phone not knowing what to say and waited for him to continue. "Are you still there?"

"Yes, yes … go on," Elsie replied.

"Please sit down if you aren't already." Another pause. "I've made the diagnosis. Ernest is in the final stages of syphilis." It was as if a bomb went off. Elsie asked him to repeat what he just said. "He has an aneurysm in his heart that is inoperable and fatal. He probably has no more than six months to live."

"Does he know?" Her mind was reeling. Syphilis. Final stages. Syphilis?

"Of course he knows he has syphilis, but he doesn't know about the aneurysm. I haven't told him. I thought you might break the news. I'll give him medication to ease his discomfort, but there is no cure at this stage of the disease. He could die at any time by a sudden strain or pressure. The aneurysm would break and death would be instant. Something as simple as riding a cable car where a sharp turn or some such movement occurred could cause his death."

She set the phone on the cradle and sat in the empty room with her hands limp in her lap, immobile with shock. She told her boss she wasn't feeling well and took the afternoon off. On her way home, she stopped at the library and read everything she could find on syphilis. Then, sitting in her apartment alone, she tried to come to terms with the doctor's revelation. Ernie was dying of a disease caused by a bacterium that could have been cured by penicillin in the first two stages. She learned that syphilis had three stages, and by the time it reached the last stage, it was terminal. It was the great imitator, known to copy other diseases like influenza. How long had he had this disease?

Then she thought of the subtle signs early on in their marriage—like the time he grabbed his heart and sat down on the curb during the march in Seattle, or the times he refused medical treatment when he was stabbed at the dance hall surrounded by Filipinos. He was obviously afraid his secret would be discovered. Then there was the time she questioned the scars on his back, and he told her it was from a bout of scarlet fever as a child. In reality, it was the result of the chancre sores that broke out in the initial stage of the disease. Then she remembered Ernie's friend who had gone to visit him at Angel Island and looked at Elsie so strangely, wondering if she knew Ernie's secret. He later told Elsie the full story about finding Ernie on the streets of New York and nursing him back to health. But why hadn't Ernie gotten medical help? Syphilis can be cured in the first two stages. Surely he knew he had the disease. Nauseating waves of betrayal swept over her. Then she thought … was she at risk?

"My god! Am I at risk?" Elsie panicked. She phoned Kaiser Health Clinic to make an appointment. Before she talked to Ernie, she wanted to ensure her good health. The blood tests came back negative and the doctor assured her she was not infected. She didn't believe him and insisted on a spinal fluid test. Eventually, Dr. Garfield sat her down and reasoned with her. She did not have syphilis. The disease is only contagious in the first two stages when the bacteria are present in open sores and rashes. By the time Elsie came into Ernie's life, his syphilis had been untreated and had lapsed into a latent stage where he was no longer contagious. But during the end of the second stage and the third stage, the infection lodges itself onto nerve endings somewhere in the body—the heart, brain, eyes, joints—lying dormant for sometimes decades before complications develop in the late or tertiary stage. Ernie was in the fatal tertiary stage.

Humiliation colored Elsie's days. She stopped seeing close girlfriends, not wanting to risk having to tell them about Ernie. She worked long hours and went home exhausted. She continued attending CP meetings as well as other progressive organizations, but mostly she kept to herself. Dr. Garfield was her confidante and listened to her vent her anger. As far as Ernie and his friends knew, he had a heart condition. Somehow, Elsie still felt they blamed her.

Elsie knew she would help him through the final stage of life, yet she drew the line when Doctor Garfield suggested she move back in with him. Instead, she left work every day and stayed with Ernie until early evening. One day, when she arrived at his apartment, he didn't answer the door. She let herself in and waited. When the minutes turned into hours, her imagination took over. By the end of the first hour she decided he had taken a cable car, and it had lurched as it turned, unleashing the aneurysm. Maybe he was lying dead and unidentified in a morgue somewhere in the city. Just when she was convinced he was dead, he walked in the door, and she uncharacteristically burst into tears. He had met some buddies, and they had stopped by a bar. "Do you know something I don't know?" Ernie asked puzzled by her emotions. Elsie finally told him about the aneurysm. He knew the score, but they never discussed the disease. Elsie never asked him the questions that haunted her years later. "Why? Why didn't you tell me? Why didn't you get help? Did you knowingly risk my health, my life?" The unasked questions settled like stones in her heart. His relief in living apart, she speculated fifty years later, was the freedom from guilt—guilt he must have felt every day of their married life. While Elsie coped with caring for Ernie, she did not know how close the FBI was to arresting her.

> **FBI REPORT:** Office Memorandum to Director, FBI
> Date: 2/19/62
> Re: Internal Security Act of 1950 – Labor
> The following individuals are in possible violation of Section 5 of the Internal Security Act of 1950 as amended by the Communist Control Act of 1954 by virtue of their holding office or employment with a labor organization and being a member of the Communist Party subsequent to 10/21/61: Elsie Fox
>
> **FBI REPORT**: 9/24/62
> Administrative: Departmental opinion has not yet been rendered on this case.

Elsie worked days at Local 6 and cared for Ernie in the evenings before retiring to her own apartment. Her Communist club activity was on hold simply because she didn't have time. In August of 1963, Ernie became bedridden, and Elsie went to his apartment before and after work taking care of his every need, but she always returned to her own apartment for the night. One evening, Ernie told her he could not stand it any longer. As the aneurysm expanded, it put pressure on his aorta. It was a painful condition that inhibited his ability to breathe. She called Dr. Garfield, and he met them at the hospital.

After Dr. Garfield left, Ernie rested in his hospital bed with Elsie sitting in the gray chair next to him. She asked if he needed anything more. A water glass with a straw sat on a tray, and the nurse had given him pain medication. "I could never have made it without you. Thank you for taking care of me." In the following days, he rallied somewhat, and his merchant marine buddies, comrades, and union friends trailed in to see him. One afternoon, he muttered, "I wish I could go to the bars one more time, Elsie." Elsie wondered if he meant that a drink would make the telling of his guilt easier. But it was only speculation. Then his condition worsened, and Elsie never left his side. "Elsie, will you forgive me?" Even on his deathbed, she felt his betrayal.

"Yes, Ernie, I forgive you." But in her heart, she did not forgive him.

His last words to her were, "I'm going. Let me go, Elsie." It was August 31, 1963. He was fifty-seven years old. Elsie kept the article announcing his death, printed by an unidentified newspaper—quite possibly the *Dispatcher*— for over forty years. Yellowed and brittle with time, it was tucked behind the only photo she had of Ernie. The article was headlined: 'Fox mourned as stalwart of coast labor'. It went on to list his accomplishments as a rank and file trade union leader "who participated in all and led some of the historic maritime strikes laying the ground for Congress of Industrial Organizations unions on the West Coast." It reported on his successful efforts—with no mention of Elsie— in fighting the Department of Immigration in their efforts to deport him during the war. The article quoted George Valter, the secretary-treasurer of Local Six of the ILWU: "His death is a loss to the labor movement in general and to Local Six in particular."

Ernie's union affiliations were listed starting when he went to sea at seventeen years of age and joined Local 510 of the International Workers of the World. The article recognized his role in the 1934 maritime strike where he led his crew ashore and took an active part in the general strike. He joined the Sailors Union of the Pacific and was the Northwest chairman of the 1937 strike committee. The article acknowledged his appointment as a CIO organizer of the Cannery and Packinghouse Workers in Washington State and Alaska. "(He) was taken off a ship and interned for three and a half years. His internment resulted in one of the largest protests ever organized among West Coast trade unions." It never mentioned who instigated that protest and kept it fueled when the country's attention was turned elsewhere.

The article recognized his numerous arrests under the McCarran Act and that he was one of the fifteen Communists and trade union members arrested under the Smith Act. "The government lost the case and the trial marked a partial lessening of Smith Act prosecutions," the article reported. It ended by stating, "His death was caused by an aneurysm of the aorta. He is survived by his wife, Elsie."

Ernie's death finally closed the matter of deportation under the McCarran Act when the "potentially dangerous alien" was laid to rest. Elsie arranged for cremation and decided not to have a memorial service, according to Ernie's wishes. She was exhausted physically and mentally, so she took a few days off work. Informants noticed and reported to the FBI:

> **FBI Report** - Memorial for ERNEST FOX
> ELSIE FOX contacted one of the staff writers at the "People's World" Office, 81 Clementina Street, San Francisco, on Sept. 4, 1963, and stated she was greatly disturbed because ——, who had never been a close friend of her husband ERNEST FOX, called ELSIE wanting to arrange a memorial service for ERNEST. ELSIE said she told —— that ERNEST FOX stated before he died that he did not want a memorial service or a funeral. ELSIE added that —— apparently had then contacted HARRY GLIKSOHN because GLISKSOHN called ELSIE shortly thereafter to see if they might arrange a memorial service regardless of the wishes of ERNEST. ELSIE related that she told

GLIKSOHN she would do everything in her power to prevent such a memorial service being held. The PW writer reportedly promised ELSIE that there would be no mention of any memorial service in the story the PW was going to publish.

(GLIKSOHN is a current member of the Warehouse Section, San Francisco County CP).

After Ernie's death, Elsie punched the time clock at Local 6 and withdrew from social engagements, Communist club activities, and other liberal causes that would ordinarily draw her out. Due to her lack of radical activity, the Department of Justice in a September 1964 report decided "not to prosecute Fox unless there is additional proof of current CP membership." The tumultuous decade of the sixties had arrived, and there were causes aplenty, but Elsie had her own turmoil to fight. She called it "the dark time of my life," otherwise known as depression.

FBI REPORT: 9/30/64 Investigative Period: 7/24/64 to 9/24/64

Sources who are familiar with CP and CP Front Group activities in the San Francisco area were contacted during September, 1964 and each was unable to state that ELSIE FOX participated in any left-wing activities other than reported herein.

CHAPTER 22:

China and Marco Polo

Meeting with Elsie

"I've been thinking of a cover for my book. I see this book with a black cover and silver lettering. The title would be something like this: *This Woman Has Seen the Rise and Fall of Capitalism*. You realize, don't you, that I was born at a time when capitalism was reaching its zenith? And now, in 2006, I'm seeing it go down." Elsie was updating me on the latest economic situation in the United States—rising fuel costs, a muddle of war, bigger gaps between the rich and the poor, and healthcare costs gone amuck. "My understanding of the basic workings of the capitalist system and the corruption that comes with it remains untouched, dear. Democratic socialism is the only answer to the problems of our society, but it *must* be based on democracy, not democratic centralism or dictatorship or totalitarianism. Capitalist economies are based on warfare, not peace. Despite the failure of Communism, I am more convinced than ever that a true, just society evolves from the collapse of capitalism!"

As she talked, I recalled the movie, *Good Night, and Good Luck,* directed by George Clooney, which Elsie had instructed me to see—one of her first assignments for me. While I sat in the darkened theater and the plot unfolded, I was stunned at how familiar, how real, the characters and situations were to me. There were Elsie and Ernie secretly discussing the loyalty oath. I felt the fear of the cleaning lady sitting before the congressional committee. My heart jumped to my throat when I *knew* the man who chose suicide instead of appearing before HUAC—the "sweetest man I had ever known." The past was no longer dull commentary in the history books or entertainment on the big screen. The past was whispering in my ear—alive and vividly present.

Elsie smiled, closed her eyes for a moment, then continued her end of the conversation. "*My Life Captures a Century of Capitalism* … what do you think about that for a title?" She sat on the edge of the orange sofa and looked at my face for a reaction. I held my pen in hand and didn't respond. I was just trying to wrap my head around simply living a whole century. "Well, we may have to shorten up the title somewhat, make it catchy." Then she added, "I think my life story would make one hell of a movie."

* * * * *

Between 1962 and 1964, Elsie quit attending meetings of the organizations she belonged to. She stopped seeing friends. Even a therapeutic shopping spree for new clothes did not help. In the summer of 1964, some caring friends, Jack and Lee, invited Elsie on a trip to Mexico.

She accepted the invitation—recognizing a vacation might help abate her depression. Elsie's excitement grew when Jack told her about the deep-sea fishing they would be doing off the coast of La Paz. Lee got sick at the sight of a boat and embraced the idea of lying by the pool during the day while Elsie and Jack fished.

They met on the dock early in the morning for the four-hour boat trip to the marlin sightings. Jack and the crew instructed Elsie about the mechanics of catching a marlin as she sat on a chair with a safety belt strapped around her. They handed her heavy-duty rigging as the boat arrived at the fishing site. Elsie remembered the thrill of catching her first marlin. "I spotted a fin breaking through the waves, and a marlin hit my line, jerking it taut. I focused on the moment, feeling the power of the fish through the line. It was a lot of work. At one point, I considered pulling the helpless woman act, but the crew would have none of that. One of the crewmembers adjusted my line while another person made sure my safety belt was tight. Otherwise, they stood by and cheered me on. I had to haul that fish in all by myself!"

Elsie's self-assuredness had crumbled under the circumstances of Ernie's death. Depression was robbing her of the very independence that had defined her personality. But knowing that no one would help her land the marlin rekindled a sense of determination.

Elsie continued, "The fish leapt out of the water and on the return, slapped water onto the deck, soaking the crew and myself. I kept up a rhythm of reeling, relaxing, reeling, and getting the fish closer and closer to the boat. Then the line went limp. I thought the fish had gotten away, and my heart just sank, but all of a sudden, the marlin jumped into the air, and the struggle resumed with even greater vigor. Finally, the fish quit—the struggle was over. The crew finally came to my aide and helped pull the fish into the boat. It seemed like it took several hours, but from the time I hooked him to landing him on the deck was just under an hour. It weighed as much as I did—one hundred twenty-two pounds. According to custom, the crew ran a flag up indicating that a marlin had been caught. I was absolutely ecstatic. The crew asked me if I wanted it mounted, and of course, I didn't. I opted to donate the meat to the poor people. Later in the evening, before dinner, I bought a round of drinks for everyone to celebrate!"

December 1963 - La Paz, Mexico

Even though she felt stiff and sore "from my hips to my armpits," she went fishing with Jack a few days later. She hooked another marlin almost immediately but turned her rod over to Jack, who was not having any luck. The rest of their trip centered on celebration. "Mexico is such a happy place—the music, the bright colors, the people. I felt that trip lifted me out of my depression, and I was able to go on with my life." Elsie, never one to be down for long, regained her focus.

While Communist membership waned, Elsie regained her vigor through her renewed activism. There were few viable Communist clubs left by the midsixties, yet Elsie continued going to meetings. Discussion centered on raising funds for the area left-wing newspaper and discussing social problems of the day—women's rights, civil rights for African Americans, workers' rights, and the peace movement. She went door-to-door campaigning for third-party progressive candidates in local and national elections. An FBI report filed in 1966 reported that Elsie attended a CP conference in 1965. The report stated, "There were about 40 or 50 people present including ELSIE FOX. The agenda at this conference included making plans for the fund drive to raise money for the *People's World* (a left-wing newspaper) and for the party, the work of the party during the preceding year, discussion of local politics, report on peace activities and the election of a new County Committee of the CP." The FBI reports filed in the sixties reflected the inactivity of the Communist Party. The reports became shorter and shorter.

During the sixties, Elsie started traveling. Mexico offered many enticing places to visit: Guadalajara, Lake Chapalla, Patzcuao, Mexico City, Oaxaca, and Guanaquato. Elsie also visited Copper Canyon. "The Cradle of Independencia, where Father Hidalgo gave out the cry for Mexican independence from Spain, was an honor to visit." The thrill of liberation from tyranny still coursed through her veins.

> FBI REPORT; 04/07/1971
> Memorandum to: Director, FBI
> From: SAC, San Francisco
> Subject: ELSIE MARY FOX
> The residence and employment of the Subject were verified as of 3/26/ and 3/30/71. FOX last attended an open CP meeting in 1966. The following sources were

> contacted with negative results re any CP activity on the part of FOX in the past six years. It is recommended that the Subject's name be removed from the Security Index.

Elsie also traveled as a guest of the ILWU to Hawaii. "I was treated like a queen. The only time in my life I've been treated like a queen." Union officials and rank and file workers arranged for her every need—a nice hotel, interesting places to eat, tours of the island and the docks. The ILWU did the same for a subsequent trip to Mexico. Elsie was intrigued with the docks in Mexico. "It was owned and run simultaneously by the owners and the union. Now that's cooperation!" In all of her travels, she made note of the status of the workers and the conditions they worked under.

In 1972, after almost twenty-seven years with the ILWU Local 6, Elsie retired due to mandatory retirement at the age of sixty-five. She began to plan and think beyond the constraints of punching a time clock. The FBI had closed their file on her … almost.

Elsie's retirement party was hosted at the San Francisco Rowing Club. She received letters from union officers, the California State Legislature, and the Employers' Association. The letters—from both sides of the fence—spoke of respect and hinted of love.[78]

Elsie had planned the logistics of her retirement a year ahead of time. Her good pension, Social Security, and excellent health care from the ILWU provided her with living security. She had fought for those benefits—gathering signatures for petitions, marching on the streets, knocking on doors in boarding houses, and raising money to support newspapers and organizations that furthered the cause of the workers.

Now she could reap the benefits. After years of listening to stories about foreign ports from the ILWU sailors, merchant marines, and the union rank and file and after getting a taste of travel in Mexico and Hawaii, Elsie decided to further her travels. She would spend a portion of her life savings on a trip around the world.

Elsie contacted a travel agent and booked herself a Marco Polo trip—a seventy-two-day bus trip beginning in Katmandu, Nepal, progressing through Asia and the Middle East—including India, Pakistan, Afghanistan, and Iran—and culminating in London. In the midst of planning for the trip, her boss strolled into Elsie's office and sat on the edge of her desk. "What do you want for your retirement, Elsie?" It did not take her long to consider the question. She had been thinking of this for some time.

"I'd like to visit China!" Very few Westerners had ventured across its borders. Cold War memory of Communists versus capitalists still lingered. Richard Nixon visited in 1972, but diplomatic relations with the United States had yet to be established. Still, Harry Bridges wrote to the officials in China, and they waited for a response.

In the meantime, Elsie booked passage from San Francisco to Japan on a Russian Communist freighter. After sightseeing in that region, she would then meet up with the bus tour in Nepal. Elsie made arrangements to send selected furniture and belongings to be put in storage in Miles City, Montana, where she would move upon her return to help her sister take care of their mother, who was in a nursing home. While awaiting word of the freighter's arrival, Elsie moved in with a friend.

Freighters didn't have tight schedules, so her departure time was rather nebulous. Her friends threw a bon voyage party for Elsie, and with her luggage packed and ready to go, she checked the freighter itinerary every day. It seemed like it would never get to San Francisco, and she began to have doubts. "And my friends got tired of wishing me bon voyage."

Then the cablegram from the Chinese government arrived, inviting Elsie to visit and instructing her as to the time and date to be in Hong Kong, where an escort would take her to Canton. "It was a thrilling piece of news," said Elsie. "My travel agent had to scramble to make the arrangements and cancel my plans to visit Malaysia, Indonesia, and Bali. We worked it out, and I made sure I had that cablegram secure in my bags."

Finally, the freighter arrived in Oakland. A friend who was not yet worn out with all the good-byes came to the dock and gave Elsie a going-away bottle of champagne. Elsie shared the bottle with other passengers, which caused a spontaneous party to erupt into a series of toasts with more bottles of champagne. She toasted her progressive friend willing to see her off. She toasted Harry Bridges and the ILWU. "I knew a lot of longshoreman working on the ship next to us. We hollered back and forth." They wished her well, and Elsie raised her glass high in appreciation as a broad smile spread across her face. Tugboats bellowed from a distance, and seagulls swooped and screed. Ships hummed across the bay, leaving a glistening path in their wake. "I'll never forget sailing under the Golden Gate Bridge and out into the open sea. I was on top of the world."

The last FBI report was dated May 6, 1973. It was issued from Hong Kong and sent to the Washington DC field office. The instructions were to check records of U.S. Department of State Passport Office for pertinent background information regarding Elsie Gilland Fox and forward the information to the office of origin in Hong Kong. On the left margin, the report was stamped, "No Action desired unless information in your files indicates otherwise."

CHAPTER 23

Retirement in Montana

Fifty years after her high school graduation and one month after her trip abroad, Elsie moved back to Miles City in November of 1973. Girlie, Elsie's sister, convinced her that if she wanted to maintain her independent lifestyle, she needed to get a driver's license. Having lived in large cities with convenient public transportation, Elsie had never gotten a license or owned a car, so she promptly went to the main office of the high school.

"I'm here to sign up for driver's training."

The secretary looked at her and said, "And who are you signing up for?"

The clerk thought Elsie was registering her grandchild. Elsie explained her intentions. So Elsie, a sixty-five-year-old, joined the fourteen- and fifteen-year-olds and began driving lessons. She passed her test, got her drivers' license, and bought a yellow Gremlin.

Elsie may have retired from a nine-to-five job, but she never retired from a life of activism. She stayed informed of relevant issues and kept an eye out for social injustice. Elsie summed it up: "That is my life, dear. Whenever I see a problem, I look for a solution. When I came back to Montana, I became part of the senior citizens statewide organization. Reagan wanted to do away with Medicare and Social Security. We had those benefits because the people demanded them by becoming involved. So I knew us senior citizens needed to protect these rights. I discovered through senior organizations like the American Association of Retired Persons (AARP) in Montana that under Medicare, doctors were given a list of procedures they would receive reimbursement for, and the doctors were charging much more than the Medicare assignment." Elsie helped organize a local chapter of senior citizens in Miles City. Butte and Miles City were the only two communities in the state with local chapters. "Our mission was to convince doctors that they must accept Medicare assignments for the poor people in full, instead of adding additional charges."

"I remember the board at the senior center—a social group that met in a building in downtown Miles City—wouldn't allow us to have a meeting in their building. I guess they thought we were just a bunch of old rabble-rousers! So we met in the Methodist church. I led the meeting and explained what was doin'. I called for volunteers to circulate petitions. Well, the first arm that shot up was draped in black. It was a Catholic nun, Sister Ruth. At that point, I knew we had it made. She was my most enthusiastic volunteer, and we developed a close friendship. We organized a demonstration walk down Main Street in Miles City. Of course, we had picket signs, and Sister Ruth pushed a white haired friend in a wheelchair.

"We also drove to Helena, the state capitol, which was a six-hour drive one-way from Miles City, to testify at hearings. I drove around the state talking at different senior citizens functions, convincing people to act. And we were successful!"

There were other issues as well—Elsie and crew successfully worked to require annual, unannounced inspections of nursing homes, and they convinced the two nursing homes in Miles City to let residents keep pets.

After telling the story of actively engaging the senior citizens of the community, she sat back and said, "One of my greatest pleasures in life is to have known such wonderful people like Sister Ruth and the union leader who led the Hawaiian Dock Strike, Frank Thompson, and Paul Robeson. They were such self-less, dedicated people, and my life is richer for them."

In 1985, at seventy-eight years of age, Elsie won the Montana Senior Citizen of the Year Award. When she was in her midnineties, Elsie was on the local community health board, which initiated a health care clinic for low-income people in the region.

Elsie worked part time at a travel agency, keeping up her love of traveling to exotic places like Greece, Turkey, France, Italy, and Germany. After returning from her trips, she gave travel talks and slide shows for clubs and organizations in the community. To add to her agenda, Elsie joined the local country club not to golf, but to play bridge weekly—something she continues to do at the age of one hundred.

And as always, she championed activism whenever the opportunity arose. Prior to the November 2006 election, Elsie wrote a letter to the editor of the local newspaper. She was just one month shy of her ninety-ninth birthday.

Dear Editor,

VOTE TUESDAY, NOVEMBER 7! It's not just a mid-term election; it's a referendum on our government's policies, most importantly ending the Iraqi War, facing our healthcare issues and economic issues such as equitable taxation, global warming, poverty, racial discrimination and illegal immigration.

A fence along the Mexican border as a "solution" to the illegal immigrant problem ignores penalizing the employers who hire them. There has got to be a better way.

Regarding the war, even President Bush admits his decision was based on some false assumptions, and yet the premise is based on two more years of occupation. This is after more than 2,800 of our best young men and women have been killed, thousands of our soldiers wounded and more than 635,000 of Iraqis killed—a figure just released. Also, our country changed from a most-loved status to a disliked status.

I know it is unpopular to be an "I told you so," but before we got into this war, I wrote a letter to the Star quoting the Bible: "What shall it profit a man if he gains the whole world and loses his soul?"

Let's get back our soul by giving new leadership a chance. Let's send people to Washington who will not check their promises at the door and only think about getting re-elected.

To Quote Judge Learned Hand: "Liberty lies in the hearts of men and women; when it dies there, no constitution, no law, no court can save it; no constitution, no law, no court can even do much to help it."

Let's vote for new leadership next Tuesday. Sincerely,

Elsie Fox

A month before her one hundredth birthday, in November of 2007, the American Civil Liberties Union (ACLU) of Montana honored Elsie with its highest honor—the Jeannette Rankin Civil Liberties Award. Rankin was the first woman elected to the U.S. Congress and cast her vote against going to war for both WWI and WWII. She was a lifetime activist in support of women's suffrage, peace, and civil rights. As Elsie accepted the award, the words from her 2006 Mother's Day Speech seemed to echo, "We, the people, must have solidarity ... unity! The voice of action must be heard ... by the people, for the people, from the people. We, the people, can take back our country! We can win!"

November 2007 - Elsie, 100 years old, receiving the Jeanette Rankin award

How fitting! Elsie Gilland Fox—with a rebellious heritage, her independent spirit born on a hard-scrabble ranch in Eastern Montana, which, along the way, combined with the impact of economic and political events, which evolved into a life of activism in two centuries—still carried the torch after one hundred years of living.

"Perhaps, dear, the title of the book could be called, *Elsie—A Shining Light!*"

Chapter 24

Garlands of Roses

I met weekly with Elsie for almost two years. Like the ink on the pages of an old diary, certain parts of Elsie's story had faded with time. She clearly described her life in headlines taken from a newsreel, newspaper, or the top-of-the-hour-report on the radio. Yet a smell, a photograph, a letter, or just digging in the past would suddenly bring a forgotten memory to light, revealing a buried truth—a bouquet of prairie daisies or a long-forgotten song. I puzzled over memory—what is held on to, what lies under the surface, and what is completely forgotten—and how that shapes a life.

One meeting that stood out more than any other was the day we went through the box of photographs and discovered the forgotten pictures of Ernie. After we tucked them back into the box, I started to read aloud some of Ernie's POW letters with the hope of loosening more of Elsie's memories. As I spoke his words in the quiet of her trailer, she sat very still, not interrupting me with her usual comments of recalled details. I read, "You can't imagine how much your weekly visits mean to me, darling," and "Darling, despite our present difficulties we really have a solid future to look forward to. I can only offer you my deepest love and profound admiration. Words, darling, are so inadequate to express my love for your steadfast loyalty and love," then "Now Elsie, don't you worry about me making any melodramatic sacrifices … I'm too much in love with you for that."

He wrote before Christmas in 1942 of his faith that the hope of the new United Nations "would be a splendid xmas gift for all of mankind." Finally, I read the letter that ended our session. "Honey, I hope above everything else the dame fortune reunites us again. I miss you terribly, darling." All of his letters were signed, "With deepest love, Ernie."

Occasionally, I stopped and asked her questions about a name or event mentioned in Ernie's letters. She answered my questions with little elaboration. Her excitement from when she met me at the door dissolved into what I thought was exhaustion. I reasoned, she had gone swimming that day, so maybe she was tired. I cut our session short, and we arranged for our next meeting.

The following week when I visited, Elsie seemed more refreshed. She wore a purple top, her favorite color, a purple, flowered skirt, and, as always, matching earrings and necklace. "Now, I want to tell you something," she said in her business voice. She sat still, almost statuesque, steeling herself for what was coming next. "I put in a very emotional last couple of days. I even shed tears." I immediately thought of someone dying in her family.

"What, Elsie? What happened?"

"Those pictures of Ernie. And his letters. It made me think about him … us." Silence. Then she continued purposefully. "It made me realize the great guilt he must have had. I believe he was consumed with that powerful guilt of not telling me about his disease." She pressed on, "We were both raised in poverty, and then our lives converged when, through a chain of circumstances, we met, and we were both looking to make our lives count for something before we died. I reasoned a long time ago that, because he knew the consequences of that disease, it explained Ernie's fearlessness and energy in working for the party. He knew he might die anytime. For some reason, he couldn't, or wouldn't, tell me. I thought it was guilt, and it will remain a mystery forever why he didn't seek treatment. That's where I have always felt the betrayal." She sat still as if gathering strength to go on with this conversation.

I remembered her words from an earlier interview—"I married him so he could be a full-time functionary. He was my alter ego. It was my sacrifice to the Communist Party." In the name of basic civil rights, she fought for his release from the prison camps. In the name of basic civil rights, guaranteed by the First Amendment, she tirelessly raised money, circulated petitions, and attended legal hearings to fight the Smith Act Trials on behalf of Ernie and all the defendants—the people across the nation whose lives were being ruined.

When she first told me about Ernie months earlier, she tried to explain her feelings. "When he died, I felt a horror, like the world was horror. I got over that, but periodically, I relive that time. I feel horror in the world—it comes back after all this time, and it leaves me weak and exhausted."

I listened as she continued, her professional voice softened, "This time, when it all came back to me after hearing you read his letters … well, I spent an emotional weekend thinking about it. I realized … he really did *love* me."

By the tone of her voice, the soft way in which she spoke, I had to ask, "And you realized something else, too, didn't you?" She nodded her head slowly, her hands clasped in her lap.

"You loved him, too," I said with a lump in my throat. For several moments, the only sound that filled the trailer was a lawnmower's whine next door. Mia could have been there on the sofa with Elsie or not. I don't remember. Tears filled my eyes and hers.

"And all those years of bitterness I had for him …" the words were almost inaudible. I had to lean in to hear. Shaking her head slightly, she continued, "All that bitterness I've held for him for so long was just washed away." The heavy stones in her heart dissolved.

Then her voice brightened. "He used to sing to me. Ernie had a beautiful baritone voice." Her arms danced as she sang, "Garlands of roses to lay at your feet. I'd climb the highest mountain …" I sat and listened. Elsie's eyes closed as she continued singing. At that moment, she was in a different place and time. I waited for her to come back. Then she opened her eyes, sat up straight, and continued, "Even though we were radicals … well, we were romantic. Ernie was very romantic." Her dark, penetrating eyes studied my face for a reaction. Then her voice blasted me out of my reverie, "So that changes everything, dear. You realize that." She followed me to the door. "The main theme of the book is a love story! The title can be *Elsie—A Great Love Story.*

As I stepped off the deck, she waved from the door, her voice singing with enthusiasm, "And now we have a great love story to write about!"

"Yes, Elsie, we do—a great love story!" I glanced at Kokopilau—the trickster, the storyteller—dancing on the railing. Was he winking as I walked toward my car?

At home, I stared at my time line of Elsie's life, strung out on brown paper across the wall above my computer. Scribbled notes in blue marker showed Elsie's life tangled with major historical events of the twentieth century. Notebooks, piles of papers, books, and cassette tapes with hours of interviews cluttered my desk. A yellowed newspaper clipping was stuck on the brown newsprint. It had fallen out of some papers I had unpacked from the box Elsie had sent home with me the first day of the beginning of our journey. I leaned closer to read it again:

> Man's dearest possession is life, and since it is given to him to live but once he must so live as to feel no torturing regrets for years without purpose: so live as not to be seared with the shame of cowardly and trivial past; so live, that dying he can say: "All my life and all my strength were given to the finest cause in all the world—the liberation of mankind."[79]

A noble purpose, indeed—to live for the finest cause in the entire world and love along the way.

EPILOGUE

When I arrived at her trailer, Elsie had a chore for me: "I lost one of my favorite earrings, dear. I think it fell behind my bed. Would you look and see if you can find it?" As I followed her down the hallway to her bedroom, she feigned a sorrowful look and said, "I regret to say your impression of me will likely change for the worse when you see the state of my bedroom." We both laughed.

It was not the piles of clothes, shoes, hats, and scarves on the floor or stacked high on chairs, nor was it the bureau top strewn with piles of makeup—bottles of foundation, rouge, mascara, eye shadow, tubes of lipstick, and jewelry tangled in the mix—that initially attracted my attention. It was the large poster in a simple black frame on the wall above her bed. The subject was evocative, stunning—a naked woman kneeling on the ground facing a woven basket mounded tall with calla lilies. Her brown body, exquisite in simplicity, contrasts with the white lilies heaped above her. The woman's arms stretch out from her lean body and embrace the billow of flowers before her. A name is scrawled boldly across the bottom of the poster—Diego Rivera. I wanted to study the poster and try to grasp the provocative statement the artist intended, but I remembered the task at hand, and, lying down on the floor, I reached my arm under Elsie's bed and fished out three books and the lost earring. "Oh, thank you, dear. I couldn't have found it without you!"

It is not without help from a team of friends that Elsie maintains her independence in her very old age, but then, she is always adept at rallying people for a good cause. Alene, her niece, checks in most every day and organizes Elsie's birthday celebration each year. Friends, Debra and her husband, Terry, take Elsie to political functions and invite her to their home where Terry coaxes the blues out of his harmonica, cooks gourmet food, and mixes drinks that rival Elsie's speakeasy days. Every spring, Debra and Elsie drive to the pine-covered hills east of Miles City where they gather purple crocuses—a wildflower of the prairie. Her friend Sharon plants daisies, geraniums, herbs, and tomatoes in clay pots, which line the deck of Elsie's home. Annie, another friend, cleans her trailer. A next door neighbor shovels snow from her walk, and if something is broken—her television or hearing aide—there is always someone willing to fix it in a flash. Her friend Betty takes Elsie swimming, to Friday night open mike, and on overnight shopping trips to Billings—a city of substantial size for Montana, 150 miles away. Betty also made sure Elsie met Bill Clinton when he campaigned in Miles City in May of 2008. Each charmed the other. "I just met an old Wobbly!" the former president told someone back stage. When Elsie heard that, she was delighted to be referred to as a radical, whatever the stripe.

Her good friends—generally women who were daughters of Elsie's contemporaries—telephone regularly and travel from Denver or New York to Miles City, where Elsie would arrange dinners, horseback rides, drives to the Gay Ranch, and other jaunts throughout eastern Montana. For Elsie's one hundredth birthday, ninety-five-year-old Irene—the San Francisco Green Street roommate and woman whom Elsie threw a birthday party for on the day Pearl Harbor was attacked—took the train from Ann Arbor, Michigan, to Miles City to help Elsie celebrate. It is not just the fact that Elsie is one hundred years old—people *like* being around Elsie, any time, any age. There is just something about Elsie.

Elsie is not a saint nor is she a heroine—Elsie is simply a woman who is active and passionately engaged in the issues and the times in which she lives. She is a champion of causes—universal health care, better working conditions on the docks, highway maintenance and construction, better working conditions for the immigrants who toil in the farmers' fields, equality for women and for all races, accountability for corporate owners and politicians. Elsie knows that change originates with one person wondering, asking questions, and demanding answers. Elsie knows power emanates from "we, the people" united in purpose.

After finding the earring, we returned to the living room to drink the lime coolers I brought to "cheer us up in this hot weather." I told Elsie I had volunteered at the nursing home earlier in the day, helping the residents play bingo. "Most of the people there are ten, fifteen, even twenty years younger than you, Elsie." Then I had to ask, "Elsie, why aren't you living in the nursing home? You're older than most of the residents." She sat still, taking an occasional sip from the neon green straw. "Why aren't you sitting in a wheelchair playing bingo?" I shot the questions at her like bullets and she didn't dodge them.

"Because I'm at the country club playing bridge that day, dear." She smiled slyly at me, and then we both laughed before she continued, "Well … I've always taken care of my health, thanks to Kaiser Health Insurance and my pension I get from the ILWU." I smiled. She never missed a chance to plug the union. "And I eat healthy; I get some physical activity like walking and swimming, and … I'm just lucky."

"But there's more, Elsie. There's a reason you keep on living," I added before she could reply, "… besides waiting for the demise of capitalism!" I wanted specifics, a recipe for not just longevity but quality longevity.

She replied in a very patient voice. "At this age, it doesn't come without effort, my dear." She took another sip from her cooler and continued, "but every day that I get up, I'm interested in life, in politics, in people. I want to know what's doin'!" She looked at me, raised her eyebrows, lifted her glass in a toast and said, "And honey, I love life."

A simple enough recipe—good genes, good attitude mixed with a strong dose of independence and determination, peppered with curiosity. As I listened to Elsie talk, I didn't see an old woman sitting on a worn orange sofa. I saw a young girl standing on the prairie where cumulus clouds of calla lilies bloomed on an eastern Montana horizon—an idealistic vision, which refuses to fade with time. I saw a singleness of purpose, unity, and beautiful purity—a vision for a better world.

I asked, "Elsie, what do you want people to come away with after reading your book?"

She replied without hesitation, "Hope."

Elsie-94 years old-near Miles City, Montana
(Courtesy Scott Andrews, photographer)

APPENDIX A:

China And Marco Polo Remembered

by Elsie

The officers on the ship spoke English, so I was able to get acquainted with the chief engineer, who was an author and had several books published. The first mate was the commissar, a party representative, on the ship. They had meetings while on board, and it was the same style of meetings I was used to. I told them about my activities in the party, and as a result, I got special treatment. They took me on tours of the engine room, where the big, steam turbines were operating. They called me an old revolutionary. I had never been categorized as a real revolutionary, and I was thrilled.

There were eight or twelve other passengers—an interesting bunch. Four or five were young people just out of college. There was a middle-aged man, an engineer married to a Japanese woman. She did not want to move to the United States, so he worked six months in this country and then went back to Japan to be with his family for six months. We shared our chocolate and booze and had some great conversations. After spending twenty days or so on the ship, we had become like a family.

When we arrived in Tokyo, where the ship would be docked for ten days, the engineer, took all of us on tours of Tokyo before he went home. I sailed with the ship and crew to their next stop—Osaka—and took a train to Kyoto. I stayed there several days exploring before going to Tokyo. From Tokyo, I flew to Hong Kong to make arrangements to go to China. I took my cablegram to a travel agency, and the agent simply told me to give him my hotel phone number, and he would contact me in a week or so. I got the feeling I was not high on his priority list. My feathers had fallen. You can't imagine how disappointed I was.

To cheer myself up, I checked into the hotel and proceeded to shop. I went to a tailor's and picked out material for clothes. Then I got new glasses, and I bought a silk dress. When I got back to my hotel in late afternoon and walked into the lobby, I sensed people were staring at me. I went to the desk, and the attendant said, "Oh, Mrs. Fox, we're so glad to see you." He handed me my phone messages, which were many. The travel agent had been calling every hour on the hour—evidently, he got in touch with Beijing and was told to make the necessary arrangements immediately. I was happy to get a taxi and go to the travel agency. He took care of all the paperwork, and I would leave the next morning. I was even given special treatment at the hotel when they learned I was going to China.

The next morning, I was met by a Chinese man who put me on a train to China. Everywhere I went, someone met me to make sure I was on the right train. At my last stop, I got off the train, which, by the way, was quite dirty and grungy. Then I literally walked across a small bridge from Hong Kong into China. It was like walking into a different world. As I walked across the bridge, I saw a red and white billboard which translated to "Long Live the Friendship Between the Chinese Peoples Republic and the Peoples of the World." There were many billboards like that across China, I discovered.

The train depot on the other side of the bridge was immaculate. It was like a living room with beautiful oriental rugs, paintings, sofas, and chairs. Young girls in blue uniforms—a uniform worn by most of the women—had their black hair braided and wore no makeup. They served tea in porcelain cups. This train was such a contrast from the trains in Hong Kong. There were lace curtains on the windows and more tea in porcelain cups. People of all nationalities, except American, were on the train going to Canton for the trade fair—an huge, exquisite display of Chinese art and products for sale.

In Canton, a woman met me and escorted me to my hotel. I was aware that people were staring at me and mentioned it to my guide. She assured me that it was a compliment—the women were fascinated by my short, curly, white hair!

Before leaving Canton, my guide took me to the Martyrs' Memorial where five thousand people were murdered because of the betrayal of Chiang Kai-shek. Then I flew to Peking. It was interesting to note that the "stewardesses" were middle-aged women, very gracious and helpful, wearing those blue uniforms. In Peking, a committee of eight very important individuals met me. I was a little intimidated. "I'm just an office worker for the big union in San Francisco. I'm overwhelmed and feel unworthy of your attention." These men were from The Chinese People's Association for Friendship with Foreign Countries—the same committee that the ILWU and Harry Bridges had contacted to get permission for a visit to China. They had officially invited the union in 1972 and were working out the details of the visit.

"No, no! Do not worry! We are very happy you are here." While driving to the hotel in a chauffeured limousine, we drove down a boulevard of beautiful flowering trees. One of the men said, "We are welcoming you and the flowers are welcoming you, too!" I was assigned a driver, Cho, and a woman who acted as an interpreter. The woman, despite having a family of her own, slept down the hall from me and was available at all times to make me feel secure in a strange country.

The tour began the next day. We went to a silk factory where I heard the thunderous sound of the huge looms moving, cranking out reams of the blue material you saw all the women wearing. I was impressed that a woman was in charge of the factory. I discovered that all factory workers had paid medical care, extra rest periods, and full pay when they were away from their job for things such as maternity leave. In this particular factory, there were apartments with kitchens for the workers to use if they wanted.

There was also a kindergarten at this factory for the workers' children. When I walked in, the children and their teacher would stand and applaud. The children were adorable with their black, shiny hair and pink cheeks. Even though all the women wore the Mao costume—blue smock and pants— the children's clothing was very colorful, like a bouquet of flowers against a dull background. They introduced me as an American grandmother, and then the children put on a little performance for me. Through an interpreter, one of the children asked me how many grandchildren I had in America. I was sorry to tell them I had none. They felt very sorry for me and told me excitedly that if I were to move to China, I would have lots of grandchildren!

Shanghai was my favorite city, despite its size of ten million people. It had beautiful tree-lined streets, and the buildings were architecturally interesting. I was especially interested in the waterfront. I talked to a woman who was a longshoreman and whose job was operating equipment. The huge port had ships from everywhere except the Soviet Union, they were quick to add.

I saw evidence of what things had been like before 1949. A sign still remained at a park we went to that said, "No Dogs or Chinese Allowed." An older man I talked with who ran a rickshaw before the "liberation" said inflation was so bad at that time—he would buy a bowl of rice in the morning, and by evening, it would be triple in price!

I realized that China was making reforms in health care, and doctors were sent to remote areas to help people. They were called the barefoot doctors. Part of the reform was to do away with prostitution by rehabilitation. As a result, venereal disease was almost eradicated. I felt like I got to see a little glimpse of how socialism could work. Of course, China did not follow the route of democracy and, to my great disappointment, has presently given way to capitalism and corruption.

I was able to visit communes where everyone was assigned a job. The older peoples' jobs' were to shop and cook meals for people who were sick. There were communes that just raised vegetable and others that raised angora rabbits. The commune produced a variety of products but used rather backward, agricultural methods. They weren't very mechanized, but they had an abundance of workers.

I saw masses of workers riding their bicycles in the streets, so I asked Cho if I could see how the labor unions functioned. I was told they were in a state of reorganization. The leadership of the Communist government was too clever to permit me to go any further in regards to unions. I didn't know it at the time, but there were developments regarding the ILWU visit that became contentious. The ILWU received a telegram from the Friendship group stating, "After you accepted our invitation we learned you are planning to send delegates to visit Taiwan. Please clarify immediately by telegram whether this is true. It is well known that the Chinese people adhere to the principled stand of opposing any activities creating 'two Chinas.' We do not invite foreign trade unions that have contacts with Taiwan trade unions." I had no idea this exchange had been going on.

It was toward the end of my two-week trip when I got into the limousine for another day of sightseeing, and inside the limo were the same important men I had met when I arrived in China. I was a little surprised. Cho was not his usual, informal, friendly self. He was very serious. We started driving when one of the men held up the *Dispatcher*, the local union paper of the ILWU. The article was reporting on the visit of the union to Taiwan, where Madame Chiang Kai-shek greeted them. "What do you say to this?" I explained to them that the union had a program where rank and file delegates are sent to different countries all over the world to study the working conditions and to increase labor solidarity between workers in that country and the United States. They said, "Well, what about going to Taiwan?" They looked perturbed. A little trickle of fear went down my backbone as I sat in the back seat of the limo. I felt very small in this great big country, and I remember thinking that it wouldn't be very pleasant ending up in jail here.

"Look, the delegates of our union go to all sorts of countries. They go to Fascist countries and to England and Africa ... all of these different places. Going to Taiwan was simply a part of this overall picture." I looked at Cho. At that time, the Cultural Revolution was winding down and Cho had survived it. He was not going to come to my defense and throw away his political future by befriending a little old American lady. I was pretty scared. "Do you remember when you met me at the plane, and I told you I was not a union official. I have nothing to do with union policy. I simply am an office worker in this union. I agree with union policy, but I have nothing to do with formulating it." Well, that did it. They seemed satisfied, and the confrontation was ended. My relationship with Cho was definitely chilled, and it was rather sad saying good-bye to him after that incident. The ILWU received a letter from the Friendship Committee a couple of months later rejecting their visit because of their visit to Taiwan, where Soong Mei-ling, wife of Chiang Kai-shek, had made comments against the Chinese people. They also accused Harry Bridges of distorting the facts in an article he wrote for the *Dispatcher*. The ILWU finally withdrew their request for a visit in 1974. Harry Bridges wrote in a April 19, 1974, *Dispatcher* article, "It seems just too damned bad, in view of this union's long record of support for the People's Republic of China, that we have received such shabby treatment." While I was there, I was treated well, and I don't regret the experience, but I have to say, I was glad to leave China.

From Hong Kong, I flew to Bangkok. I did the usual tourist things, and I bought wonderful jewelry at fantastic prices. I found traveling alone had its advantages. People will approach you in a friendly manner if they realize you are alone. I had good experiences meeting people. I also had various opportunities for romantic situations on this trip, but I turned them all down. I had determined when I set out that I was going to be cautious so nothing would jeopardize the experience.

After exploring Bangkok, I flew to Katmandu, Nepal, to meet up with the Marco Polo bus trip to London. That began a seventy-two-day trip through Asia and the Middle East—where we spent most of our time before racing through Europe to London. This bus route originated in London, and I discovered it was a drug route for youths at that time. They would come to Nepal because you could buy hashish openly in the stores. It's a known fact that after smoking hashish, a person has a desire for sweets. I found it amusing that an entrepreneurial pastry-shop owner had a flourishing business next to the shops that sold hashish!

I befriended some of the travelers that came from London and inquired as to where the good shopping was along the route. Several people told me Suffering Moses in Kashmir was something not to be missed, so I added that to my list of places to go. While in Katmandu, we saw the monks dressed in their saffron robes and visited a monastery. We got up at some ungodly hour one morning so we could see the sunrise over Mt. Everest. Seeing this grand mountain range and Mt. Everest framed in the delicate, pink sky is still etched in my memory.

The majority of the people on our bus to London were young people from Australia. They were delightful travel mates. One of the young men, named Bon, would go with me on my shopping trips. Not only do I love shopping, but it really is the way you get to see the local culture, and I enjoyed Bon's company. Someone asked him, "Why do you go with Elsie on these shopping trips?" He answered, "She buys me beer!"

Traveling through India with the Himalayas stretched out before us was a sight to see. Arrangements were made for hotels all along the way, and sometimes those accommodations were pretty scroungy. I became a fast friend with the young Australian women on the tour over one particular incident: While we were still traveling in the mountains where the nights could be rather cool, our hotel room beds had no sheets—they simply had rough woolen blankets. Now these girls had taken up with the fashion of not wearing anything to bed—no pajamas, no nighties—and here were these rough scratchy wool blankets! I happened to have some extra kimonos I had bought in Japan, so I loaned them to the girls. From then on, I was in like Flynn! They adopted me as their little mama, and we had such fun together!

I fell in love with India! We visited the Taj Mahal, where we walked through rooms with beautiful jewels inlaid in the white, marble walls. We went to Vanarsi, where we saw the bodies being cremated on the Ganges River. I bathed in the Ganges because that is what you're supposed to do there, but I wouldn't recommend it as a regular, cleansing operation!

In one of the towns, the girls and I decided to find another hotel that had a swimming pool. There were a bunch of young Indian army officers at that hotel, and they were so delighted to see these young girls. So I got to visit with these young fellows. They were very interested in the fact that I went to China and wanted to know all about it. India had socialistic ideas at the time, so we talked. One of these young fellows said he wanted me to meet his family, who lived in Delhi. When we arrived in Delhi, I got in touch with them—he had written ahead of time about me. I was invited to their home, which was a real privilege at the time. They had invited a big group of people, their family and friends, to hear me talk about China.

Our trip continued to Kashmir in northern India. It is beautiful beyond imagination. We arrived in Srinagar, the capitol, and stayed on various houseboats at Dal Lake. This area has been called a pearl (the lake) surrounded by emeralds (the mountains), and the description is quite apt. We lived on the houseboats, a definite influence from the English occupation of the country.

One day, Bon and I decided to find the Suffering Moses that had been recommended to me at the beginning of the tour. I found it rather odd that when I inquired about Suffering Moses to shop owners and some of the locals, they wouldn't tell where it was and simply ignored me. Finally, we got a taxi and told him, "We want to go to Suffering Moses." He immediately told me while driving around, that no, I didn't want to go there!

"I'll take you to my uncle's shop. His is much better. You will like it much better than that store." We argued back and forth while he was driving, and I began to wonder why in the world I had so much trouble finding this store, which made me all the more determined to go there! I finally told him to stop the taxi, and I got out and went to the back and wrote down his license plate. He knew what I was doing, and when I got back in, he finally took us straight to Suffering Moses. It turned out that the store was a Hindi store, and our cab driver was Muslim. There was, and still is from what I understand, a great clash between these two religions, and Bon and I experienced that in a very small way.

The bus tour continued on over Khyber Pass into Afghanistan, and we stayed briefly in Kabul. After being used to the mountains in Montana and the western United States, where trees and snow capped peaks soften their profile, the mountains of Afghanistan were such a contrast. The road over the pass was dramatic—winding its way around the mountains of rock and earth. There were no trees, just bare rock, which is a certain, stark kind of beauty. As we drove along, you could see the road we had been on below us on another side of the mountain.

In Iran, we stayed in Tehran, and, of course, I continued my shopping spree at the wonderful bazaars in the city. I absolutely fell in love with Iran, the history and culture. Turkey, Greece—so many things to see and experience. I felt such a sense of history and different cultures through all of the sights and the people I met. I was especially thrilled to go through the town in Greece named Demitrias, where democracy had its beginnings.

When we hit Europe, we didn't stop at the sights very much and just beelined it for London. We all arrived at our destination very bedraggled after seventy-two days on the road. All of us had been smitten with dysentery at some point, my hair was dirty, and my clothes were dirty. Fortunately, I had reserved a room at the YWCA and had a place to go. I spent five weeks in London and managed to explore the area before finally returning to the United States.

After I moved to Miles City, I received a lot of publicity because of my travels—particularly the China trip. As a result, I gave a series of talks and slide shows regarding my trip. I also got a part-time job with the local travel agency, The Blue Caboose. I really worked very little but did give talks to groups of middle-aged and older people about travel, the advantages of travel, and encouraged older, single women that they, too, could travel. Because of my affiliation with a travel agency, I was able to continue my travel experiences and went back to many of the locations I had been on the Marco Polo trip—India, Spain, Monte Carlo, Cannes, Genoa, Rome, Florence, Greece, Egypt, Crete.

I have been blessed with many things in my life—a loving family, a wonderful career, good health, good friends, and the experience of world travel. Despite her struggles, I think the greatest gift my mother gave to each of her children was the capacity to enjoy life.

Since writing this, I have decided to forgive Ernest. I know a little of what he suffered with his terrible secret, and I know he loved me. It is better to forgive.

May the world be peaceful and a happy place to live.

APPENDIX B:

Labor Victory Letter

LABOR'S UNITY FOR VICTORY COMMITTEE

AFL • CIO • RAILROAD BROTHERHOODS • INDEPENDENT UNIONS

Co-Chairmen
JOHN F. SHELLEY, President, San Francisco Labor Council
GEORGE WILSON, Secretary, San Francisco C. I. O. Council

Co-Secretary-Treasurers
JOHN E. BYRNES, Business Representative, Production and Aeronautical Lodge 1327, I. A. M.
MERVYN RATHBORNE, Secretary, California Industrial Union Council

Vice-Chairman
ALEXANDER WATCHMAN, President, San Francisco Building Trades Council

WAR PRODUCTION PUBLICITY DIVISION
ROOM 1710 CENTRAL TOWER
703 MARKET STREET • SAN FRANCISCO
PHONE EXBROOK 5282

October 4, 1942

TO WHOM IT MAY CONCERN:

Miss Elsie Gilland worked in this office during the summer of 1942, and I found her to be an alert, intelligent and capable person. She is reliable, and has initiative, resourcefulness and decided administrative ability.

I cannot recommend her too highly.

Sincerely,

Charles D. Raudebaugh
Publicity Director

PRINTED ON UNION-MARKED PAPER BY UNION LABOR

APPENDIX C:

Machinists Letter

PHONE MARKET 8911

Lodge 1327, International Association of Machinists

AFFILIATIONS
SAN FRANCISCO LABOR COUNCIL
BAY CITIES METAL TRADES COUNCIL
UNION LABEL SECTION OF S. F.
CALIF. STATE FEDERATION OF LABOR
PACIFIC COAST METAL TRADES DISTRICT COUNCIL
CALIF. STATE CONFERENCE OF MACHINISTS

LODGE 1327 SAN FRANCISCO
AMERICAN FEDERATION OF LABOR

ROOM 315
2940 SIXTEENTH STREET
SAN FRANCISCO 3, CALIFORNIA

ANTHONY BALLERINI
BUSINESS MANAGER

JOHN BYRNES
BUSINESS REPRESENTATIVE

IVY HAYS
RECORDING SECRETARY

EMMETT CAMPION
FINANCIAL SECRETARY

March 17, 1944

TO WHOM IT MAY CONCERN:

For approximately one year and a half, Elsie Gilland has been employed by Lodge 1327, International Association of Machinists.

During this time she has acted as my secretary. In addition she has handled contracts and all the various phases of local union office work.

She is a capable, responsible secretary, and I cannot recommend her too highly.

Yours very truly,
Anthony Ballerini
ANTHONY BALLERINI
Business Manager

OEA:13188
AFL;61

PRINTED ON UNION LABEL WATER MARKED PAPER

APPENDIX D:

FBI Report - Elsie Fox

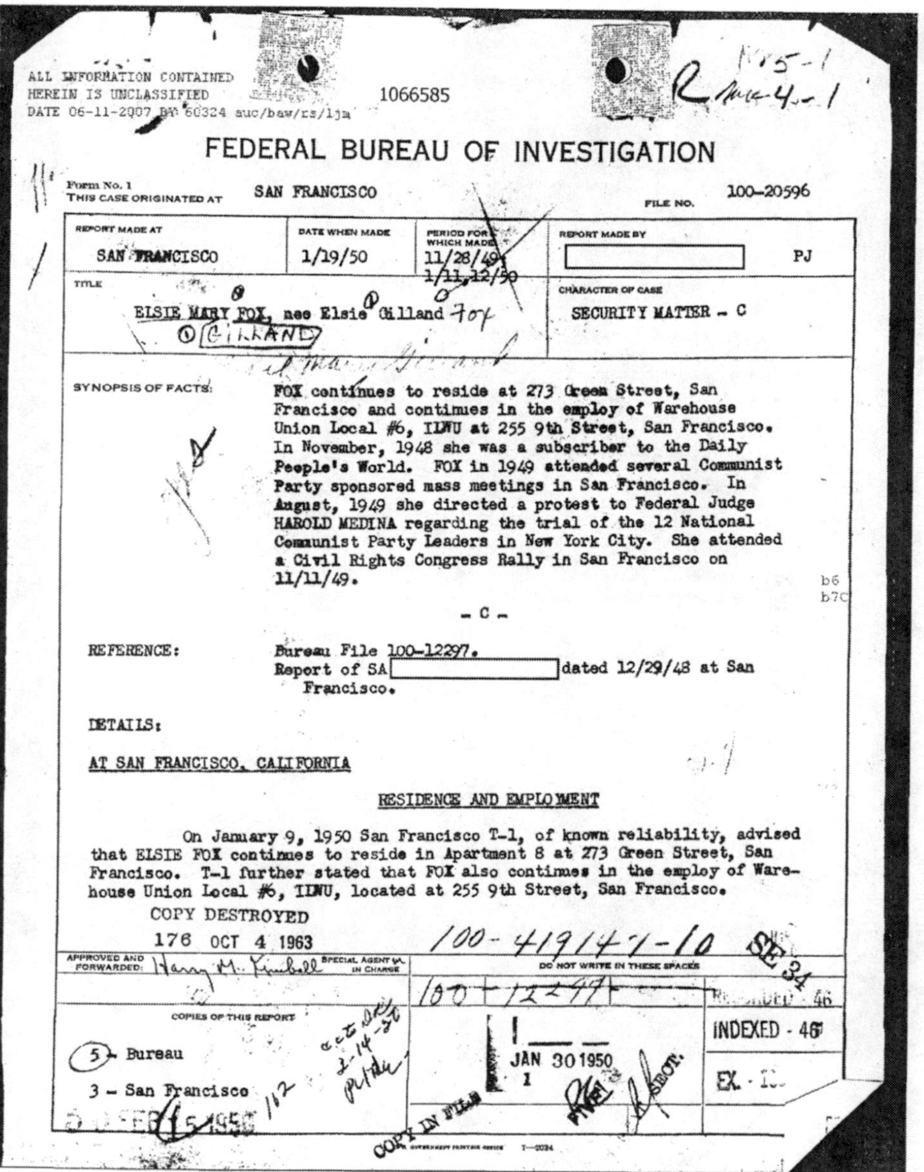

ALL INFORMATION CONTAINED
HEREIN IS UNCLASSIFIED
DATE 06-11-2007 BY 60324 auc/baw/rs/ljm

1066585

FEDERAL BUREAU OF INVESTIGATION

Form No. 1
THIS CASE ORIGINATED AT SAN FRANCISCO FILE NO. 100-20596

REPORT MADE AT	DATE WHEN MADE	PERIOD FOR WHICH MADE	REPORT MADE BY
SAN FRANCISCO	1/19/50	11/28/49; 1/11,12/50	[redacted] PJ

TITLE	CHARACTER OF CASE
ELSIE MARY FOX, nee Elsie Gilland	SECURITY MATTER - C

SYNOPSIS OF FACTS: FOX continues to reside at 273 Green Street, San Francisco and continues in the employ of Warehouse Union Local #6, ILWU at 255 9th Street, San Francisco. In November, 1948 she was a subscriber to the Daily People's World. FOX in 1949 attended several Communist Party sponsored mass meetings in San Francisco. In August, 1949 she directed a protest to Federal Judge HAROLD MEDINA regarding the trial of the 12 National Communist Party Leaders in New York City. She attended a Civil Rights Congress Rally in San Francisco on 11/11/49.

b6
b7C

\- C -

REFERENCE: Bureau File 100-12297.
Report of SA [redacted] dated 12/29/48 at San Francisco.

DETAILS:

AT SAN FRANCISCO, CALIFORNIA

RESIDENCE AND EMPLOYMENT

On January 9, 1950 San Francisco T-1, of known reliability, advised that ELSIE FOX continues to reside in Apartment 8 at 273 Green Street, San Francisco. T-1 further stated that FOX also continues in the employ of Warehouse Union Local #6, ILWU, located at 255 9th Street, San Francisco.

COPY DESTROYED
176 OCT 4 1963

100-41914-10

APPROVED AND FORWARDED: Harry M. Kimball SPECIAL AGENT IN CHARGE

DO NOT WRITE IN THESE SPACES

100-12297

INDEXED - 46

COPIES OF THIS REPORT

5 - Bureau
3 - San Francisco

JAN 30 1950

EX. -

COPY IN FILE

ALL INFORMATION CONTAINED
HEREIN IS UNCLASSIFIED
DATE 06-12-2007 BY 60324 auc/baw/[redacted]

FD-376 (3-8-65)

1066585

UNITED STATES DEPARTMENT OF JUSTICE

FEDERAL BUREAU OF INVESTIGATION

WASHINGTON, D.C. 20535

In Reply, Please Refer to
File No. 100-20596

July 30, 1965

Chief
United States Secret Service
Department of the Treasury
Washington, D. C. 20220

Dear Sir:

The information furnished herewith concerns an individual who is believed to be covered by the agreement between the FBI and Secret Service concerning Presidential protection, and to fall within the category or categories checked.

1. ☐ Has attempted or threatened bodily harm to any government official or employee, including foreign government officials residing in or planning an imminent visit to the U. S., because of his official status.

2. ☐ Has attempted or threatened to redress a grievance against any public official by other than legal means.

3. ☒ Because of background is potentially dangerous; or has been identified as member or participant in communist movement; or has been under active investigation as member of other group or organization inimical to U. S.

4. ☐ U. S. citizens or residents who defect from the U. S. to countries in the Soviet or Chinese Communist blocs and return.

5. ☐ Subversives, ultrarightists, racists and fascists who meet one or more of the following criteria:

   (a) ☐ Evidence of emotional instability (including unstable residence and employment record) or irrational or suicidal behavior:
   (b) ☐ Expressions of strong or violent anti-U. S. sentiment;
   (c) ☐ Prior acts (including arrests or convictions) or conduct or statements indicating a propensity for violence and antipathy toward good order and government.

6. ☐ Individuals involved in illegal bombing or illegal bomb-making.

Photograph ☐ has been furnished ☒ enclosed ☐ is not available
☐ may be available through ______________________.

Very truly yours,

J. Edgar Hoover

John Edgar Hoover
Director

1 - Special Agent in Charge (Enclosure(s) (2)
U. S. Secret Service, San Francisco

Enclosure(s) (2) *(Upon removal of classified enclosures, if any, this transmittal form becomes UNCLASSIFIED.)*

REGISTERED MAIL

APPENDIX E:

California Legislative Resolution #47 and ILWU Retirement Letter

Assembly Rules Committee-California Legislature RESOLUTION
By the Honorable John L. Burton , Twentieth Assembly District
RELATIVE TO COMMENDING ELSIE FOX
FOR OUTSTANDING SERVICE ON THE OCCASION OF
HER RETIREMENT

WHEREAS, The Members of the Assembly have learned that Elsie Fox, Office Manager of Local 6, ILWU, is retiring after 26 ½ years of devoted service to that organization; and

WHEREAS, Elsie Fox has worked diligently and conscientiously with the officers of Local 6 to help to carry out the aims and policies of the union; and

WHEREAS, Although she is not a member of the union, she has been steadfastly dedicated to the union's policies, and that dedication has carried over into the community in which she lives; and

WHEREAS, She has consistently held to the principles and ideals of the ILWU although at great personal sacrifice; and

WHEREAS, She remains a fighter for peace and justice for all mankind and will be missed by her many friends and co-workers; now, therefore, be it

Resolved by the Assembly Rules Committee, That the Members congratulate Elsie Fox on her outstanding service to Local 6, ILWU, and wish her success and happiness in her retirement; and be it further

Resolved, That the Chief Clerk of the Assembly transmit a suitably prepared copy of this resolution to Elsie Fox.

Resolution No. 47
Approved by the Assembly Rules committee
By
John L. Burton
Chairman
Subscribed this 23rd day of January, 1973
Bob Moretti
Speaker of the Assembly

INTERNATIONAL
LONGSHOREMEN'S & WAREHOUSEMEN'S
UNION

150 GOLDEN GATE AVENUE, SAN FRANCISCO, CALIFORNIA 94102 • 775-0533

HARRY BRIDGES, President — WILLIAM H. CHESTER, Vice-President — GEORGE MARTIN, Vice President — LOUIS GOLDBLATT, Secretary-Treasurer

February 2, 1973

Dear Elsie:

I had hoped I could make some other arrangements for the meeting I must preside over tonight in Berkeley so that I could join your many friends at the party for you tonight, but unfortunately it did not work out that way.

Since I can't be there in person, Elsie, I want to take this means to let you know that I think you deserve much, much commendation for all your years of service to the union as a capable, devoted bookkeeper and office manager of Local 6, as well as being a force that enhanced the stability of the entire union.

Although I am speaking as an individual, I am sure the whole membership of the ILWU would want to join me in wishing you many happy, healthy years of retirement.

We will always remember you with affection and respect.

Sincerely,

William H. Chester

William H. Chester

ENDNOTES:

Introduction

1. George Manz, "First it was." *Briarpatch* 32.4 (December 2002): 12(1), GeneralOneFile, Gale Document Number: A101448325, Montana State Library, http://find.galegroup.com/ips/start.do?prodId=IPS (accessed October 8, 2008).

Chapter Eight

2. Samuel McCracken, "Beerly Legal" Book review of *Dry Manhattan: Prohibition in New York City,* by Michael A. Lerner. *Columbia Magazine* (Summer 2007), http://www.columbia.edu/cu/alumni/Magazine/Summer2007/Reviews/html#beerly (accessed July 25, 2008).

3. Cyndy Bittinger, "The Business of America is Business?" Calvin Coolidge Memorial Foundation, http://www.calvin-coolidge.org/html/the_business_of_america_is_bus.html (accessed July 29, 2008).

4. Carolyn Kott Washburne, *America in the 20th Century: 1930–39* (New York: Marshall Cavendish Corporation, 1995), 442.

5. Ibid., 450

6. Bettina Miller, ed., *From Flappers to Flivvers: We Helped Make the '20s Roar* (Greendale: Reiman Publications, 1995), 8.

7. Carolyn Kott Washburne, *America in the 20th Century: 1920–1929* (New York: Marshall Cavendish Corporation, 1995), 296.

Chapter Nine

8. Kathleen London, "The History of Birth Control," Yale Web site, http://www.yale.edu/ynhti/curriculum/units/ 1982.html (accessed March 14, 2007).

9. Cindy Kuzma, "Contraception and the Law," Planned Parenthood Web site, http://www.plannedparenthood.org/ news-articles-press/politics-policy (accessed March 14, 2007).

10. Gloria Steinem, "The Ten Most Influential People of the 20th Century," http://www.time.com/time/time100/ leaders/ profile/ sanger3.html (accessed March 14, 2007).

11. *Griswold v. Connecticut,* 381 U.S. 479 S. Ct. (1965), http://www.law.umkc.edu/faculty/projects/ftrials/conlaw/ griswold.html (accessed June 5, 2008).

Chapter Ten

12. The American Experience, ed., *People & Events: The Bonus March (May-July, 1932)*, http://ww.pbs.org/ wgbh/ amex/ macarthur/peopleevents/pandeAMEX89.html (accessed July 16, 2006).

13. United States Department of Veterans Affairs, ed., "History of the Department of Veterans Affairs: Part 3," http://www1.va.gov/ opa/feature/history/history3.asp (accessed June 5, 2008).

14. "Martin Declares Bank Holiday" *Seattle Post-Intelligencer,* March 3, 1933.

15. "Library Board of Seattle: Minutes of Proceedings, 1920-1933," 4: 347, Seattle Public Library Archives.

16. Karl Marx and Friedrich Engels, with introduction by Vladimir Pozner. *The Communist Manifesto* (New York: Bantam Books, 1992), 58.

Chapter Eleven

17. *Voice of Action*, November 29, 1935, Microform and Newspaper Collections, University of Washington Libraries.

18. *Voice of Action*, January 1, 1934, Microform and Newspaper Collections, University of Washington Libraries.

19. Sarah Falconer, "Revels Cayton: African American Communist and Labor Activist," *Voice of Action,* February 27, 1934, http://depts.washington.edu/civilr/revels_cayton.htm (accessed April 20, 2006).

20. Sarah Falconer, "Revels Cayton: African American Communist and Labor Activist," *Voice of Action,* February 27, 1934, http://depts.washington.edu/civilr/revels_cayton.htm (accessed April 20, 2006).

21. Jennifer Phipps, "Washington Commonwealth Federation & Washington Pension Union," http://faculty.washington.edu/gregoryj/cpproject/phipps.htm (accessed, January 28, 2006).

Chapter Twelve

22. Eugene V. Dennett, *Agitprop: The Life of An American Working-Class Radical* (Albany: State University of New York Press, 1990), 48.

23. *Voice of Action,* August 16, 1935.

Chapter Thirteen

24. Harvey Schwartz, ed., ILWU Oral History Collection, "The Union Takes Hold and the Coming of the Big Strike, 1933-1934," *Dispatcher*, October 2000.

25. Ibid.

26. Ibid., November 2000.

27. Ibid.

28. Ibid., October 2000.

29. Max Schactman, "Radicalism in the Thirties," in *As We Saw the Thirties* ed. Rita James Simon (Chicago: University of Chicago Press, 1967), 37.

30. Judith Stepan-Norris and Maurice Zeitlin, *Left Out: Reds and America's Industrial Unions* (Cambridge: Cambridge University Press, 2003), 27.

31. Ibid., 41.

Chapter Fourteen

32. *Voice of Action*, May 1, 1934

33. "Library Board of Seattle: Minutes of Proceedings, 1920-1933," 4: 374, 379, 380, Seattle Public Library.

Chapter Fifteen

34. The Harry Bridges Project, November 2002 Newsletter, http://www.pbs.org/moyers/journal/blog/ 2007/08/my_fellow_texan.html (accessed July 25, 2008).

35. Stephen Fox, *America's Invisible Gulag: A Biography of German American Internment & Exclusion in World War II* (New York: Peter Lang Publishing, 2000), 5.

Chapter Sixteen

36. Ibid., xv.

37. Ibid., 71.

38. Ernie Fox to Elsie Fox, August 27, 1942. Elsie Gilland Fox Papers.

August 27, 1942

Darling Elsie, No new developments. Haven't rec'd anymore letters, except the one you wrote. I'm feeling fine and sincerely hope you feel likewise. Gee, I miss you tremendously darling. It takes this sort of a climax to drive home the full realization of what a wonderful person you really are. I read a very interesting article in the August 8th issue of Colliers about the activity of the National Maritime Union in the war effort and it made me extremely happy to know that some of my personal friends are playing an important role (in the war effort). With Deepest Love, Ernie

39. Charles D. Raudebaugh, Recommendation letter for Elsie Gilland, October 4, 1942. Elsie Gilland Fox Papers. See Appendix B.

War Production Publicity Division Room 1710 Central Tower, 703 Market Street, San Francisco, CA, October 4, 1942

To Whom It May Concern: Miss Elsie Gilland worked in this office during the summer of 1942, and I found her to be an alert, intelligent and capable person. She is reliable, and has initiative, resourcefulness and decided administrative ability. I cannot recommend her too highly. Sincerely, Charles D. Raudebaugh, Publicity Director

40. See Appendix C.

41. Unidentified newspaper clipping, Elsie Gilland Fox Papers.

42. Ernie Fox to Elsie Gilland Fox, November 1942 and January 1943. Elsie Gilland Fox Papers.

Internee of War, Camp Forrest, November 1942

Darling Elsie, Rec'd your belated cookies, and to state that they resembled the wreck of the '99 is putting it mildly but just like Maxwell House Coffee, they were good to the last broken crumb. Don't feel badly, darling, I enjoyed them. Tuesday an inspector from the Immigration Dep't. cross-examined and questioned me for two hours, the interview was a repetition of my Sharp Park investigation. I was informed that the investigation was to determine my immigration status, and had no bearing on my appeal for reconsideration of my original hearing. Otherwise, my life follows the same dull routine. Well, sweetheart, until the next letter. Love, Ernie

Prisoner of War, Camp Forrest, Tennessee, January 1943

My Dear Darling, Your New Years telegram and the information it contained made me extremely happy. I sincerely hope for a favorable decision, which would permit me to sail again and play a useful role in the war effort. I hope the local board has the authority to make a final decision which would expedite matters and save considerable time. The tremendous drive of the Soviet Union is certainly wonderful news darling. Your steadfast loyalty and the continued support of organizations and friends keeps me filled with hope and encouragement. Please extend my most sincere wishes to Irene for a happy successful marriage. I miss you terribly, darling. With deepest love, Your loving husband, Ernest

Chapter Seventeen

43. Fox, *America's Invisible Gulag*, 90, 150–151.

44. Karen E. Ebel, "WWII Violations of German American Civil Liberties by the US Government," http://www. foitimes. com/ internment/gasummary.htm (accessed October 9, 2006).

45. Ernie Fox to Elsie Gilland Fox, March 20, 1943. Elsie Gilland Fox Papers.

Prisoner of War, Camp Forrest, Tennessee, March 20, 1943

My Darling Elsie, Received your letter. I imagine you've already contacted George regarding the latest development in my case. As I stated before, don't become unduly alarmed. If my present status is strictly an immigration case, I wonder if it's possible to be released on bond. Yes, Elsie dear, this has been the acid test, and it makes me exceedingly happy to know that this whole unfortunate incident will tend to make our understanding of each other more profound and lasting. Happy to know you enjoyed the Gershwin Concert. I think very highly of his music, unfortunately he died quite young. With deepest Love, Your Loving Husband, Ernest

46. Ernie Fox to Elsie Gilland Fox, May 1943, Elsie Gilland Fox Papers.

May 1943, Ft. Lincoln, Bismarck, N.D.

My Darling Elsie, Well, sweetheart, we finally arr'd at our new home after three weary train days. I don't think it necessary to describe this particular part of N.D. It reminds me very much of Western Montana. I'm extremely happy to be out West again, God, how I hate the South. General conditions in this camp are very satisfactory. Compares very favorably to Camp Forrest. I sincerely hope I find some kind of a job here similar to my work at Camp Forrest. Seems rather strange to use ordinary stationery again, and thank God the old address is no longer necessary. Rumors are being circulated that three hearing boards from Washington DC are due to hold hearings here starting June 1st. The international situation continues to look good. Honey, did you receive my telegram? With Deepest Love, Ernest

47. Ernie Fox to Elsie Gilland Fox, May 1943. Elsie Gilland Fox Papers.

May 1943, Prisoner of War, Camp Forrest, Tennessee

My Darling Elsie, Well, sweetheart, my prediction in my last letter proved correct. We're being moved to a different camp, destination unknown, so please don't be perturbed because of my delay in mail. I understand we're being placed in the custody of the Department of Justice. I sincerely hope we're segregated, unconfirmed rumors point in that direction. Rec'd your smokes and latest book, thank you most kindly, darling. The African campaign finally culminated in a complete Allied victory, now for the invasion of the continent and the complete destruction of Fascist reaction. Glad to hear that my immigration hearing was postponed, more time to prepare my case. Yes, I've read a number of articles regarding the Spanish Vets. Hope the situation is corrected. Love, Ernest

48. Ernie Fox to Elsie Gilland Fox, May and December 1943. Elsie Gilland Fox Papers.

October 1943, Ft. Lincoln, N.D.

My Darling Elsie, Congratulations, Elsie, dear, for the splendid organizational campaign you're building up in my behalf. I'm positive that ultimately this will produce the desired results. The editorial in the New World regarding my case, and the recent action of the Fisherman's Union made me very happy. The international situation continues very favorable for the United Nations. Honey, you certainly picked a swell radio, excellent reception and the volume is very good. My net earnings from Sept 15th to the 30th was $35.00. I paid a $17.50 Federal Tax alone. We also pay a 4% railroad tax, $1.25 a day for room and board. Well, Darling it's getting rather late so goodnight darling, until next week. With Deepest Love, Ernest

Christmas 1943

My Darling Elsie, A merry xmas and a happy new year, Elsie dear. I was fervently wishing to be home by xmas but that's out, I imagine, darling. I hope you rec'd the $10 money order for your xmas gift. I'm very happy to hear that continued progress is being made on my case, it's a slow, tough uphill fight, but we must not become discouraged. Well, honey, we rec'd our first baptism in fire Tues. The temperature was 14 below zero. Lord, what a tough working day! Recently we were placed on a 9 hr. day, which reduced my earnings considerably. I manage to clear about $50 per month. If the weather becomes too tough we always have on alternative, and that is return to Camp Lincoln, which I'm not particularly keen about. (In October some internees reportedly pro-Nazi staged a revolt against internees who worked outside the camp.) We were granted permission to mail five xmas cards. Sorry I had to miss some folks. The international situation looks better each day. The recently concluded Teheran conference and the Cairo meeting made me exceedingly happy. Well, darling, enjoy the holidays and best Seasons greetings to my many friends. Deepest Love, Ernest

49. Fox, *America's Invisible Gulag*, 148.

50. Fox, *America's Invisible Gulag*, 147.

51. Ernie Fox to Elsie Gilland Fox, April 1944. Elsie Gilland Fox Papers.

April 1944, Ft. Lincoln, Bismarck, N.D.

My Darling Elsie, Your recent visit made me happy beyond words, Elsie darling. I think I'm the most fortunate man alive in being married to such a wonderful person as you. I wish it were possible to express with mere words my love for you. The splendid help of our many friends will be cherished to my dying day. How was your return trip home? Not too tiresome, I hope. I shall write the letters we discussed as soon as possible. Well, little girl, let's hope for a favorable decision on our recent re hearing. If I should get an adverse decision on our recent re hearing, I shall apply for a job on the Idaho project. I'd be more happy in the surrounding country and much closer to you, and regular visits would be possible. Elsie, dear, lately I've been dreadfully lonesome and yearning for you. I sincerely hope we're united again in the immediate future. With Deepest Love, Your Husband, Ernest

52. Fox, *America's Invisible Gulag*, 148.

Chapter Eighteen

53. Ann Fagan Ginger and David Christiano, *The Cold War Against Labor* (Berkeley, CA: Meiklejohn Civil Liberties Institute, 1987), 1:200.

54. Ibid., 1:205.

55. Ibid., 1:234.

56. Ibid., 1:240.

57. Ibid., 1:243.

58. Ibid., 1:246.

59. Ibid., 1:249.

60. Ibid., 1:250, Subversive List (partial list): Abraham Lincoln Brigade, American Committee for Protection of Foreign Born, American League Against War and Fascism, American League for Peace and Democracy, American Women for Peace, Chopin Cultural Center, Committee for the Negro in the Arts, Committee for the Peace and Brotherhood Festival in Philadelphia, Committee to Uphold the Bill of Rights, Community Party, U.S.A., Congress for the Unemployed, Finnish-American Mutual Aid Society, Hollywood Writers Mobilization for Defense, Idaho Pension Fund, League of American Writers, Nature Friends of America, People's Institute of Applied Religion, Pittsburgh Arts Club, Protestant War Veterans of the United States, Inc. ,Samuel Adams School, Boston, Mass, Santa Barbara Peace Forum, Silver Shirts of America, Veterans of the Abraham Lincoln Brigade, Washington Pension Union.

61. See Appendix D.

62. Harvey Schwartz, ed., "Oral History of Lou Goldblatt: May 18, 2004," http://www.ilwu.org/history/oral-histories/lou-goldblatt.cfm?renderforprint=1 (accessed October 6, 2006).

63. Ginger and Christiano, *The Cold War Against Labor,* 1:211

64. Ibid., 1:304.

Chapter Nineteen

65. James Gregory and Jennifer Phipps, *Communism in Washington State History and Memory Project, Chapter 4: Washington Commonwealth Federation & Washington Pension,* http://faculty.washington.edu/gregoryj/ cpproject/phipps.htm (accessed January 28, 2006).

66. *ACA v. Douds,*339 U.S. 382 (1950).

67. Ginger and Christiano, *The Cold War Against Labor,* 1:311.

68. U.S. Congress, *McCarran Internal Security Act Public Law 831*, 81st Congress (September 23, 1950): "There exists a world Communist movement which, in its origins, its development, and its present practice, is a world-wide revolutionary movement whose purpose it is, by treachery, deceit, infiltration into other groups (governmental and otherwise), espionage, sabotage, terrorism and any other means deemed necessary, to establish a Communist totalitarian dictatorship in the countries throughout the world through the medium of a world-wide Communist organization.... The Communist movement in the U.S. is an organization numbering thousands of adherents, rigidly and ruthlessly disciplined ... and is a present danger to the security of the U.S.

69. Michael Barson, *Better Red Than Dead: A Nostalgic Look at the Golden Years of RussiaPhobia, Red-baiting, and Other Commie Madness* (New York: Hyperion, 1992), http://www.writing.upeen.edu/~afilreis/50s/mccarran-act-intro.html (accessed October 24, 2006).

70. Ginger and Christiano, *The Cold War Against Labor,* 1:420–422.

71. Elsie Gilland Fox, FBI Report Files: "FBI REPORT—Date: 1/19/50, Period for which made: 11/29/49 – 1/12/50. Synopsis of facts: FOX continues to reside at 273 Green Street, S.F. and continues in the employ of Warehouse Union Local #6, ILWU at 255 9th St., San Francisco. In Nov. 1948 she was a subscriber to the Daily People's World. FOX in 1949 attended several Communist Party sponsored mass meetings in S.F. In August, 1949 she directed a protest (by circulating a petition) to Federal Judge HAROLD MEDINA regarding the trial of the 12 National Communist Party Leaders in New York City. She attended a Civil Rights Congress Rally in San Francisco on 11/11/49."

72. "Elizabeth Flynn," http://www.spartacus.schoolnet.co.uk/usaflynn.html (accessed on January 19, 2006).

73. "Smith Act and Related Cases," *The Norman Leonard Collection*, Accession #1985/006, *Yates, et al. v. United States*, Records, 1951–1962, University of San Francisco Library (accessed June 25, 2007).

74. Elsie Gilland Fox, FBI Report Files: "FBI REPORT—Date: Sept.1953, Period for which made: 8/53. Synopsis: In 1952 active in raising funds to defend Smith Act defendants in Los Angeles. Attended meetings sponsored by the Civil Rights Congress in 1949, 1950 and 1951. In 1951 was Secretary of the Northern California Committee for the Protection of the Foreign Born. Subject's husband, ERNEST FOX, was convicted in 1952 in Los Angeles for violation of the Smith Act. Description set forth."

Chapter Twenty

75. "Smith Act and Related Cases," *The Norman Leonard Collection,* Accession #1985/006, *Yates, et al. v. United States*, Records, 1951–1962, Labor Archives and Research Center, San Francisco State University.

76. Elsie Gilland Fox, FBI Report Files: "FBI REPORT Oct. 21, 1954. Connections with the Communist party and all party

front groups: A. COMMUNIST PARTYSF T-2 advised that he had observed the subject's name and phone number in the papers maintained by a member of the CP of District 13 Communist Party. SF T-3 advised that ELSIE FOX was present at an executive board meeting of the North Beach Section. B. CIVIL RIGHTS CONGRESS, SF T-4 advised that on Oct. 9, 1953, he observed ELSIE FOX at a rally for the benefit of ___. C. COMMITTEE FOR THE PROTECTION OF THE FOREIGN BORN, SF T-5 advised that on Oct.5, 1953, ELSIE FOX was present at a fiesta held at Finnish Hall, 10th and Santa Barbara, Berkeley, Cal. The fiesta was sponsored by CPFB. On March 5, 1954, a dinner, proceeds which were for the benefit of the CPFB was held at Garibaldi Hall and ELSIE FOX was present. T-6 advised ELSIE FOX was at Hotel Bellevue, to a dinner sponsored by CPFB and ELSIE FOX presented ___ with a gift for her work on this committee. D. INDEPENDENT PROGRESSIVE PARTY (IPP). In the Fourth Report of the Senate Fact-Findings Committee on Un-American Activities of the 1949 Cal. Legislature, pg. 317, the IPP of Cal. Was cited as one of the most important Communist front groups. E. CALIFORNIA LABOR SCHOOL (CLS). Observed by T-6, T-7, T-9 ELSIE FOX attended a lecture entitled "Africa and Colonial Liberation." Subject acted as chairman. Attended lecture 6/9/54, lecture "McCarthy and McCarthyism." Attended lecture 8/8/54 lecture "Dare Schools and Colleges Teach the Truth?" Subject acted as chair. F. JAPAN LETTER: The articles which appear in this publication are translations from Japanese newspapers but generally consist of articles which criticize the U.S. or the Far Eastern Policy of the U.S. Subject was present at a dinner, the proceeds of which were for the benefit of "Japan Letter". G. DAILY PEOPLE'S WORLD (DPW). The DPW is a West Coast Communist Party newspaper. T-13 advised on Aug. 13, 1954 that ELSIE FOX had a yearly subscription to DPW. T-14 advised that ELSIE FOX on Sept. 7, 1953 was present at a picnic which was held for the benefit of the DPW in Paradise Park, to honor outstanding People's World Workers.

77. "Justice Hugo L. Black Quotes/Quotations" http://quotes.liberty-tree.ca/quotes_by/justice+hugo+1.+black, (accessed June 19, 2007).

Chapter Twenty-two

78. See Appendix E.

BIBLIOGRAPHY

Books

Dennett, Eugene V. *Agitprop: The Life of An American Working-Class Radical.* Albany: State University of New York Press, 1990.

Fox, Stephen. *America's Invisible Gulag: A Biography of German American Internment & Exclusion in WWII.* New York: Peter Lang Publishing, Inc., 2000.

Ginger, Ann Fagan and David Christiano, eds. *The Cold War Against Labor, Volume One and Two*, Berkeley, CA: Meiklejohn Civil Liberties Institute, 1987.

Miller, Bettina, ed., *From Flappers to Flivvers: We Helped Make the '20s Roar*. Greendale, WI: Reiman Publications, 1995.

Schactman, Max, "Radicalism in the Thirties." In *As We Saw the Thirties,* edited by Rita James Simon. Chicago: University of Chicago Press, 1967.

Stepan-Norris, Judith and Maurice Zeitlin. *Left Out: Reds and America's Industrial Unions*. Cambridge: Cambridge University Press, 2003.

Washburne, Carolyn Kott, *America in the 20th Century: 1930–39,* New York: Marshall Cavendish Corporation, 1995.

Works Consulted

Lieberman, Robbie. *My Song Is My Weapon.* Chicago: University of Illinois Press, 1995.

Starobin, Joseph R. *American Communism in Crisis, 1943–1957.* Cambridge, MA: Harvard University Press, 1972

Stegner, Wallace. *Joe Hill: A Biographical Novel.* New York: Penguin Books, 1950.

Pozner, Vladimir with Brian Kahn. *Parting with Illusions*. New York: The Atlantic Monthly Press, 1990.

Marx, Karl and Friedrich Engels, with introduction by Vladimir Pozner. *The Communist Manifesto*. New York: Bantam Books, 1992.

Electronic Sources

The American Experience, eds. *People & Events: The Bonus March (May-July, 1932)*. http://ww.pbs.org/ wgbh/ amex/macarthur/ peopleevents/pandeAMEX89.html (accessed July 16, 2006).

Ebel, Karen E. "WWII Violations of German American Civil Liberties by the US Government." http://www. foitimes. com/ internment/gasummary.htm (accessed October 9, 2006).

"Elizabeth Flynn." http://www.spartacus.schoolnet.co.uk/usaflynn.html (accessed on January 19, 2006).

Falconer, Sarah. "Revels Cayton: African American Communist and Labor Activist." *Voice of Action,* February 27, 1934. http://depts.washington.edu/civilr/revels_cayton.htm (accessed April 20, 2006).

Gregory, James and Jennifer Phipps. *Communism in Washington State History and Memory Project, Chapter 4: Washington Commonwealth Federation & Washington Pension.* http://faculty.washington.edu/gregoryj/ cpproject/phipps.htm (accessed January 28, 2006).

Griswold v. Connecticut. 381 U.S. 479 S. Ct. (1965). http://www.law.umkc.edu/faculty/projects/ftrials/conlaw/ griswold.html (accessed June 5, 2008).

The Harry Bridges Project, November 2002 Newsletter. http://www.pbs.org/moyers/journal/blog/ 2007/08/my_fellow_texan.html (accessed July 25, 2008).

"Justice Hugo L. Black Quotes/Quotations." http://quotes.liberty-tree.ca/quotes_by/justice+hugo+l.+black (accessed June 19, 2007).

The Huguenot Society of America: History. http://www.huguenotsocietyofamerica.org/history.html (accessed April 3, 2007).

Kuzma, Cindy. "Contraception and the Law." Planned Parenthood Web site. http://www.plannedparenthood.org/ news-articles-press/politics-policy (accessed March 14, 2007).

London, Kathleen. "The History of Birth Control." Yale Web site. http://www.yale.edu/ynhti/curriculum/units/ 1982.html (accessed March 14, 2007).

Phipps, Jennifer. "Washington Commonwealth Federation & Washington Pension Union." http://faculty. washington.edu/gregoryj/cpproject/phipps.htm (accessed, January 28, 2006).

Schwartz, Harvey. "Oral History of Lou Goldblatt: May 18, 2004." http://www.ilwu.org/history/oral-histories/lou-goldblatt.cfm?renderforprint=1 (accessed October 6, 2006).

Steinem, Gloria. "The Ten Most Influential People of the 20th Century." http://www.time.com/time/time100/ leaders/ profile/sanger3.html (accessed March 14, 2007).

United States Department of Veterans Affairs, ed. "History of the Department of Veterans Affairs: Part 3." http://www1.va.gov/opa/feature/history/history3.asp (accessed June 5, 2008).

Collections

Elsie Gilland Fox Papers. Loaned to author by Fox.

Labor Herald Photograph Collection. Labor Archives and Research Center. San Francisco State University.

"Library Board of Seattle Minutes of Proceedings: 1920-1933." Seattle Public Library Archives.

"Smith Act and Related Cases." *The Norman Leonard Collection*. Accession #1985/006. *Yates, et al. v. United States*. Records, 1951–

1962. Labor Archives and Research Center, San Francisco State University.

Voice of Action (1933-1935). Microform and Newspaper Collections. University of Washington, Seattle.

Laws and Legal Documents

U.S. Congress. *McCarran Act or Internal Security Act, Public Law 831*. 81st *Congress* (September 23, 1950*)*. http://www.writing.upenn.edu/~afilreis/50s/mccarran-act-intro-html.

Electronic Sources Consulted

Ebel, Karen E."WWII Violations of German American Civil Liberties by the US Government." February 24, 2003. http://www.foitimes.com/internment/gasummary.htm (accessed October 9, 2006).

Fresco, Crystal. "Cannery Workers' and Farm Laborers' Union 1933–39: Their Strength in Unity." Seattle Civil Rights and Labor History Project. http://www.depts.washington.edu/civilr/cwflu.htm (accessed May 1, 2007).

Manz, George, "First it was." Briarpatch 32.4 (December 2002): 12(1). GeneralOneFile. Gale Document Number: A101448325. Montana State Library. Http://find.galegroup.com/ips/start.do?prodId=IPS (accessed October 8, 2008).

McCarthyism. http://www.spartacus.schoolnet.co.uk/USAmccarthyism.html (accessed November 11, 2006).

"The Great Hawaii Dock Strike: Rice and Roses." Center for Labor Education and Research, Pearl City, HI. http://homepages.uhwo.hawaii.edu/~clear/1949.html (accessed January 17, 2006).

Paul Robeson. http:// www.pbs.org/wnet/americanmasters/print/robeson_p.html (accessed November 10, 2006).

Schwartz. "The 'Old Left' and the union: Jack Olson, activist and educator." June 9, 2004. http://www.ilwu.org/ dispatcher/2004/04/ jack-olson-oral-history (accessed October 6, 2006).

Schwartz, "The 'Old Left' and the union: Keith Eickman of warehouse Local 6." http://www.ilwu.org/dispatcher/ 2004/03/2004-03-eickman-oral-history (accessed October 6, 2006).

Smith, Michael Steven. "About the Smith Act Trials." http://www. english.uiuc.edu/maps/poets/g_l/jerome/smithact.htm (accessed November 7, 2006)

The Protocols of the Elders of Zion. http://www.jewishvirtuallibrary. org/jsource/anti-semitism/protocols.html (accessed July 31, 2008).

Printed in the United States
147464LV00002B/1/P

9 781440 109096